Energy in the Caspian Region

Euro-Asian Studies

General Editor: **Christoph Bluth**, Visiting Professor, Centre for Euro–Asian Studies, University of Reading, and Professor in International Studies, University of Leeds

The transition of the countries in Euro-Asia is one of the most important developments affecting the international system since the end of the Cold War. The development of market economies after decades of central planning, the formation of new states and national identities, the creation of new, democratic institutions of state and the reintegration into the world economy pose enormous challenges. While some countries have progressed relatively well and are in the process of joining the European Union, others have experienced several economic and social dislocations, to the point of political disintegration and armed conflicts. The Centre for Euro-Asian Studies at the University of Reading is dedicated to the academic study of the political, economic, social and cultural aspects of this process. This series presents the most recent contributions from leading academics in the field. With an interdisciplinary focus, it seeks to provide a substantial, original and ongoing contribution to our understanding of the region which is of vital importance for academics and of high policy relevance for governments and business.

Titles include:

Yelena Kalyuzhnova and Dov Lynch (*editors*)
THE EURO-ASIAN WORLD
A Period of Transition

Yelena Kalyuzhnova, Amy Myres Jaffe, Dov Lynch and Robin C. Sickles (*editors*)
ENERGY IN THE CASPIAN REGION
Present and Future

Yelena Kalyuzhnova and Michael Taylor (*editor*)
TRANSITIONAL ECONOMIES
Banking Finance, Institutions

Euro–Asian Studies
Series Standing Order ISBN 978-1-349-42568-6
(*outside North America only*)

You can receive future titles in this series as they are published by placing a standing order. Please contact your bookseller or, in case of difficulty, write to us at the address below with your name and address, the title of the series and the ISBN quoted above.

Customer Services Department, Macmillan Distribution Ltd, Houndmills, Basingstoke, Hampshire RG21 6XS, England

Energy in the Caspian Region

Present and Future

Edited by

Yelena Kalyuzhnova
Director
The Centre for Euro-Asian Studies
The University of Reading

Amy Myers Jaffe
Senior Energy Advisor and Research Coordinator
James A. Baker III Institute for Public Policy
Rice University

Dov Lynch
Lecturer in War Studies
King's College London

and

Robin C. Sickles
Professor of Economics
Rice University

Foreword by

James A. Baker

palgrave
macmillan

Softcover reprint of the hardcover 1st edition 2002 978-0-333-92959-9

Published by
PALGRAVE MACMILLAN
Houndmills, Basingstoke, Hampshire RG21 6XS and
175 Fifth Avenue, New York, N. Y. 10010
Companies and representatives throughout the world

PALGRAVE MACMILLAN is the global academic imprint of the Palgrave Macmillan division of St. Martin's Press, LLC and of Palgrave Macmillan Ltd. Macmillan® is a registered trademark in the United States, United Kingdom and other countries. Palgrave is a registered trademark in the European Union and other countries.

ISBN 978-1-349-42568-6 ISBN 978-0-230-50122-5 (eBook)
DOI 10.1057/9780230501225

This book is printed on paper suitable for recycling and made from fully managed and sustained forest sources.

A catalogue record for this book is available from the British Library.

Transferred to digital printing 2001

For the Nations of the Caspian Region

Contents

List of Figures

List of Tables

Foreword

James A. Baker, III

When I was asked to write this foreword, I accepted with pleasure for two reasons. First, this is the first volume of its sort issued by the Baker Institute's Energy studies program. It is the product of a unique international collaborative venture with the Centre for Euro-Asian Studies at the University of Reading in the United Kingdom. Its publication is an event of which I, as the Institute's Honorary Chair, take great personal pride. Second, its subject – Central Asia and the Caucasus – is one that is close to my heart.

During my tenure as Secretary of State few trips compared, in exhaustion or exhilaration, to the two whirlwind visits I made to Central Asia and the Caucasus in late 1991 and early 1992. It was an extraordinary time, not just for the region but indeed for the world. Communism had collapsed. A popular revolt that had begun just two years before in the capitals of Central and Eastern Europe had spread with dizzying speed to Moscow itself. There, on Christmas Day, 1991, the hammer and sickle flew for the last time over the Kremlin. The Soviet Union was no more – and gone with it was much of the empire that the Bolsheviks had inherited from the Tsar. Not just the Baltics were now independent. So too were Belarus, Ukraine and Moldova. And, to their east lay a whole range of new states – Georgia, Armenia, Azerbaijan, Turkmenistan, Uzbekistan, Tajikistan, Kyrgyzstan and Kazakhstan – to which independence had come almost overnight. My visit to regional capitals was, first and foremost, a symbol of the Bush administration's support for that independence – a support that remains to this day the linchpin of US policy towards Central Asia and the Caucasus.

Like most Americans, I knew little about the region. What I discovered there was a mix of excitement and uncertainty. The excitement was tangible – and, for me at least, infectious. After laboring a century or more under Tsarist and Communist rule from Moscow, the peoples of the region were now finally free to forge their own destinies. But with this freedom had come uncertainty. Would the states of Central Asia and the Caucasus be able to maintain their sovereignty in the face of a possible Russian effort to re-exert dominance in the region? Would national leaders be willing or able to create the enduring political and economic institutions necessary to ensure democracy and prosperity? Would the countries of the region prove capable of overcoming the internal and external conflicts that already threatened stability?

A decade later, the worst fears I heard articulated when I first visited the regions have gratifyingly gone unrealized. Though a number of nations in Central Asia and the Caucasus have troubled relations with Moscow, all remain independent. And, with the exception of Tajikistan, none has descended into chaos. But the high hopes of the early days of independence have also proven elusive. Economic reform has been, by and large, disappointing. Political progress has been similarly spotty. Only a few states in the region can be termed truly democratic; others range from the autocratic to the dictatorial. And conflict – whether we are speaking of the dispute between Azerbaijan and Armenia, the civil war in Tajikistan, or separatist movements in Georgia – remains an abiding threat to stability.

In short, Central Asia and the Caucasus present a complex picture. This is especially true of one area of great interest to the outside world: energy. The region is rich – perhaps very rich – in both oil and gas. Even when I first visited the region, its energy potential was the subject of immense interest and great hope. The development of oil and gas reserves was viewed not just as a boon to the individual countries fortunate enough to possess them, but as a means to bind the entire region together economically.

This dream has yet to become a reality. Despite keen interest and major investment by international energy companies, development of the region's oil and gas has been frustratingly slow. Technical difficulties, local instability, international rivalry – these are just a few of the impediments that have faced those inside and outside the region who have sought to bring its oil and gas to international markets. As I have mentioned, the region is complex. And the development of its energy resources both reflects–and, indeed, deepens–that complexity.

This book, "Energy in the Caspian Region: Present and Future", accepts, even embraces this fact. Rather than look at the issue from a strictly technical or even economic point of view, it seeks to place energy in the broader context of the geo-strategic, political, social and cultural factors in play. This emphasis upon context is reflected not just in the wide range of subjects this volume addresses but in the varied background the authors bring to them. Through the unique collaboration of the Institute and the Centre for Euro-Asian Studies it has been possible to assemble a team of authors from the United States, UK and Russia. Some are distinguished economists, political scientists and sociologists; others foreign policy analysts; still others are energy industry experts.

While the first essay in this volume attempts to bring together much of the later material in a summary fashion, it does not pretend to be comprehensive. Our individual authors have their own perspectives, their own points of views. But those perspectives, I believe, are useful and those points of view informed. That is why they are included in this book – and why I urge you to read them.

Reading this volume, I was struck by how much had happened in the years since I first visited Central Asia and the Caucasus. But I am also reminded of just how new these states still are. Ten years after independence, their prospects are still exciting, their futures still uncertain. If we in the United States are to help them fulfill their promise – and I believe we should – we will require a foreign policy better grounded in a rich understanding of region.

I congratulate editors, Yelena Kalyuzhnova, Amy Myers Jaffe, Dov Lynch and Robin Sickles for overseeing such a remarkable international research project and making the publication of this book possible. This book is a step – and, I hope, an important one – in that direction.

Preface

Yelena Kalyuzhnova

This book is the first product of the collaboration between the Centre for Euro-Asian Studies at the University of Reading (UK) and the James A. Baker III Institute for Public Policy of Rice University (USA)'s Energy Studies program. Drawing on both institutions' interdisciplinary expertise in economics, political science, geology, and engineering, the book seeks to contribute significantly to studies of energy policy issues around the Caspian basin. It has focused on the geological, political and economic hindrances to the speedy development of Caspian oil reserves and has concluded that these reserves are unlikely to serve as a cheaper, more secure alternative to Persian Gulf oil in the coming decade but rather will represent only 3 percent of world oil supplies.

The idea for writing such a book came to us in 1999 when I visited Rice University. After the presentation of my work on "The Kazakstani Economy" at the James A. Baker III Institute, Amy Myers Jaffe raised the idea of joint book. We realized that for the "merging" topic of Caspian energy we should join efforts together and to incorporate the work of academics and professionals in one study. Only through this approach may the world of action and the world of ideas be brought closer together.

The terrorist attack on New York and Washington occurred just as this book was preparing to go to print. It is clear, even at this early date, that the tragic events of September 11, 2001 will dramatically alter the international landscape in ways that we today cannot fully fathom. This is certainly true of the place of the Caspian Basin – and its energy resources – in world affairs. There is little doubt that the region – with its large Muslim population and proximity to Afghanistan and the Persian Gulf – will loom larger in the consideration of policymakers in major world capitals.

It is with this in mind that we decided to go forward with publication sooner rather than later. While lacking direct discussion of the historic events of September 11, we believe that this volume's essays nonetheless provide, a rich and much-needed analysis of one of the most complex and least understood regions of the world. We will consider this book a success if it helps inform international debate about the role of countries of the Caspian Basin in world economic and political affairs. In the wake of the September 11 tragedy, it is a debate more urgent than ever before.

The work on the book has been done in a spirit of collaboration and we are sincerely grateful to all contributors of the volume for their cooperation and talent. We especially thank Andrei Kalyuzhnov, Julian Lee and Julia Nanay for their support and cooperation in the most difficult period of writing this book. Our sincere gratitude goes to all referees for their helpful comments and encouragement. The Editors also thank the Center for International Political Economy (CIPE) of New York for its generous support towards the initial research on energy, politics and culture in the Caspian basin. Thanks are also extended to Natasha Shevchik for helping with statistics for this book and Linda Auld our proof editor. We appreciate all encouragement and guidance of Christoph Bluth, the general editor of the Euro-Asian series. We are extremely grateful to Evelyn McDonald, Administrator at the Centre for Euro-Asian Studies, for all the help and care given during the whole process of our project. We dedicate this volume to the people of the Caspian region.

Yelena Kalyuzhnova
Reading, UK

Abbreviations

AIOC	Azerbaijan International Operating Company
ANAP	Motherland Party
b/d	barrels per day
bcf/d	billion cubic feet per day
bcm	billion cubic metres
bcm/yr	billion cubic metres per year
BCSIA	Belfer Center for Studies in International Affairs, Kennedy School, Harvard University
BLACKSEAFOR	Black Sea Cooperation Naval Task Group
BOTAŞ	Turkish State Pipeline Corporation
BSEC	Black Sea Economic Cooperation
CAEC	Central Asian Economic Community
CAOPP	Central Asian Oil Pipeline Project
CAU	Central Asian Union
CEE	Central and Eastern Europe
cf	cubic feet
cf/d	cubic feet a day
CGES	Centre for Global Energy Studies
CIPCO	Caspian International Petroleum Company
CIS	Commonwealth of Independent States
CNPC	China National Petroleum Corporation
CPC	Caspian Pipeline Consortium
CSIS	Center for Strategic and International Studies
CSRE	Caspian Sea region economies
DSP	Democratic Left Party
EBRD	European Bank for Reconstruction and Development
EIU	Economist Intelligence Unit
Exim Bank	Export-Import Bank of the United States
FOB	freight on board
FP	Virtue Party
FSU	former Soviet Union
GDP	gross domestic product
GMM	Generalized Method of Moments
GUUAM	Georgia, Ukraine, Uzbekistan, Azerbaijan, Moldova

IDU	Islamic Movement of Uzbekistan
IEA	International Energy Agency
ILSA	Iran – Libya Sanctions Act
IMF	International Monetary Fund
IMO	International Maritime Organization
IRP	Islamic Revival Party
IV	Instrumental Variable
JBIC	Japanese Bank for International Cooperation
km	kilometres
kW/h	kilowatts per hour
LNG	liquefied natural gas
LPG	liquefied petroleum gas
LSDV	least squares dummy variable
mcm/day	million cubic metres per day
mDarcy	miliDarcy
MFA	Ministry of Foreign Affairs
MHP	Nationalist Action Party
MITI	Ministry of International Trade and Industry
MLE	Maximum Likelihood Estimation
mmb/d	million barrels per day
MMG	Mangistaumunaigas
NAOC	North Absheron Operating Company
NATO	North Atlantic Treaty Organization
NBR	National Bureau of Asian Research
NIOC	National Iranian Oil Company
NMP	Net Material Product
NSC	National Security Council
OIEC	Oil Industries' Engineering and Construction
OKIOC	Offshore Kazakhstan International Operating Company
OLS	Ordinary least squares
OPEC	Organization of Petroleum Exporting Countries
OPIC	Organization for Security and Co-operation in Europe
OSCE	Organization for Security and Co-operation in Europe
PEC	primary energy consumption
PFP	Partnership for Peace
PIW	Petroleum Intelligence Weekly
PSA	production sharing agreement
RP	Welfare Party

RPI	Russian Petroleum Investor
ShNOS	Shymkentnefteorgsyntez refinery
t/yr	metric tonnes per year
tcf	trillion cubic feet
TCP	Trans-Caspian Pipeline
TPAO	Turkish Petroleum Corporation
TRACECA	Transport Corporation Europe Caucasus Asia
UK	United Kingdom
UN	United Nations
USA	United States of America
UTO	United Tajik Opposition

Contributors

James A. Baker, III has served in senior government positions under three United States presidents. From 1988 to 1992, he served as US Secretary of State under President George Bush and was the first US Secretary of State to visit the newly independent states of Central Asia. In 1995, Mr Baker published *The Politics of Diplomacy*, his reflections on those years of revolution, war and peace. He is presently a senior partner in the law firm of Baker Botts, and Senior Counselor to The Carlyle Group, a merchant banking firm in Washington, DC. Mr Baker is Honorary Chairman of the James A. Baker III Institute for Public Policy at Rice University and serves on the boards of Rice University and the Howard Hughes Medical Institute.

Joe Barnes is a Research Fellow at the James A. Baker III Institute for Public Policy at Rice University. Prior to joining the Institute he was an Associate with Carlyle International, a division of the merchant banking firm Carlyle Group. Barnes served for many years as a Foreign Service Officer with the US State Department.

Andrei Belopolsky currently works as a geophysicist at BP America Inc., in the Deep Water Gulf of Mexico Production Business Unit. He received his PhD in Geology and Geophysics from Rice University in Houston, Texas, in 2000. While at Rice, he was involved in the Caspian region study at the James A. Baker III Institute for Public Policy.

Edward P. Djerejian is the founding Director of the James A. Baker III Institute for Public Policy at Rice University. He is one of the US's most distinguished and experienced diplomats. His career has spanned the administrations of eight US presidents. A leading expert on the complex political, security, economic, religious and ethnic issues of the Middle East, Ambassador Djerejian has served as US Ambassador to Israel and Syria.

Mehrdad Haghayeghi is Associate Professor of Political Science at Southwest Missouri State University. He has published a book on Islam in Central Asia and numerous articles that have appeared in *Central*

Asian Survey, Central Asia Monitor, Middle Eastern Studies, The Journal of Iranian Studies, World Affairs, and *Muslim World.* During 1997–2000, Dr Haghayeghi was a regular contributor to the Economist Intelligence Unit of London on Kyrgyzstan, Tajikistan, and Kazakhstan. He has been a consultant to the United States State Department, the National Intelligence Council, United States Agency for International Development, Soros Foundation, British Broadcasting Corporation, and Radio Free Europe.

Patrik T. Hultberg is Assistant Professor in the Department of Economics and Finance at the University of Wyoming. He also holds an adjunct position in the International Studies Department and teaches and conducts research in the field of international economics.

Amy Myers Jaffe is Senior Energy Advisor and Research Co-ordinator at the James A. Baker III Institute for Public Policy at Rice University and principal author of the Institute's first four energy security studies that cover the Persian Gulf, Caspian basin, China and Japan. She also serves as Project Director for the Baker Institute/Council on Foreign Relations task force on "Strategic Energy Policy."

Andrei Kalyuzhnov is a mechanical engineer and a consultant in London, UK. He has experience in engineering and procurement for process plants, design, manufacture and assembly of machines employed in both petrochemical and general fields. Andrei holds an MSc degree in mechanical engineering from Kazak State Technical University.

Yelena Kalyuzhnova is the Director of the Centre for Euro-Asian Studies and a lecturer in the School of Business at the University of Reading. Her research interests include the planning process and industrial policy in the transitional economies, and macroeconomic issues in transition. Dr Kalyuzhnova is the author of the first major study of the Kazakhstani economy (1998) as well as an editor of *The Euro-Asian World. A Period of Transition* (2000) *and Transitional Economies:* Banking, Finance, Institutions (2001).

Julian Lee is Senior Energy Analyst at the London-based Centre for Global Energy Studies (CGES), where he directs research on the oil and gas industries of the former Soviet Union. He is also heavily involved in the oil market analysis carried out by the CGES.

Dov Lynch is Lecturer in War Studies at King's College London. He is also a member of the Centre for Euro-Asian Studies. He has been a Research Fellow at the Royal Institute of International Affairs, and also at St Antony's College, Oxford. His book on *Russian Peacekeeping Strategies towards the CIS* was published in 2000. He is currently working on a research project examining "de facto states in the former Soviet Union" funded by the United States Institute of Peace.

Michael Margelov is a member from Pskov of the Council of Federation (Upper Chamber) of the Federal Assembly of the Russian Federation. He is also a member of the Committee for Foreign Affairs. Since 1995, Michael Margelov is one of the leading political consultants in Russia.

Fred R. von der Mehden is Albert Thomas Professor of Political Science Emeritus at Rice University. He is presently doing research at the James A. Baker III Institute of Public Policy. He has written widely on issues related to Islam in Asia.

Julia Nanay is a Director at the Petroleum Finance Company in Washington, DC, where she provides clients with risk analyses for investments in the oil and gas industry. She has worked in the petroleum industry in various capacities since 1976. Over the last two years, she has devoted a large share of her time to advisory work on the Caspian region.

Martha Brill Olcott is a Senior Associate at the Carnegie Endowment for International Peace in Washington, DC. She also co-directs the Carnegie Moscow Center's Project on Ethnicity and Politics in the former Soviet Union. She is also a professor of political science at Colgate University.

Robin C. Sickles is Professor of Economics at Rice University and holds Adjunct Professorship positions in the Statistics Department at Rice University and at Baylor College of Medicine. Professor Sickles is Director of the Graduate Program in Economics and the Center for the Study of Institutions and Values at Rice University. He has published over 70 articles and is currently serving on the editorial boards of the *Journal of Econometrics, Journal of Business and Economic Statistics, Communications in Statistics,* and *Empirical Economics.*

Ronald Soligo is a Professor of Economics at Rice University with a speciality in development and energy economics. He has authored a number of studies on energy-related topics for the James A. Baker III Institute for Public Policy at Rice University. These include the relationship between the level of economic development and the level and composition of energy demand and issues of energy security.

Manik Talwani is Schlumberger Professor of Geophysics at Rice University He has held this position since 1985. In addition, he was the director of the Geotechnology Research Institute, Houston Advanced Research Center (HARC) until 1998. He is presently engaged in establishing cooperative research projects involving the energy industry. A major area of his interest is the use of gravity gradiometry in exploration and production projects.

Gareth M. Winrow is a Professor in the Department of International Relations at Istanbul Bilgi University. He is a member of the Royal Institute of International Affairs (UK) and works on the editorial board of the journal Turkish Studies. He is also the representative in Turkey for the Centre for Euro-Asian Studies at the University of Reading.

Introduction

Amy Myers Jaffe and Edward Djerejian

The Caspian region is considered by many to be the next oil and gas frontier. The region's sizable energy reserves, combined with its unique political stature as eight newly independent states emerging from the break-up of the former Soviet Union, have catapulted these countries into the limelight of Western media and policy debate. Beyond energy, Central Asia and the Caucasus's location between Russia, China, Iran and Turkey make it a magnet for foreign powers and a flash point for potential conflict between them. In addition to these neighboring countries, the US, Europe, Japan, Pakistan, Saudi Arabia and Israel have all shown interest in the region.

With so large a number of major powers viewing the region in terms of a broader contest for spheres of influence, there is heightened risk of a geopolitical competition that could aggravate existing instability. Central Asia and the Caucasus already suffer from localized conflicts, economic distress, and environmental disasters. Divisive ethnic tensions simmer beneath the surface in many of the countries of the region, and few, if any, boast an institutional framework for smooth succession of leadership. Security arrangements are also ill-defined, leaving the region prone to instability and threatening its economic development.

For regional powers, interest extends well beyond commercial considerations. Historical factors play a role. To some extent, regional powers seek to reach into Central Asia and the Caucasus to help control ethnic movements in their own hinterlands, including Russia's southern regions, Kurdish borderlands in Turkey, ethnic Azeri borderlands in northern Iran and the Xinjiang province in western China. And, the re-emergence of Islamic practices in the region is a magnet for attention from Islamic countries such as Saudi Arabia and Iran. But commercial considerations remain strong, and prolific resources of oil and natural gas are a prime attraction.

Breaking new ground: The Caspian region in the 21st century

Indeed, the hydrocarbon reserves of the Caspian region are significant. The range of total proven reserves of the four largest hydrocarbon-rich Caspian countries – Azerbaijan, Kazakhstan, Turkmenistan and Uzbekistan is 14.7 to 31.3 billion barrels of oil and 242.6 to 373 trillion cubic feet (tcf) of natural gas. These figures represent about 2.7 percent of total world oil proven reserves and 7 percent of proven natural gas reserves. While oil production in Central Asia and the Caucasus will never match the Persian Gulf, where there are five major oil powers and several smaller producers, the region will nonetheless be a prime oil and gas producing area. As Andrei Belopolsky and Manik Talwani discuss in their chapter "Geological Basins and Oil and Gas Reserves of the Greates Caspian Region" the region has the potential to produce almost 4 million barrels perday (b/d) by 2015. Estimated possible reserves are assessed at high levels of 60 – 100 billion barrels of oil, most of it located in Kazakhstan, and 260 – 665 tcf of gas. Its remoteness from world markets, political risks, and environmental concerns, however may delay peak production.

Despite its oil and gas wealth, a host of complex geopolitical, social, religious, and cultural factors will influence the future of the Caspian Basin region in the years to come. The countries of Central Asia and the Caucasus, having achieved independence from the Soviet Union a mere seven years ago, are in their relative infancy. They have hardly begun the task of building new institutions or creating new national identities. In the chapter "Confronting Independence: Political Overview," Martha Brill Olcott looks at the cultural, religious, demographic and ethnic challenges facing the new states and discusses how these factors will create strains in intra-regional relations and international relations.

Olcott contends that since the outset of independence, the region's leaders have been struggling with the task of strengthening the weak sense of nationhood among the Central Asian peoples. Three pillars of identity have been utilized, including the resuscitation of the indigenous languages, revival of religion and the reinterpretation of history. But all three have presented serious challenges to the underlying societies and to the legitimacy of the ruling elite. While the region's current leaders may be coping for the time being with the risks of their countries' ethnic and social diversity, the problem of leadership succession looms large as a future challenge throughout the Caspian Basin region. The national political discourse in the region almost without exception lacks meaningful competitive elections and adequate division of powers. Vigorous attempts to stamp out political opposition in Central Asia has preserved macropolitical stability in the short run but may lay the ground work for violent, revolutionary change down the road. Socioeconomic problems and rampant corruption at the elite level loom large, increasing the chances for future instability.

The economic challenges for the region are elaborated in Yelena Kalyuzhnova's chapter "Economies and Energy." Kalyuzhnova discusses the acute problems that face the region as it attempts to reduce strong dependence on trade with Russia and reform backward, inefficient state-run industries. All the countries in the region remain at low levels of economic development. Kazakhstan has the highest per capita income in the region at only $1230, followed by Uzbekistan at $720, Turkmenistan at $660 and Azerbaijan at $550. Moreover, the region's economies were adversely affected in the late 1990s by the Russian financial crisis and fluctuations in prices for export commodities such as energy and metals.

In addition, Kalyuzhnova argues that structural problems will be difficult to overcome. For example, the size and distance influence the potential for economic growth in the Caspian region. The Caspian region is a large landlocked area with low population density and low GDP per capita. These factors limit domestic markets and make economic development in the region difficult. Kalyuzhnova argues that economic cooperation can help to eliminate these obstacles by providing expansion of the domestic markets for local producers as well as opportunities for increasing economies of scale in production, effective use of resources and increasing trade opportunities. However, the oil-bearing countries in the region will have to work hard to avoid Dutch oil disease and protect the development of a diversified economic base.

It must be noted that if current trends prevail, the internal stability of the region could come under threat. Mehrdad Haghayeghi and Fred von der Mehden argue in their chapter "Islam and Energy Security" that delayed economic progress and political repression will increase the risks of a rise in Islamic radicalism in Central Asia in the coming years. The authors note that the current Islamic revival in post-independent Central Asia includes the formation of Islamic parties and organizations aimed at gaining access to the political process and the introduction of Islamic fundamentalist ideology that rejects secular belief and aims to establish an Islamic state in the region.

So far, however, Central Asian Islamic movements have differed from their Middle Eastern neighbors by lacking anti-Western ideological overtones and rejecting violence as a method of achieving statehood.

For now the revival of interest in Islam among the peoples of Central Asia and Azerbaijan is highly decentralized and remains relatively distinct from the political arena. No organized, broadbased, monolithic fundamentalist movement exists in the region and it is likely that the process of reclaiming Islam and reconstructing a viable Muslim civil society will take generations. Indeed, the secularized nature of most of the Central Asian people and the relative weakness of Islamic organizations have limited the impact of radical Islam in the region.

The authors note, however that to the extent that outward political expression and dissent are repressed by authoritarian regimes and driven underground, the growing network of mosques and religious schools will provide an alternative framework for organization of opposition movements and a forum for mobilization. A high incidence of political repression and a lack of democratic process; visible corruption and nepotism among members of the ruling elite; an increasingly younger population with diminishing employment and educational opportunities; and the creation of a network of mosques and religious centers could eventually lead to a greater radicalization in the region, if Islam is utilized as a rallying cry for those perceiving themselves as economically and politically oppressed by an "anti-Islamic" regime. A rise in radical Islam, such as is spreading from Afghanistan into the Fergana valley, could create a more serious threat to energy exports and political stability in the region than seen today.

Reaching a world market: Pipelines, transit routes and processing plants

The huge distance of Central Asia and Caucasus hydrocarbon reserves from the world's major energy consuming regions requires a considerable financial investment to bring them to market. The countries of the region are landlocked. Unlike competitors in other large oil-rich regions such as the Middle East, South America, and even Russia, the region's producers cannot simply ship oil by tanker from domestic ports. Instead, they must rely on expensive pipelines constructed through foreign territories as the chief means for transport.

In their chapter, "The Economics of Pipeline Routes: The Conundrum of Oil Exports from the Caspian Basin" Ronald Soligo and Amy Myers Jaffe discuss how the landlocked geography of the Caspian Basin has created serious logistical impediments to speedy exploration and development. The region is distant from major supply centers for exploratory equipment and faces a crippling shortage of modern drilling platforms and other material that is slowing oil development in the region.

Similarly, the development of pipeline corridors from the Caspian Basin to international oil markets has been a slow and painstaking process. Many possible routes through Russia, Georgia, Turkey, China, Afghanistan, and Iran have been discussed, and the negotiating process for each alternative route has been shaped by the ambitions of various participants to capture both the economic and geopolitical benefits of sponsoring the transport of oil from the region. However, Jaffe and Soligo argue that there might not be enough oil to justify construction of numerous export pipelines to the West. Caspian oil production is not expected to exceed 3.4 million b/d over the next decade, and increased export sales into the Black Sea littoral states such as Romania, Ukraine, Bulgaria and Turkey could be expected to handle at least one-third to half of the expected volume. So far, Russia seems to have a lock on oil export routes from the Caspian countries, with the exception of a small amount of oil moving through Georgia. But the US government continues to support the construction of a major pipeline via Turkey from Baku to the Mediterranean port of Ceyhan.

China made its first investment in Central Asia in June 1997. The China National Petroleum Corporation (CNPC) agreed to purchase 60 percent of Kazakhstan's Aktyubinsk Oil Company for US$4.3 billion and announced plans to build a US$3.5 billion, 3000 km pipeline linking western Kazakhstan with its own Xinjiang region. In announcing its investment, China said it hoped to secure significant, long-term supplies of crude oil which would not only make a proposed Kazakh-Xinjiang pipeline more economically feasible, but also render economically attractive planned eastbound pipelines which would link Xinjiang province with China's energy demanding, industrial heartlands. However, actually building the pipeline would prove to be more problematic than expected.

Jaffe and Soligo investigate the economics of moving Kazakh oil to China. In the case of a Bosporus route to Europe, transport costs to Asia are generally higher than transportation costs for Kazakh oil to Europe, implying that Kazakstan producers would need a considerable subsidy before they would shift oil from the more profitable Mediterranean market to the Chinese market. This will be true despite the fact that Asian oil markets generally carry a price premium to Mediterranean prices. Only in the case of the Baku–Ceyhan route versus an Iranian route, would the existence of an Asian price premium mean that Kazakh producers could earn more profits selling their oil to China via Iran.

The domestic energy industries of the Caspian countries are also thwarted by the twin burdens of geography and history. Refineries in the Caspian region are struggling to overcome their legacy of outdated technology and the fact that they had previously operated as just a part of a broader, integrated regional network. There are 12 refineries in Azerbaijan, Kazakhstan, Georgia, Turkmenistan and Uzbekistan but almost all suffer from inadequate oil supplies, poor product quality, and unstable payments for their output. By the same token, the natural gas processing, transportation and distribution infrastructure inherited by the Caspian region countries from the Soviet Union reflected the needs of that union, rather than those of the individual countries as sovereign territories. In their chapter "Domestic Use of Energy: Oil Refineries and Gas Processing" Andrei Kalyuzhnov, Julian Lee, and Julia Nanay discuss the struggle of the region's countries to realign their domestic energy industries to meet their own domestic needs and to allow any surplus natural gas or refined products to reach foreign markets. The newly independent countries are only moving slowly towards refurbishing, rationalizing and updating their domestic natural gas transportation and processing infrastructure. Countries such as Kazakhstan and Azerbaijan have identified the need to utilize their own gas resources locally and are beginning to take steps to make this desire a reality. But as the authors discuss, the refurbishment and extension of local natural gas networks and refining facilities are hampered by a lack of funds locally and the difficulty of attracting foreign investment into sectors plagued by non-payment and aging equipment.

Despite the enthusiasm internationally about the potential of the Caspian Basin's oil industry, even under the most optimistic assessments, Caspian oil production is unlikely to reach more than 3.5 million b/d by 2010. In the chapter "Convergent Economies: Implications for World Energy Use" Patrik Hultberg and Robin Sickles demonstrate that this will represent only 3 – 4 percent of anticipated global oil use. By contrast, Venezuelan oil is expected to account for as much as 7 – 8 percent while Middle East oil will still dominate with a 25 – 35 percent share, depending on market conditions.

In short, the Caspian Basin is not going to be the ace in the hole for international energy security. The region is by no means the only major oil and gas province in play that can help diversify world oil supplies and reduce reliance on the volatile Persian Gulf. Substantial reserves remain to be exploited in Africa, South America and offshore

Asia. In particular, the payoff may be higher in terms of magnitude of incremental to global markets if greater efforts were applied to other regions than the Caspian.

National interests in the Caspian Basin

Despite the limits to the Caspian region's near term oil production potential, geopolitical considerations still loom large. While talk of a new "great game" may be exaggerated, a number of major powers clearly view the region as important for their spheres of influence. Russian leadership is highly sensitive to the activities of the West in the Caspian Basin. Under Vladimir Putin, Russia has set forth a new foreign policy that emphasizes Russia's integration into the world community in a manner that is consistent with the country's overall state and national interests. President Putin's visit to Baku, Azerbaijan in early January 2001 marked a clear shift in Russian policy with Russia constructively supporting new efforts at resolving the conflict between Azerbaijan and Armenia over the disputed territory of Nagorno-Karabakh and reasserting itself in the Caspian Basin as a whole.

Putin has given clear instructions for the Foreign Ministry and other relevant state agencies, as well as Russian energy companies, to step up their activities in the Caspian Basin, in an attempt to pre-empt US efforts to promote American influence in the region, Michael Margelov argues in his chapter "Russia's National Interests in the Caspian Region." But Russia would like to avoid confrontation and pursue a pragmatic approach for the development of multilateral ties with all countries in the region. Margelov discusses Russia's attempts to make Azerbaijan a key partner in the region and elicit its support in the Chechen problem. Similar efforts with Georgia have not been successful – Georgia, for example, has refused to cooperate on border issues – and discussions with Georgia continue.

The effective development of the Caspian natural resources is seen by Russia as being pivotal for the region's economic growth and stability. Because of economic links and common borders, regional stability in the Caspian Basin is of great importance for Russia, which has placed a strong priority on countering the rise of terrorism in the region. Russia would like to create a zone of stability around the Russian Federation that would allow it to concentrate on crucial domestic concerns. Still, Russian foreign policy will still assert its interests in the Caspian Basin, potentially bringing it into rivalry with the US, which is viewed by Moscow as using Caspian energy diplomacy to enhance Washington's own geopolitical and economic importance and strengthen the position of American transnational companies.

Regardless of Russian and US intentions, it is clear that no single great power will be able to maintain any exceptional degree of influence across the Caspian region. From the US perspective, it will serve Western interests to pursue policies that undermine, rather than embolden, neo-imperialists in Moscow. In particular, in absence of real resources and guarantees, US talk of containing Russia in Central Asia and the Caucasus can only be counterproductive. While US policy finds its roots in the premise that energy export revenues can play a central role in buttressing the legitimacy of local regimes and enhancing their continued independence and sovereignty, the region remains remote from the heart of Europe, and US strategic interests in the region, minus energy, are modest. In his chapter "US National Interests: Getting Beyond the Hype" Joe Barnes discusses why the US must exercise caution as it reassesses American policy towards the region under the new Republican Administration.

The US will continue to view the region in some measure through the prism of its policies towards Russia and the Persian Gulf and US interests in the Caspian Basin pale in comparison to Washington's vital interest in working towards a continued orderly reduction in Russia's nuclear arsenal. Moreover, even under the more reasonably optimistic assessments of Caspian oil potential, the Persian Gulf will remain by far the most important supplier of petroleum to world markets. Barnes argues that while the new Bush Administration may be tempted to exert a firmer hand with perceived Russian meddling in the Caspian region, the Administration will similarly take care not to overextend American resources by engaging in a dramatically heightened involvement in a remote region tangential to the traditional set of strategic American interests.

US policy also in good measure caters to its alliance and close relations with Turkey, a NATO member. Turkey's interests in the region are multi-fold. The region holds the cultural attractions of pan-Turkism, and Ankara seeks influence over the area to help control ethnic movements and conflicts that could threaten Turkey's own hinterlands. Economic considerations also loom large – the region is a major trading partner with Turkey as well as an important source for energy supply. Finally, geopolitical factors come into play as discussed in Gareth Winrow's chapter "Turkish National Interests." In spite of new regional security initiatives, Turkey continues to be suspicious of Moscow's intentions – militarily or other – and has sought to ensure that not all energy pipelines from the Caspian Basin will be routed through Russia. Concerns about Russia expanding Russian influence, combined with worries about safety along the congested Bosporus Straits, have prompted Turkey to push for an onland pipeline route through its territory, beginning at Baku and ending at the Mediterranean port of Ceyhan. This route has been the cornerstone to Turkish policy in the region and the symbol of the US–Turkish alliance to limit the influence of other countries, notably Russia, Iran and China, in the Caspian game.

Rather than serve as a zone for geopolitical rivalry and confrontation, all parties would benefit from seeing Central Asia and the Caucasus converted to a zone of cooperation. Greater international attention, through multilateral organizations, could be helpful in reducing Central Asia's mounting problems – problems that will affect all the great powers actively engaged in the region. Attention should be given not only to conflict resolution in the Caspian region but also to social welfare issues such as poverty, environmental crises, sweeping disease epidemics, malnutrition, and power shortages. Participation of international organizations in conflict resolution, regional arms control, humanitarian assistance, and cooperation on a broad-range of economic issues, including economic reform, should be the cornerstone for devising constructive, multinational policies towards this region of newly independent states.

Part I

Breaking New Ground: The Caspian Region in the 21st Century

1

Geological Basins and Oil and Gas Reserves of the Greater Caspian Region[1]

Andrei V. Belopolsky and Manik Talwani

Introduction

The part of Central Asia around the Caspian Sea, commonly referred to as "the Caspian region", has been a subject of tremendous attention in the past few years. After the collapse of the Soviet Union this area, known as one of the oldest and most prolific petroleum provinces in the world, became open to foreign investors who were eager to pursue oil and gas exploration and production in the region. The estimates of hydrocarbon reserves in the region varied significantly, and it has even been speculated that the undiscovered Greater Caspian reserves rival those of the Persian Gulf countries. Since the time when the doors were first open to foreign investors, the prognosis for hydrocarbon exploration and production changed from highly optimistic to cautious. While some companies have already exited the region, others have been successful in pursuing production from the existing fields and discovering new ones.

This study focused on the evaluation of the different geological basins within the Greater Caspian region and assessment of the proven oil and gas reserves.

Geological basins of the Caspian region

Five countries surround the Caspian Sea: Azerbaijan, Iran, Kazakhstan, Russia, and Turkmenistan. Uzbekistan does not border the Caspian Sea but is usually considered to be a part of the "Caspian block". The Caspian Sea and surrounding areas are not a single geological basin. In fact, this area encompasses five different geological basins with different basin history, rock age and type, and hydrocarbon types and reserves. The political borders commonly do not follow the boundaries that separate the geological basins. In order to assess the existing reserve base and reserve potential, we have evaluated five geological basins with the Greater Caspian. These basins are: South Caspian, North Caspian, North Usturt, Mangyshlak, and Amu-Darya.

South Caspian basin

The South Caspian basin occupies the area of Azerbaijan, western Turkmenistan, and part of Iran (Figure 1.1). A significant portion of the basin lies offshore, with water depths varying from shallow (less than 20 m) to relatively deep (maximum depth 900 m). In contrast, the northern part of the Caspian Sea which belongs to the North Caspian basin separated from the South Caspian basin by The Absheron sill, is shallow with an average depth of 10 m. The South

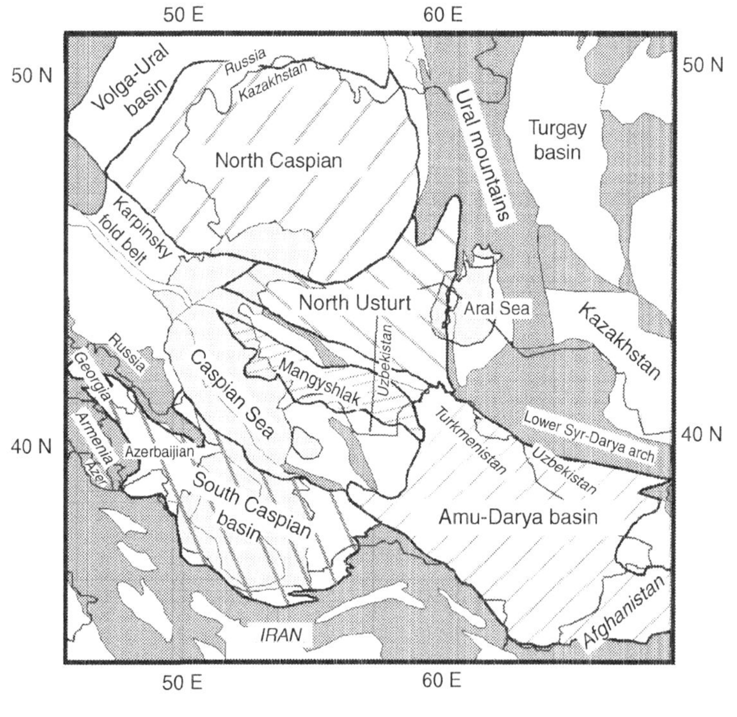

Figure 1.1 Sedimentary basins of the Caspian

Caspian basin is 400 km across in the northwest to southeast direction. It is located in the central part of a broader depression, which includes the Kura trough to the west and the coastal lowland of Turkmenistan to the east.

South Caspian is considered a Tertiary back-arch basin (Zonenshain and Le Pichon, 1986). It is suggested that an oceanic type crust underlies a 20-km thick sedimentary package. Oceanic crust has fast rates of subsidence that made possible the deposition of the extremely thick sedimentary package in a relatively short time. The low geothermal gradient (about 1.5°C per 100 m) provides favorable conditions for the preservation of hydrocarbons at significant depths (potentially up to 10 km).

Drilling on the South Caspian shelf in Azerbaijan and Turkmenistan (Alikhanov, 1978) revealed a 2500 – 3000 m, thick package of shallow water sediments that accumulated from the Late Jurassic to the Early Pliocene time. Mesozoic shales and sandstones with flysh-like intervals comprise most of the section. Tertiary deposits are represented by shales including carbonate-bituminous shales of the Maikopian suite (Oligocene–lower Miocene) which are considered to be a regional source rock, middle and upper Miocene shales and marles, and Meotic and Pontian (lower Pliocene) shales. The Turkmenistan shelf section consists mainly of shales, locally interbedded with evaporites.

A major change in sediment accumulation occurred in Middle Pliocene when sandstones and siltstones started being deposited in the basin. In Azerbaijan, these sediments lie transgressively on the Pontian (lower Pliocene) shales. The middle Pliocene sandstones and siltstones form oil reservoirs that are known as the "Productive Series." The thickness of the oil-bearing Productive Series varies from 1500 to 3500 m. It has been suggested (Alikhanov, 1978) that these sands and silts are deltaic deposits of the paleo-Volga River whose buried valley was disclosed by seismic surveys in the central part of the Caspian Sea (Clark, 1993). Upper Pliocene and Quaternary sediments up to 2000 m overlay middle Pliocene deposits. They are composed of clastic sediments brought in by the Volga and small mountain rivers.

The full thickness of sedimentary packages in the deeper parts of the basin is unknown because it has not been penetrated by drilling. Estimates from seismic profiles show the thickness of upper Pliocene-Quaternary deposits varying between 3 and 6 km and middle Pliocene oil-bearing deposits between 5 and 6 km. Seismic profiles also show significant deformation within the sedimentary package. A 100–120 km wide fold system with penetrating mud volcanoes occupies the western part of the basin (Abrams and Narimanov, 1997).

Most of the known South Caspian hydrocarbon fields are contained within structural traps. The traps vary from anticlinal folds to monoclines with various degree of reverse faulting and fracturing. Mud diapirs and mud volcanoes penetrate many structures. Structures are commonly located along clearly identifiable trends associated with underlying deep-seated Mesozoic faults reactivated during Cenozoic.

South Caspian is a mature basin from the exploration standpoint with over 150 years of commercial oil production. The deeper waters offshore (>50 m), however, remain a frontier area. The most prolific offshore trend is the Absheron sill that extends from Baku to the Turkmenistan shelf across the Caspian Sea. Many of the structures on the Absheron sill have been drilled and billion barrel fields discovered including the Azeri-Chirag-Guneshli field that is presently being developed by the Azerbaijan International Operating Company (AIOC) – a partnership between BP, Unocal, Devon, ExxonMobil, TPAO, Itochu, Statoil, Delta Hess, Ramco, LUKoil, and Socar. The reserves are estimated at 4.3 billion barrels of oil and 3.5 trillion cubic feet of gas. Current production (July 2000) is 100 000 barrels/day.

Other significant fields are located onshore or in the proximity of the shoreline. Many of the onshore fields have passed the point of maximum production but enhanced recovery techniques are expected to extend the lifespan of these fields. Deep water (>80 m) structures have certain potential but their drilling is slowed by technical difficulties such as availability of deep water drilling rigs in the landlocked basin. The area offshore of Turkmenistan has been underexplored and remains an attractive exploration target.

Recent drilling in the South Caspian basin has not yet yielded new oil fields but a large gas field, Shah Deniz, was discovered in 200 m of water by a BP-operated consortium. The field is estimated to contain 15 – 25 tcf of gas. The development of the field is complicated by the lack of infrastructure for gas export. Some of the other recently signed production sharing agreements (PSAs) include Inam (BP-Shell-Socar), Absheron (Chevron-TotalFinaElf), and Nakhichivan (ExxonMobil-Socar). Two large consortia – the Caspian International Petroleum Company (Pennzoil, Agip, LUKoil, and Socar) and The North Absheron Operating Company (BP Amoco, Unocal, Itochu, Delta Hess, and Socar) – were dissolved after disappointing drilling results.

Total proven reserves of the South Caspian basin are estimated at 6.5 billion barrels of oil and 16.5 tcf of gas.

North Caspian basin

The North Caspian basin (also known as Pri-Caspian) is located on the southeastern margin of the Russian Plate and extends to the northern coast of the Caspian Sea (Fig. 1.1). Approximately two-thirds of the basin are located on the territory of Kazakhstan; the rest remains within the territory of the Russian Federation. A large portion of the Russian Caspian shelf, however, is off limits for hydrocarbon exploration because it is a sturgeon spawning ground.

The North Caspian is considered a passive margin basin of the Late Proterozoic–Paleozoic age. The basin is bounded by the Ural Mountains to the east, and the Volga-Ural platform to the north. Two super giant onshore fields exist in the basin: Tengiz (estimated recoverable reserves of 4 – 6 billion barrels of oil) and Karachaganak (estimated recoverable reserves of 2.4 billion barrels of oil and condensate and 16 tcf of gas). There is also a number of smaller fields in the basin.

The most recent discovery in the North Caspian basin is the Kashagan field drilled by the Offshore Kazakhstan International Oil Company (OKIOC), a consortium of BG, BP, Agip, ExxonMobil, TotalFinaElf, Statoil, Shell, Inpex, and Phillips. The discovery well, Kashagan East-1, announced in July 2000, tested at 3775 barrels/day and 7 million cf/day. The secondary appraisal well, Kashagan East, is planned to be spud in the Fall of 2000, 40 km away from the discovery well. The enormous size of the structure and very encouraging results of the discovery well foresee a new true super giant field capable of affecting significantly the economy of the region.

Tengiz, Kashagan, Karachaganak, as well as the smaller but still significant Kenkiyak and Zhanazhol fields are all carbonate platforms that consist of stacked sequences of middle Devonian to Lower Permian carbonate rocks. Kungurian (lower Permian) salt provides the seal for the hydrocarbons. The depth to reservoir of Karachaganak, Tengiz, Astrakhan, and Zhanazhol fields varies from 3 to 5.2 km (Bagrintseva and Belozerova, 1990). Rocks forming the reservoirs are shallow-water marine carbonates. The complex facies architecture of Tengiz and Karachaganak fields results in abrupt changes in porosity and permeability, a patchy distribution of reservoirs, and significant thickness changes within the reservoir. Many reservoirs are fractured.

The intensive karstification in the upper part of the section caused the development of high-capacity cavity porosity.

The main hydrocarbon migration paths were updip from the faster subsiding parts of the basin. The reservoir fill occurred in multiple stages. First, the oil pools formed at the end of Paleozoic. Later, with further subsidence of the basin, gas was generated and entered oil-filled traps changing the pools into gas-oil, gas-oil-condensate, and gas. The hydrocarbon migration path patterns explain why northern, western and southwestern parts of the basin are gas-prone while the east and southeast are oil-prone.

A significant portion of the North Caspian basin that lies offshore under the shallow waters of the Caspian Sea remains relatively unexplored. The proximity of the Tengiz super giant field makes that portion of the basin even more attractive. Technical difficulties such as very shallow (< 5 m) waters and the coastal transitional environment impaired previous exploration efforts. The discovery of the supergiant Kashagan field in 3 m of water, the largest structure in the area, gives hope that more fields of significant size are going to be discovered.

The important recent discovery well Khvalynskaya-1 on the Severny block was drilled in 2000 by LUKoil, a major Russian oil company, in the Russian sector of the Caspian Sea. The company announced the recoverable reserves of the field to be 2.2 billion barrels of oil.

North Usturt basin

The North Usturt Basin is located on the territory of Kazakhstan and Uzbekistan and occupies 240 000 sq km. It is located south of the North Caspian basin and is bounded by the Mugodzar and Chelkar downwarps on the northeast, by Aral-Kyzylkum zone of highs on the east, and by the Mangyshlak-Central Usturt system of highs (Fig. 1.1). On the west, the basin extends under the Caspian Sea.

The North Usturt basin is a foreland basin. Seismic data and drilling in the North Usturt basin revealed folded basement covered by a package of sedimentary rocks up to 12 km thick. The sedimentary cover consists of the following sequences: Carboniferous–lower Permian, middle and upper Triassic, Jurassic, Cretaceous, Paleogene and Neogene.

The distribution of reserves among the plays is the following: middle–upper Jurassic rocks contain over 60 percent of oil and gas, Triassic have 10 percent, the lower Cretaceous section contains 21 percent, and 8 percent are contained within the Eocene rocks.

Carboniferous–lower Permian carbonates and clastic rocks comprise the lower part of the sedimentary cover in the eastern part of the basin. The average thickness of the section is 1000 m. Lower Triassic redbeds and local volcano-clastics are 3000 m thick on the Buzachi Peninsula. The section contains argillites within the redbeds that may serve as a regional seal for lower reservoirs. The middle Triassic section is mainly clastic with a thickness up to 2 km. Two reservoirs with porosity up to 20 percent are present in the Kalamkas area. The Upper Triassic section is made of clastic rocks up to 600 m thick. They are similar to the Upper Triassic of the Prorva area of the North Caspian basin. Overlying sediments have the following thickness: Jurassic (150 m), Cretaceous (2500 m), Paleogene (1200 m), and Neogene (500 m).

The Triassic oil and gas play is composed of alternating sand-silt and clay beds 3–5 m thick. Sandstone reservoirs have up to 17 percent porosity and up to 30 mDarcies permeability. Oil has been found in the Triassic sediments in the Koltyk area.

The Middle–Upper Jurassic play is made of clays, argillites, siltstones, and sandstones. The thickness varies from 200 to 1000 m. Siltstone and sandstones form reservoirs and have high 28–32 percent porosity and 1.5–2 Darcy permeability. Upper Jurassic clay-carbonate unit forms a hydrocarbon seal. Commercial discoveries in the Jurassic have been made in the Karazhanbas, Severo-Buzachi, Kalamkas, Arman, Arystan, Karakuduk, Koltyk, Komsomol, and Vostochno-Karaturun fields.

The lower Cretaceous (Neocomian) play is represented by interbedded sands, silts and clays, which range in thickness from 150 to 850 m. The reservoirs are largely siltstones, and Aptian clays act as a seal. Commercial amounts of hydrocarbons have been discovered in the Karazhanbas, Severo-Buzachi, and Kalamkas fields.

The Eocene play is in the upper part of the strata locally known as "Kuma Horizon" and is represented by marls, siltstones, and clays. The reservoirs are siltstones which display porosity of 36 percent and 30 mDarcy permeability. The thickness is 10–30 m, and Eocene clays form the seal. Gas has been found in the five fields of the Chumyshty-Bazay group.

Recent drilling in the North Usturt basin included Ostrovnaya #1 well drilled in 1998 by Oryx in the Mertvyi Kultuk area. The well found a subcommercial (30–50 million barrels) oil accumulation in the upper Jurassic section. Kerr McGee, the company that took over Oryx, still has a number of PSAs in the area and is expected to drill their Salkenskaya prospect with expected reserves of 1 billion barrels in 2000.

Total estimated proven reserves of North Usturt basin are 2.2 billion barrels of oil and 1.41 tcf of gas. The possible oil reserves are estimated at 3.4 billion barrels of oil and 2.22 tcf of gas.

Mangyshlak basin

The Mangyshlak basin lies almost entirely within the territory of Kazakhstan with a small part of the basin extending into the Uzbekistan territory (Fig. 1.1). It is located on the western part of the Turan epi-Paleozoic platform.

Tectonic activity in the Riphean-Vendian time led to crustal tension and rifting with development of the Central Mangyshlak and Tuarkyr-Karaaudan rift systems (Murzagaliyev, 1996). The Central Mangyshlak rift formed in the Early Paleozoic time. Deep drilling showed that Paleozoic sediments consist of the upper-middle Devonian and lower Carboniferous clastics and lower Permian–Carboniferous carbonate rocks. The Mangyshlak and Usturt plates collided with the East European continent during the Early Cimmerian tectonic event. Tangential compression in the collision zone led to formation of inverse highs with upthrust-overthrust activity. The result was a series of linear mega-anticlines and mega-synclines. The rocks of the Permo-Triassic age are strongly deformed.

The Tuakyr-Karaaudan rift formed probably in the Early Paleozoic. Middle Paleozoic deposits are strongly deformed and contain basic and ultra-basic rocks of Devonian and Early Carboniferous age (Murzagaliyev, 1996). These rocks are interpreted as ophiolites that were probably fragments of older oceanic crust. They are overlain by the red Permo-Triassic molasses formation composed of conglomerates with tuff and lava beds. The total thickness of the molasse formation is 4–5 km.

Exploration activity in the 1980s in the Mangyshlak basin was focused on Triassic and Jurassic rocks of the Zhetbay-Uzen structural step, and Triassic rocks of the Peschanomys-Rakushech, Karadin, and Zhazgurlin tectonic zones of South Mangyshlak. Exploration targets were mainly anticlinal structures identified on seismic profiles. Despite years of exploration in the central part of the South Mangyshlak basin, no significant hydrocarbon discoveries have been made. The exploration activity since 1990 was targeting Upper and Middle Triassic in the eastern part of the Sedendyk depression and the northern part of the Karagin saddle (Popkov *et al.*, 1992). Paleozoic rocks of Mangyshlak also may contain oil. A commercial discovery in Paleozoic reservoir rocks has been found in the Oymash area. Other areas of the basin, such as Eastern Mangyshlak, the Uchkuduk depression, and the continuation of the Mangyshlak basin offshore Caspian have not been explored for oil and gas. Exploration in the Eastern Mangyshlak and South Usturt has been disappointing – a single gas field (Kansuy) was discovered. Thick Jurassic and Cretaceous reservoirs and seals are commonly disrupted at the crests of anticlines; the Triassic section is also strongly deformed.

Recent seismic surveys showed a connection between the Uchkuduk depression and the Zhazgurli depression of the southern Mangyshlak. This suggests that the Uchkuduk depression contains Middle and upper Triassic oil and gas reservoirs similar to those in the southern Mangyshlak (Popkov, *et al.*, 1992).

There is an increasing amount of interest in the northern part of the Buzachi Peninsula and offshore on the Caspian Sea shelf. Seismic surveys demonstrate that many onshore structures on the Buzuchi Peninsula extend into the Caspian Sea. A large structure of the Jurassic-Cretaceous age has been identified north of the Kalamkas anticlinal zone and west of Karazhanbas (Popkov, *et al.*, 1992).

Amu-Darya basin

The Amu-Darya basin extends over an area of 370 000 sq. km of eastern Turkmenistan and western Uzbekistan. Another 57 000 sq. km are located in the neighboring countries, in particular, northern Afganistan (Fig. 1.1). The southwestern border of the basin lies at the base of the Kopet Dag, an Alpine age mountain range. The Amu-Darya basin is positioned within the Turan plate, a feature that extends into the Caspian Sea and farther west into Europe and is known as the Scythian platform. On the north, the basin is connected with the West Siberian platform through the Turgay depression.

The sedimentary section of the Amu-Darya basin consists of lower and middle Jurassic clastics with coal beds, Callovian-Oxfordian carbonates, Kimmeridgean and Tithonian carbonates and evaporites, lower and upper Cretaceous clastic deposits, and Paleogene carbonates and clastics (Clarke, 1994). This section is commonly referred to as the "Intermediate complex" that could be up to 10 km thick.

The Amu-Darya Basin has a complex tectonic structure. A large graben filled with 3 km of Permian-Triassic deposits is identified beneath the Khiva downwarp that has a 4–5 km thick sedimentary rock cover. The Beurdeshik structural step is located to the west of the Khiva downwarp and is a transitional feature to the Central Kara Kum arch farther west. This arch is interpreted as a microplate caught up in the Hercynian orogenic belt (Clark, 1994).

More than 130 gas, gas-condensate, and oil fields have been discovered in the Amu-Darya basin. Of these, 60 percent are in western Uzbekistan and 40 percent are in eastern Turkmenistan. There are three regional plays: lower–middle Jurassic clastic rocks, upper Jurassic carbonates, and lower Cretaceous carbonate-clastic rocks. There are also two local plays: upper Cretaceous carbonates and clastic and Paleogene carbonates.

The Lower–Middle Jurassic play consists of sandstones, siltstones, argillites, and thin coal beds. Their thickness varies from 100 to 400 m. The reservoirs are not continuous and in general have low porosity. Seals are local and are not favorable for the large hydrocarbon accumulations. Fifteen gas and gas-condensate pools have been discovered on the Bukhara, Chardzhou, and Beurdeshik structural steps and some oil pools have been found in this part of the section. The estimates show that this play accounts for 15 percent of the undiscovered resources of the province and essentially is unexplored.

The Upper Jurassic play is made of limestones with a wide range of porosity and permeability. The thickness of the play zones varies from 10 to 60 m. The thick Kimmeridgian evaporites form the seal. Where evaporites are missing, argillaceous rocks may act as a seal. In the areas where argillites or evaporites are absent, the hydrocarbons have migrated upward to form pools in the Cretaceous or to escape entrapment. Gas fields have been found on the Beurdeshik, Khiva, Zaunguz, and Chardzhou structural features. This play is assessed as carrying 56 percent of the undiscovered petroleum resources of the province.

The Lower Cretaceous–Cenomanian play includes carbonate-clastic deposits of the Neocomian–lower Aptian and predominantly clastic deposits of the upper Aptian, Albian, and Cenomanian. The section consists largely of 20–60 m thick sandstones, rare carbonates, and clays 10–200 m thick. Total thickness of the sedimentary package ranges from 700 to 1600 m. An upper Albian clay unit, 100–130 m thick, forms a regional seal for this play. In the central part of the basin, the "Shatlyk" Horizon of the upper part of the Hautervian Stage carries 90 percent of the discovered gas of this play. The reservoir rock is red sandstone with good porosity and permeability. The reservoir beds are hydrodynamically sealed. The Shatlyk Horizon rocks form the reservoir of the super giant Dauletabad-Donmez gas field. This play hosts more than 50 percent of the discovered gas of the basin and is estimated to contain 20 percent of the undiscovered petroleum resources in Amu-Darya.

A few small discoveries have been made in the Upper Cretaceous play of the Bukhara tectonic step and Central Kara Kum arch. Small pools have been found in Maastrichtian limestones in the Badkhyz-Karabil zone of highs. Four thin play zones are recognized in the Upper Cretaceous of the Central Kara Kum arch, in the Cenomanian and Turonian Stages. They consist of fine-grained sandstones. Very large pools are present in the Upper Cretaceous in the Gazli field. Two gas-bearing horizons in the Cenomanian rocks contain 70 percent of the reserves of the field.

Small amounts of oil have been found in Paleogene carbonates in the Karabil field of the Badkhyz-Karabil zone of highs. Reservoirs are both carbonates and sandstones with Eocene clay forming the seal. The play is assessed to contain less than 10 percent of the undiscovered petroleum resources of the basin.

The northern part of the Chardzhou structural step potentially contains structural traps. Here, the lower Cretaceous deposits rest on an erosional surface above Kimmeridgian-Tithonian beds. Facies changes and pinch-outs could act as potential reservoirs that trapped hydrocarbons migrating from deeper parts of the Jurassic basin of deposition.

There are a number of undrilled structures in the Bakhardok monocline and northern margin of the Cis-Kopet Dag foredeep. Three main plays are recognized here: Oxfordian, Tithonian, and Valanginian, with Tithonian being the most promising. The lower–middle Jurassic, Triassic, Permian, and Carboniferous sections also may contain commercial amounts of hydrocarbons. New discoveries are also possible in the Mesozoic section in the Central Kara Kum arch despite the mature stage of exploration in the area. Southeastern Turkmenistan may contain significant gas and condensate reserves in the upper Jurassic both below and above the upper Jurassic evaporite in the Murgab region.

The most promising area in terms of oil and gas exploration is the Yashlag area in the central part of the Murgab region. The late Jurassic basin here has adequate source beds and similar conditions to those of the northern basin's margin where the Kukdumalak field has been discovered. O'Connor and Sonnenberg (1991) assess the undiscovered resources of this area at 120 tcf of gas, 7 billion barrels of condensate and 3–4 billion barrels of oil.

The Amu-Darya basin is gas-prone. Oil is found only as small pools in the Chardzhou and Bukhara gas-oil regions. Of the total assessed hydrocarbon resources in the basin, 4 percent is oil and 96 percent is gas. The same ratio is assumed for the undiscovered resources.

Ulmishek and Masters (1993) estimate that the entire Amu-Darya basin contains 0.7 billion barrels of oil in identified reserves and 3 billion in undiscovered reserves. For gas, the cumulative production is 86 tcf, identified reserves are 200 tcf and undiscovered reserves are assessed as 75 tcf.

Comparison of the Caspian region oil and gas reserves with the world hydrocarbon reserves

The estimates of the world ultimate crude oil recovery range from 1650 to 3200 billion barrels, with most of the estimates between 2 and 3 trillion barrels (Edwards, 1997). Future discoveries are forecast to be 1005 billion barrels of oil (Marbo, 1996). World estimated ultimate recoverable conventional crude resources are the sum of cumulative production (720 billion barrels of oil), reserves (1111 billions), and future discoveries and field growth (1005 billions), totaling 2836 billion barrels of oil. World natural gas reserves are estimated to be 5171.8 tcf (BP Statistical Review).

Table 1.1 shows the range of both proven and possible petroleum reserves estimated in this study. The estimates vary significantly but one can see the scale of resources available. Kazakhstan and Azerbaijan have significant proven oil reserves while both Turkmenistan and Uzbekistan both have less than a billion barrels of discovered oil. Kazakhstan has the most potential (50–80 billion barrels), much of which is related to the size of the recent supergiant Kashagan discovery. Turkmenistan leads the four Caspian countries in gas reserves with 101–105 tcf, and both Uzbekistan and Kazakhstan are not too far behind. Azerbaijan, traditionally not considered a gas-rich country, has emerged as a potential gas-exporter with the recent large gas discovery in Shah Deniz and potential gas discoveries in South Caspian offshore structures. The range of total proven reserves of the four Caspian countries is 14.7 to 31.3 billion barrels of oil and 242.6 to 373 tcf of gas.

The daily oil and gas production rates of the Central Asia countries are given in Table 1.2 (data from Wood Mackenzie Report, McCutcheon and Osbon, 2000). Kazakhstan was the largest oil producer in 2000 with 716 000 barrels a day (b/d). Azerbaijan was second with 290 000 b/d. Uzbekistan's daily production was 172 000 b/d, and Turkmenistan produced 146 000 b/d. Combined daily production of

Table 1.1 Estimated proven and possible Caspian oil and gas reserves

Country	Estimated proven oil (billion barrels)	Estimated proven gas (tcf)	Estimated possible oil, billion (barrels)	Estimated possible gas (tcf)
Azerbaijan	3.6–7	10.6–30	7.0–14	30–60.2
Kazakhstan	10.0–22	65–83	50–80	65–200
Turkmenistan	0.5–1	101–155	1–1.4	101–277
Uzbekistan	0.6–1.3	66–105	1.0–5	66–127
Total	14.7–31.3	242.6–373	59–100.4	262–664.2

Source: Compiled from various sources.

Table 1.2 Daily oil and gas production rates

Production	Oil (thousand b/d)			Gas, (thousand cubic feet a day)		
	1990	2000	2020	1990	2000	2020
Azerbaijan	251	290	1 093	960	606	3 973
Kazakhstan	516	716	2 531	643	1009	5 729
Turkmenistan	114	146	251	8 491	4 286	12 732
Uzbekistan	68	172	97	3 935	5 253	6 421
Total	949	1 324	3 972	14 029	11 154	28 855

Source: Wood Mackenzie (McCutcheon and Osbon, 2000).

the four Caspian region countries in 2000 was 1 324 000 b/d. This indicates an increase of 375 000 b/d, or 28 percent, compared to the 1990 level (Table 1.2). Wood Mackenzie also predicts a threefold increase in production to 3 972 000 b/d by 2020 (McCutcheon and Osbon, 2000).

Uzbekistan currently leads with 5 253 000 cf/d gas production, followed by Turkmenistan with 4 286 000 cf/d. Turkmenistan's daily gas production, however, is expected to significantly surpass Uzbekistan's production with 12 732 000 cf/d in 2020 (Wood Mackenzie). Azerbaijan's and Kazakhstan's gas production is significantly smaller (Table 1.2).

Tables 1.3 and 1.4 contain data on the proven oil and gas reserves by country reported by BP Statistical Review, Oil and Gas Journal, and World Oil. The countries are listed in descending order based on their proven reserves. Kazakhstan and Azerbaijan occupy the 15th and 17ths places, respectively, and have oil reserves comparable to those of countries like Oman, Angola, Brazil, and Algeria (Table 1.3). This estimate does not take into account the recent supergiant Kashagan discovery offshore Kazakhstan that can propel this independent republic to much higher ranks. Both Uzbekistan and Turkmenistan trail with only 0.6 and 0.5 billion barrels of oil in proven reserves, respectively.

Turkmenistan has the largest amount of gas reserves out of the four Central Asia counties evaluated in this study (Table 1.4). Turkmenistan's gas reserves are estimated at 101 tcf of gas which places Turkmenistan in between Iraq (109.8–112.6 tcf) and Malaysia (81.7–85.8 tcf). Uzbekistan (66.2 tcf) and Kazakhstan (65–70.6 tcf) also contain significant gas reserves comparable to those of Indonesia and Canada (Table 1.4). Azerbaijan's gas reserves have increased substantially with the discovery of the giant Shah Deniz field and are likely to increase with the drilling of the offshore structures in South Caspian.

Conclusion

The Caspian region contains five petroleum basins with different geologic history, reservoir types, source rocks, and types of hydrocarbons. This diversity creates a wide variety of play types which makes this region a highly attractive area for hydrocarbon exploration and development.

Kazakhstan contains the largest amount of proven oil among the Caspian countries and also has the highest potential for future oil discoveries. Kazakhstan has up to 22 billion barrels of proven oil reserves, and the appraisal of the recently discovered Kashagan field could

Table 1.3. World proven oil reserves

Country	Oil, end of 1999, BP (in billions of barrels)	Oil, January 1, 1999, OGJ (in billions of barrels)	Oil, January 1, 1999, World Oil (in billions of barrels)
Saudi Arabia	263.5	261.5	261.4
Iraq	112.5	112.5	99
United Arab Emirates	97.8	97.8	63.9
Kuwait	96.5	96.5	94.7
Iran	89.7	89.7	92.9
Venezuela	72.6	72.6	45.5
Russia	48.6	48.6	55.1
Libya	29.5	29.5	26.9
USA	28.6	21	21
Mexico	28.4	47.8	28.4
China	24	24	33.5
Nigeria	22.5	22.5	22.5
Norway	10.8	10.9	11.9
Algeria	9.2	9.2	13
Kazakhstan	8	5.4	7
Brazil	7.3	7.1	7.5
Azerbaijan	7	1.2	N/A
Canada	6.8	4.9	5.6
Angola	5.4	5.4	4
Oman	5.3	5.3	5.6
UK	5.2	5.2	5.2
Indonesia	5	5	8.6
India	4.8	4	3
Yemen	4	4	1.9
Malaysia	3.9	3.9	4.6

Table 1.4 World proven natural gas reserves

Country	Gas, end of 1999, BP (in tcf)	Gas, January 1, 1999, OGJ (in tcf)	Gas, January 1, 1999, World Oil (in tcf)
Russia	1 700	1 700	1 705
Iran	812.3	812.3	812.2
Qatar	300	300	395
United Arab Emirates	212	212	209
Saudi Arabia	204.5	204.5	208
USA	164	164	164
Algeria	159.7	130.3	137.5
Venezuela	142.5	142.5	146.6
Nigeria	124	124	124
Iraq	109.8	109.8	112.6
Turkmenistan	101	101	N/A
Malaysia	81.7	81.7	85.8
Indonesia	72.3	72.3	77.1
Uzbekistan	66.2	66.2	N/A
Kazakhstan	65	65	70.6
Canada	63.9	63.9	63.9
Netherlands	62.5	63.1	62.5
Kuwait	52.7	52.7	56.4
China	48.3	48.3	42.4
Libya	46.4	46.4	46.3
Australia	44.6	44.6	28.4
Norway	41.4	41.4	43.6
Ukraine	39.6	39.6	N/A
Egypt	35.2	31.5	37.2
Mexico	30.1	63.5	30.3

Table 1.4 World proven natural gas reserves *cont*

Country	Gas, end of 1999, BP (in tcf)	Gas, January 1, 1999, OGJ (in tcf)	Gas, January 1, 1999, World Oil (in tcf)
Azerbaijan	30	4.4	N/A
Oman	28.4	28.4	29.1
UK	26.7	27	26.7
Argentina	24.2	24.1	24.2
India	22.9	19	12.9
Pakistan	21.6	21.6	21.6
Trinidad and Tobago	19.8	18.3	19.8
Yemen	16.9	16.9	17
Brunei	13.8	13.8	9.6
Romania	13.2	13.2	4.1
Thailand	12.5	12.5	14.8
Germany	12	12.3	12
Bangladesh	10.6	10.6	N/A
Italy	8.1	8.1	7.8
Brazil	8	8	8.7
Colombia	6.9	6.9	8
Vietnam	6.8	6.8	6
Papua New Guinea	5.4	5.4	14
Bolivia	4.3	4.3	5.3
Bahrain	3.9	4.2	N/A
Ecuador	3.7	3.7	3.7
Denmark	3.4	3.9	3.2
Hungary	2.9	3.1	1.4
Peru		7	7.1
Syria		8.5	8.4

Table 1.4 World proven natural gas reserves *cont*

Country	Gas, end of 1999, BP (in tcf)	Gas, January 1, 1999, OGJ (in tcf)	Gas, January 1, 1999, World Oil (in tcf)
Angola		1.6	1.7
Cameroon		3.9	3.9
Congo (Brazzaville)		3.2	4.3
Gabon		1.2	3.5
Tunisia		2.8	2.3

N/A – data not available.
Source: *BP Statistical Review* (www.bp.com), *Oil and Gas Journal* (OGJ, ogj.pennet.com), *World Oil* (www.worldoil.com).

significantly increase this number. A large part of Kazakhstan lying in the shallow waters of the North Caspian remains underexplored. The hydrocarbon prospecting in this area, however, presents a large environmental threat due to the extremely fragile ecosystem. Azerbaijan has the second largest oil reserves among the Central Asian countries. The onshore exploration is at a mature stage and new discoveries are not likely to be large. The focus in the onshore area will be on the enhanced and secondary recovery from the existing under-performing fields. Large discoveries, many of them likely to be gas and/or condensate, are expected to be found offshore in the deeper waters of the South Caspian.

Turkmenistan and Uzbekistan have small oil reserves (less than a billion barrels each) but have tremendous gas reserves (101 and 66.2 tcf respectively). A significant part of Turkmenistan offshore Caspian has substantial potential. Kazakhstan also has significant proven gas reserves, and recent discoveries in South Caspian helped Azerbaijan to emerge as a potential net gas exporter.

There is no doubt that the Caspian region has resources and potential to become one of the world's prime oil and gas producing areas. It has the potential to produce almost 4 million barrels a day by 2015 but the remoteness from world markets, political risks, and environmental concerns may delay peak production. Despite all of that, the Caspian region will play a very important role in the hydrocarbon exploration and production of the 21st century.

Notes

This chapter is based on the results of a research project which was part of a multidiscipline study "Unlocking the Assets: Energy and the Future of Central Asia and the Caucasus–A Political, Economic, and Cultural Analysis" conducted by the James A. Baker III Institute for Public Policy at Rice University in Houston, Texas (Belopolsky *et al.*, 1998).

References

Abrams, M.A., and Narimanov, A.A. (1997). "Geochemical Evaluation of Hydrocarbons and Their Potential Sources in the Western South Caspian Depression, Republic of Azerbaijan", *Marine and Petroleum* Geology, 14(4), pp. 451–68.

Alikhanov, E.N. (1978) *Geochimiya Kaspiiskogo morya* (*Geochemistry of the Caspian Sea*). Baku: Elm Publishing House, (in Russian).

Bagrintseva, K.I., and Belozerova, G.Y. (1990). Types and properties of reservoirs in sub-salt sediments of the North Caspian depression. *Petroleum Geology*, 24, 7/8, pp. 230–2.

Belopolsky, A.V., Talwani, M., and Berry, D.L. (1998). "Geology and Petroleum Potential of the Caspian Sea Region", in: *Unlocking the Assets: Energy and the Future of Central Asia and the Caucasus*. Houston, TX, Rice University.

BP Statistical Review, www.bp.com

Clarke, J.W. (1993). "Observations On the Geology of Azerbaijan", *International Geology Review*, 35, pp. 1089–92.

Clarke, J.W. (1994). "Petroleum Potential of the Amu-Dar'ya Province, Western Uzbekistan and Eastern Turkmenistan", *International Geology Review*, 36, pp. 407–15.

Edwards, J.D. (1997). "Crude Oil and Alternate Energy Production Forecasts for the Twenty-first Century: The End of Hydrocarbon Era", *AAPG Bulletin*, 81, 8, pp. 1292–1305.

Marbo, R. (1996). "The World's Oil Supply 1930–2050, a Review Article", *The Journal of Energy Literature*, 2 1, pp. 25–34.

McCutcheon, H., and Osbon, R. (2000). "Who Holds the Key to the Caspian?" in: *Caspian Key Players*, Wood Mackenzie Report.

Murzagaliyev, D.M. (1996). "Riftogenesis and Oil-gas Potential of Mangyshlak", *Geologiya Nefti i Gaza*, 5, pp. 36–9.

O'Connor, R.B. Jr. and Sonnenberg, S. (1991). "Amu Darya Liquids Potential Indicated", *Oil and Gas Journal*, June 3, pp. 104–9.

Popkov, V.I., Rabinovich, A.A., and Timurziyev, A.I. (1992). "New Directions for Oil and Gas Exploration in Mangyshlak", *Geologiya Nefti I Gaza*, 6, pp. 14–15.

Ulmishek, G.F., and Masters, C.D. (1993). "Petroleum Resources in the Former Soviet Union", US Geological Survey Open File Report 93–316.

Zonenshain, L.P., and Le Pichon, X. (1986). "Deep Basins of the Black Sea and Caspian Sea as Remnants of Mesozoic Back-arc Basins", *Tectoniphysics*, 123, pp. 181–211.

2

Confronting Independence: Political Overview

Martha Brill Olcott

After the euphoria of gaining independence settles down, the elites of each new sovereign country inevitably stumble upon the challenges of building a viable state. The inexperienced governments soon venture into unfamiliar territory when they have to formulate foreign policy or when they try to forge beneficial economic ties with foreign investors. What often proves especially difficult is the process of redefining the new country's relationship with its old colonial ruler or federation partners.

In addition to these often-encountered hurdles, the newly independent states of Central Asia – Kazakhstan, Kyrgyzstan, Tajikistan, Turkmenistan, and Uzbekistan – have faced a host of particular challenges. Some of these emanate from the Soviet legacy, others from the ethnic and social fabric of each individual polity. Yet another group stems from the peculiarities of intra-regional dynamics. Finally, the fledgling states have been struggling to step out of their traditional isolation and build relations with states outside of their neighborhood. This paper seeks to offer an overview of all the challenges that the Central Asian countries have confronted in the process of consolidating their sovereignty. Despite all the talk of a larger Caspian region, this paper argues that the five states of Central Asia form a political space distinctive from Azerbaijan and the Transcaucasian states, featuring a shared history and economic orientation, and facing common challenges for development. Although all these states participated in the Soviet experience, the five newly independent states of Central Asia differ in their pre-Soviet history, religious composition, and geographic and economic orientation.

The challenge of independence

What best distinguishes the birth of the Central Asian states from that of any other sovereign country is the incredible weakness of pro-independence movements throughout the region. In fact, both the elites and the masses were reluctant to leave the imperial union to which their homelands belonged.

The Central Asians insistence on preserving the union was a well-founded result of several realizations. First, the level of national self-awareness throughout the region was quite low. Not only did none of the Central Asian states have a history of previous statehood, but also their boundaries and even the peoples for whom they were named were, to a great extent, political creations of the Soviet period. Azerbaijan, in contrast, enjoyed a brief pre-Soviet history as an independent state, and sought independence when the demise of the Soviet Union was imminent. Secondly, the checkered demographic and religious make-up of the new entities forebode the difficulties associated with the integration of all communities into a single nation. Finally, the region constituted a common geopolitical, cultural, and religious space that did not include Azerbaijan, since the majority of Azeris belong to Shi'ia Islam rather than to the Sunni Islam which is predominant in Central Asia. The leaders recognized the great challenges that the legacy of interdependence and dependence on the former metropolis would pose to the new sovereign states.

Since the outset of independence the region's leaders have struggled with the task of strengthening the weak sense of nationhood among the Central Asian peoples. The Soviet-trained presidents took the collapse of the Soviet Union as synonymous with their republics' national liberation. Thus each of these men perceived their new states to be the national homelands of the community whose name they bore. As a result the three pillars of their nation-building strategies became the resuscitation of the indigenous languages, the revival of religion, and the reinterpretation of history.

Soon after gaining independence all Central Asian legislatures passed laws which granted the titular nationality's language the status of official language. These so-called "language laws" envisioned a gradual transition away from Russian in all spheres of public life. Non-indigenous-language speakers were given a deadline by which to master the new language (Hunter, 1996, p. 47).

In societies like Uzbekistan and Turkmenistan, where the level of mastery of the native language had always been high, the shift has pretty much taken place already. While Kazakhs and Kyrgyz also feel increasingly obliged to use their native language in preference to Russian, the transition has been much more painful. In Kazakhstan, many adults simply do not know their 'own' language. In Kyrgyzstan, many senior officials and other members of the Soviet elite had attenuated language skills, which they have been forced to strengthen since independence. Still, it is curious to note that during his last visit to the US in June 1997, President Akaev addressed his audiences in Russian, even though the interpreter, who was also Kyrgyz, could translate fluently from his native tongue into English.[1]

The return to pre-Soviet norms of self-identity has also brought back the awareness that a Central Asian perhaps ought to behave like a Muslim, even if he in actuality does not practice the religion. Most of the return to Islam which is evident today in Central Asia should thus be seen in the context of this effort to restore cultural continuity.

To a certain extent the nation-building strategies of the Central Asian governments have been successful, as increasing numbers of people choose to use their native language and know more about their history and traditions. We should not forget, however, that the Central Asian states are all multinational in composition. In the most homogeneous of them – Uzbekistan and Turkmenistan – the eponymous community makes up slightly over 70 percent of the population. About a quarter of Tajikistan's citizens are ethnic Uzbek, and about 8 percent are ethnic Russians. In Kyrgyzstan, the former account for 15 percent of the population, and the latter about 22 percent. At about 40 percent, the Kazakhs in Kazakhstan do not even hold a majority, while the Russian minority is as big as 38 percent of the population.[2]

The governments' efforts to create ethno-national communities, rather than to consolidate multi-national states, frightened and alienated the ethnic minorities. This development gave rise to new challenges to independent statehood. Some of the states have faced severe shortages of highly educated professionals. In others, the disgruntled minorities have been perceived as a tinderbox for inter-ethnic strife.

Independence left most Russians and other non-Asians with the uneasy feeling of being "stranded" in an increasingly alien society. In Turkmenistan, Uzbekistan, and Tajikistan the bulk of the Russian population consisted of Moscow's administrators, specialists working in different industries, military personnel, and other highly trained professionals. In the first couple of years of independence Russian emigration skyrocketed, as most were afraid of Islamic fundamentalism or discrimination on the basis of language and nationality (Fuller, 1994, pp. 109-10). The outstream led to severe shortages of professionals in such fields as medicine, education, and technical industry. In fact, these shortages became so severe that for a time the Uzbek government attempted to stop emigration, by a combination of blandishments, guarantees, and imposed impediments, such as the 1992 ban on private lease or purchase of shipping containers.

In both states, the presence of a large Russian population made the evolution toward ethnically defined statehood impossible. For the most part better educated than the eponymous peoples, and dominating jobs in industry, administration, and the specialized services which Soviet hiring practices made it difficult for Asians to fill, the Russians had seen themselves in the Soviet period to be part of a much larger state in which they were the numerical and cultural superiors. The collapse of the USSR left the non-indigenous populations of both Kyrgyzstan and Kazakhstan suddenly aware that they were cut off from that larger body and that, in the case of the first at least, they were now a distinct minority, linguistically, culturally, and religiously. Because of the indisputable preponderance of the Kyrgyz, as well as because of the republic's precipitous economic descent, Russians in Kyrgyzstan tended to cope with their new predicament as had their co-ethnics in Turkmenistan, Tajikistan, and Uzbekistan, by selling up and moving out.

Over time the Kyrgyz government has largely managed to ebb the flow of local Russians. Alone among the Central Asian countries, Kyrgyzstan allows the Russian language the same legal status as Kyrgyz enjoys; the government is so sensitive to the issue that Russian legislators are given translators so that they can follow the debate in the parliament when – as is increasingly becoming the case – the speakers choose to speak in Kyrgyz.

The situation in Kazakhstan is even more complex than that of Kyrgyzstan. Both because the two populations were so nearly equal in size, and also because most of the Russians were in a few highly concentrated areas quite close to the Russian border, the non-eponymous population was much more inclined than it might have been elsewhere to fight for its political and economic position in the new state. The consequent heterogeneity of the original population had the effect of forcing Kazakhstan initially to opt for developing the political institutions of a secular and multi-ethnic democracy.

Over time though, Kazakhstan's political life has come to increasingly favor the interests of the Kazakhs over those of the Russians, as well as over the other ethnic communities in the nation. The Russian language enjoys a status nearly equal to that of Kazakh, but that "near equality" is not a sufficient guarantee for the country's diminishing but still substantial Russian population. Over 1.2 million ethnic Russians have left Kazakhstan since independence, and the wave of out-migration seems far from over (Vitrovskaya, unpublished manuscript). While the Kazakh government initially tried to halt this movement, they now are at least indirectly encouraging it. The rationale behind this tacit approval is that the emigration is a mechanism of letting out the most disgruntled members of the minorities and thus reducing tensions in the country.

Over the years Kazakhstan's leadership has been confronted with several challenges, stemming from the country's sizable Russian minority. In the first years following independence, the Kazakh government feared that the Russian-dominated northern provinces would try to secede. The fiery rhetoric of the Russian government about defense guarantees for the Russians in the near abroad, and the dubious Russian involvement in the ethnic conflicts in the Transcaucasian states and Moldova incited fears of Russian interference in Kazakh affairs (Olcott, 1996, p.58). Even after Russia's interest in the welfare of "stranded" ethnic Russians had abated, the Kazakh government dreaded a separatist explosion from within, led by some ethnically based parties and movements of Russians and Cossacks. In the past couple of years, any challenge posed by the Russian minority was more likely to result from the possible failure of the economic reforms in the country, rather than from nationalistic inter-ethnic strife.

While the mightiness of their patron gives the ethnic Russians a greater leverage in the Central Asian societies, the other ethnic minorities within the Central Asian states should not be dismissed as unimportant. Kyrgyzstan's Uzbeks, who live in ethnically consolidated communities near the Kyrgyzstan–Uzbekistan border, are now estimated to account for some 15 percent of the country's population. Like the Russians, they are irked by policies that strengthen the Kyrgyz grip on power, but unlike the Russians, they do not have enough power to defend their interests successfully. As a result the Uzbeks are potentially a more explosive minority, with unclear loyalties.

Uzbekistan's biggest demographic challenge is its Tajik population. Counted as only about 5 percent of the population in the 1989 census, Tajiks are in fact said to make up closer to 20 or even 25 percent of Uzbekistan's population.[3] Fear of upsetting the precarious ethnic balance of its border region has been a constant factor influencing Uzbekistan's policy toward the conflict in Tajikistan.

Tajikistan itself is also a demographic and cultural pastiche of disparate peoples, whom the Soviets uprooted or dumped in the republic over the decades. As was mentioned earlier, a quarter of Tajikistan's citizens are ethnic Uzbek, who in alliance with some Tajik families used to dominate the republic during Soviet times. Now, nominal power is in the hands of natives of the southwestern region, which has always been a volatile and discontented province with a strong tradition of political Islamic fundamentalism. The eastern half of the state is made up of "Mountain Badakhshan" – a lightly populated, extremely poor, and very rugged autonomous region whose people practice Ismaili Shi'ism and speak a language which other Tajiks cannot understand. With so many demographic problems at hand it should not come as a surprise that the young Tajik state slipped into a seven-year civil war right after it received its independence.

Since the signing of the Tajik armistice in June 1997, the whole Central Asian region has been quite stable. The current leaders seem to have learned to handle the tasks and risks associated with their countries' ethnic and social diversity. The presidents, however, will not live forever. Their countries will sooner or later face the inevitable challenge of finding a mechanism for elite succession.

Currently, all Central Asian regimes are authoritarian, although the degree of closeness of the society varies from country to country. Turkmenistan and Uzbekistan are evolving to become south Asian states very similar to other states in their region, such as Iran, Pakistan, or (in some regards) Afghanistan. Each is ruled by one man, who essentially controls all political and economic power in his republic, despite the fig-leaves of constitutions, parliaments and other appurtenances of rule-of-law government. Turkmenistan's parliament voted in December 1999 to make Saparmurad Niyazov, who has ruled since 1985, president for life. This decision marked a definitive step away from democracy, toward an increasingly autocratic state. Both states remain officially secular, and Uzbekistan in particular has fought back hard against what might have been a push by politicized Islam soon after independence; in both, however, traditional Muslim practices and attitudes are clearly woven into the fabric of everyday life, strengthening the Muslim character of both states. Tajikistan, essentially in a state of civil war since 1991, has fared so poorly since independence that some observers suggest the state may have been still-born (Rubin, 1944).

Kazakhstan and Kyrgyzstan, each of which were more heterogeneous at independence, both made more energetic commitments to democracy and an open economy in their early years, but each has since pulled sharply back. In both states the presidents have used popular referenda and personal fiat to amend their states' first constitutions, greatly reducing the power of legislatures which had in both states begun to coalesce as genuine counter-balances to presidential power. In June 2000, President Nazarbaev of Kazakhstan was granted lifetime powers by the nation's parliament, including the right to address the nation and parliament, on key initiatives; the right to lead the Peoples' Assembly; the right to be a member of the Kazakh National Security Council; and the right to advise presidents on declaring a state of war or emergency.[4] Though not as drastic as the decision of the Turkmenistani parliament that made Niyazov president for life, the bill ensured that Nazarbaev's semi-authoritarian rule will continue far into the future.[5]

The common denominator in the region consists of the lack of meaningful competitive elections and division of powers. In Kazakhstan and Turkmenistan the presidents ran unopposed and garnered more than 95 percent of the votes. In Uzbekistan, Tajikistan, and Kyrgyzstan, however, where the presidential elections were contested, the opposition candidates gathered less than a quarter of the votes.

To a certain extent, the unimpressive showing of opposition candidates in the presidential elections might be due to outright fraud, intimidation of voters, and discriminatory electoral regulations. More importantly, however, the presidential elections have underscored the absence of viable opposition parties or movements across the region. In Turkmenistan, democratically minded figures were quickly relieved of their governmental posts and forced into exile. In Uzbekistan, Karimov summarily abolished the vice-presidential institution, when its holder Sukrullo Mirsaidov turned out to have the potential to become a political rival. Until recently, Mirsaidov served as a leader of the Democratic Opposition Coordination Council, whose aim was to coordinate the efforts of opposition groups, or what was left of them after most opposition party and movement leaders had fled the country. The council's existence was the last indication of at least a facade of democratic structures in the country, but since Mirsaidov's resignation in March 1998, the council officially ceased to exist.

The vigor with which any attempt at political opposition has been rooted up in Central Asia has without question preserved a kind of macro-political stability in most of the republics. The current emphasis upon "stability" – which really means preservation of the privileges of the existing elites and of the *status quo* – makes it all but impossible for new political figures or ideas to enter the national arena save in catastrophic and revolutionary ways. By attempting to eliminate the ups-and-downs of messy democracy, the leaders of Central Asia have made it more likely that political change, when it finally comes, will be convulsive and violent. The lack of predictability regarding the succession is likely to breed instability.

Before they are faced with the problem of succession, however, the Central Asian governments could see the stability of their states endangered by socioeconomic problems. There are certain clear advantages to this kind of "stability" – economic reforms have proceeded as the government deems they should; resources have been applied to projects which the leaders wish; foreign investors and donors have been reassured that their money is secure, and the hold of the current elite is unquestioned. At the same time, however, this stability is increasingly difficult to distinguish from stasis, as fear of change of any sort makes it ever harder for administrators to respond to changing social conditions.

The leaders of the new states have performed very poorly in keeping the social "bargain" which their constituents had come to expect from Soviet-style government. Living standards have slumped tremendously in the region, with each country plunging at least twenty-some seats down the UN-calculated ladder of human development. Run-away inflation in the early 1990s drained savings accounts. The breaking of inter-republic connections led essentially to economic collapse, which has meant an accumulation of enormous wage and pension arrears, as well as the gradual deterioration of the educational, social welfare, and healthcare systems. By 1997, Central Asians spent more than 60 percent of their income on food.[6]

At the same time, the members of a tiny business and bureaucratic elite have amassed great fortunes through corruption, graft, and preferential business conditions. Bribery has become the norm of official conduct, with officials taking money not only for performance of their routine duties, but also, at times, to stop the activities of others. Soon after independence there were reports in Kazakhstan, for example, of an official who had accepted $1 million, in return for trying to stop the Chevron oil deal (Mack, 1995, p. 58). Fraud is widespread, as businesses or favored individuals take loans on which they default, or convert taxes and other payments to their own use. In an attempted crack-down in Kazakhstan in 1996 it was reported, for example, that millions of dollars of foreign aid which the republic had incurred had simply vanished, with no records of its whereabouts or use (Bivens, 1997, p. 69). The susceptibility of the organs of justice to bribery has also brought a rise in street crime and violence, as it increasingly becomes possible to have rivals "taken care of," or to buy one's way out of difficulties. Uzbekistan and Turkmenistan, where the organs of state security have remained comparatively stronger, have not seen so vivid a deterioration of public order, but Kazakhstan and Kyrgyzstan have witnessed sharp increases in robberies, rapes, muggings, and murders. Tajikistan, which saw its social fabric picked virtually apart by social war, teeters on the brink of street anarchy, with kidnappings, armed attacks, and murders commonplace.

The spread of corruption and the concentration of wealth has created a vicious circle which is likely to keep the majority of Central Asians in poverty. The failure to create a broad property-owning class has also precluded the generation of a stable tax-paying class, thus dramatically decreasing government revenues. At the same time, unlike the political power distributed by the Soviet system of the past, which was annulled as soon as it was withdrawn, the money which the new system has brought to the tiny layer of the new rich has made them more impervious to the leaders and the system which allowed them to get rich in the first place. In fact, the people and businesses who make enough income to be able to pay taxes also have the political clout to avoid doing so. The result of this financial irresponsibility has been a spiraling crisis of the emptying of public coffers, and non-payment of wages and pensions, which have in turn led to public demonstrations and strikes in Kazakhstan, and even in Turkmenistan, while also setting off further regional liquidity crises. The longer this cycle persists, the greater the danger of social unrest. More importantly, apart from strikes and demonstrations, the disillusioned Central Asians might increasingly turn to Islam for answers (Kazhegeldin, 1999).

One way to make up for the government revenues lost in unpaid taxes would be to attract significant flows of foreign investment. All Central Asian states have unexplored natural resources and a low-cost, well-trained labor force – a combination of factors which has proven to allure foreign investors. Turkmenistan is the world's fourth largest producer of natural gas, with reserves of approximately 100 trillions cubic feet. It also has about 6 billion barrels of oil. Kazakhstan, which hopes to develop the newly discovered Kashagan formation in the Caspian Sea, as well as the Tengiz field in its northwestern part, has reserves of some 8 billion barrels of oil and 65 trillion cubic feet of natural gas (British Petroleum Statistical Review of World Energy, 2001).

Uzbekistan has lesser quantities of both fossil fuels, but probably enough oil to become self-sufficient, and enough natural gas to already be a regional net exporter. The two mountainous states, Tajikistan and Kyrgyzstan, have only token deposits of oil, but much more promising deposits of minerals, especially gold, silver, and uranium. Uzbekistan has enough gold to have accounted for 25 percent of the total production of the USSR, while Kazakhstan is rich in gold, uranium, coal, copper, aluminum and many other minerals (Beddoes, 1998).

Over the past six years a number of problems, such as the inadequate legal guarantees for foreign investors and widespread patterns of bureaucratic corruption, have somewhat cooled Western interest (Sagers, 1998, p. 125). The potential yield of the region's oil and gas deposits is so great, however, that foreign investors show no signs of tiring of the waiting game in which they have been forced to engage. Firms may drop out, but there is no shortage of interested parties willing to take their places.

Central Asia: an interconnected geopolitical region

While economic success certainly depends on the internal economic choices that the Central Asian governments take, there is also a set of intra-regional challenges that have shaped the first steps of the fledgling independent nations. As the Soviets electrified, industrialized, and irrigated the region, their developmental policies were based on the assumption that the artificially created Central Asian republics would never be independent states. Therefore, in 1991 the Central Asian states were confronted with the task of building sovereign entities, while being integrally linked into a common economic and geopolitical space.

Nowhere are the states of the former Soviet Union more closely bound with one another than in Central Asia, not only because of the strong sense of common ancestry and shared cultural and religious heritage, but also simply because of the region's geography. Precise physical boundaries were never drawn and highway and railway systems pay little attention to national borders – for example, the principal route between the Uzbek cities of Tashkent and Andizhan and that between Tashkent and Samarkand go through Kazakhstan and Tajikistan, respectively. The Kyrgyz also must pass through customs points on the main routes between Bishkek and Osh, as well as between Bishkek and Talas, crossing briefly into Uzbekistan and Kazakhstan, respectively. Southern Kazakhstan has always informally oriented itself to

Uzbekistan's capital Tashkent – less than two hours away – rather than Kazakhstan's capital, Almaty, which is a ten-hour drive. The same is true of Osh oblast in Kyrgyzstan, which is part of the Ferghana Valley, and separated from the country's capital, Bishkek, by an arduous 11-hour drive on a road which is impassable for over a third of the year. Tajikistan is also closely intertwined with Uzbekistan. Azerbaijan, located on the opposite shore of the Caspian Sea, is more closely linked through highway, railway, and pipeline systems with Russia and the other Transcaucasian states than with Central Asia.

In addition to the road infrastructure, the Central Asian states are bound together by an integrated electrical grid and common water resources. The bulk of the region's water resources are concentrated in Kyrgyzstan. The two main Central Asian rivers – Amu Darya and Syr Darya – originate from the ample snow of the Kyrgyz area of the Pamir mountains. In the upstream the two rivers cascade down the slopes, which makes the construction of hydroelectric plants possible. The Syr Darya (called the Naryn in its Kyrgyz part) currently powers six hydroelectric plants in Kyrgyzstan, which have so far generated about 140 billion kilowatt-hours of electricity. Kyrgyzstan, however, has consumed less than a third of this energy, while Uzbekistan and Kazakhstan have received 83 and 54 billion kW/h respectively, free of charge (Dorian *et al.*, 1999).

This allocation is not surprising because Central Asia has an interconnected power grid. Up until 1991, the cost and quantity of power transfers were determined through a central allocation system, devised in Moscow. Since the collapse of the Soviet Union, market rates have been introduced, which has created disequilibria and suboptimization. The shift to market prices has also been a source of contention among the member countries.

One way to renovate and optimize the electricity industry in Central Asia is to redefine the basis of cooperation within the region, but still keep the integrated power grid. The Central Asian states could turn the burdensome Soviet legacy into an asset by encouraging energy exchanges. All states could contribute financially to the renovation of the industrial base in Kyrgyzstan which is best suited to produce cheap electricity. Kyrgyz politicians have repeatedly appealed to their neighbors to help finish the construction of the two Kambaratinskiye power plants, started during the Soviet era. In return Kyrgyzstan can export electricity without tariffs and taxes to its neighbors. Such an arrangement would be beneficial for everyone, because the oil-producing states would not "waste" their potential fuel exports to power electricity generation plants, and Kyrgyzstan would have a market for its surplus electric power. In addition to financial support for its electrical power plants, Kyrgyzstan has claimed that its neighbors should assume part of the burden of maintaining fresh water reservoirs. The rationale behind the Kyrgyz demands is based on the fact that Uzbekistan and Kazakhstan use the water for their agriculture, while the Kyrgyz have sacrificed arable lands, and lose about $60 million a year from ungenerated electricity(Dorian *et al.*, 1999).

Because of the region's interconnectedness, the Central Asian leaders have also been concerned about security threats to stability, such as drugs and the spread of political Islam. The governments of Kazakhstan and Kyrgyzstan are particularly worried about the possibility of their countries' becoming part of the international opium route, which originates in Afghanistan, and the effects that such a development might have on their societies.

The civil war in Tajikistan, whose resolution has been further complicated by the civil war in Afghanistan, has served as a strong reminder to the Central Asian leaders of the destructive potential of a politicized Islamic movement, when combined with a disgruntled and divided former Communist party elite. Fear of a similar scenario certainly helps explain why Uzbekistan's president backed away from democratic reforms in 1992 and banned all religious-based parties. None of these states want to disavow their Islamic heritage, but they do not want their futures determined by their pasts.

The strong sense of common regional identity as well as the clear awareness of the region's economic and security interdependence has fostered a shared commitment among the Central Asian leaders to regional cooperation. Formal coordination of efforts dates back to 1990, when the five presidents set up a consultative forum, that was largely charged with common management issues, including water usage, hydroelectric power, trade issues and shared ecological problems. In 1994, the original inter-republican agreement was given interstate status.

Also in 1994, Kyrgyzstan, Kazakhstan, and Uzbekistan formed the Central Asian Union. The organization was envisioned as a defense, political, and economic formation, based on the structure of the European Union. The move was reportedly spurred by the inefficiency of the CIS as a venue for integration. The new organization would have an interstate council of heads of state, a council on foreign affairs and defense, and a Central Asian Bank for Cooperation and Development. The Central Asian Union members also pledged to set up a common market by the year 2000. The process towards the establishment of such a union would involve the gradual abolishment of tariffs, quotas, licenses and all other trade barriers. Progress toward such a union, however, has been slower than anticipated, and the goal of a common market by 2000 could not be met.

Regional cooperation has turned out to be a difficult undertaking (Olcott *et al.*, 1999). The Central Asian Union (CAU) – now renamed the Central Asian Economic Community (CAEC) – of which Azerbaijan and the other Transcaucasian states are not members, has held more than 15 meetings of heads of states or prime ministers on which more than 20 agreements have been signed (both interstate and intergovernmental). The organization stresses the need to "accelerate the processes linked with the economic cooperation of the region, and to implement the projects intended to revive the economies of the nations affiliated to the community (Neshrumai, 1999) The issues discussed have included the settlement of the conflicts in Tajikistan and Afghanistan, economic cooperation, and water resource management, but much in the CIS style, the adopted agreements have not yielded noticeable results. Also like the CIS, the CAU/CAEC has not been very successful as an instrument through which the members could resolve differences and disputes. One sphere in which virtually no progress has been made towards a mutually beneficial solution is water resource management. The Central Asian presidents have signed many agreements in which they pledge to resolve the thorny issue. Kyrgyzstan, however, continues to export some 80 percent of its water resources to Uzbekistan, Tajikistan, and Kazakhstan free of charge. The presidents of the latter group of countries, however, have staunchly defended the notions that all water resources in the region are common property. Moreover, they have insisted that Kyrgyzstan, even though it does not border the Aral Sea, should join the initiative to save this endangered body of water and contribute up to 1 percent of its GDP to the problem. In turn, Kyrgyzstan has threatened to cut off electricity supplies or, in one instance, to open its dams and flood thousands of acres of arable land, belonging to its defiant neighbors.

Another instance in which the CAU/CAEC failed to perform its role as a dispute-solving body has concerned late payments. In 1996 even a Presidential summit was unable to relieve relations between Kazakhstan, Uzbekistan and Kyrgyzstan that had become strained over late payments and non-delivery of gas and electricity (Lyaporov, 1998). Though interstate debts were subsequently restructured, and plans even made for coordinated foreign economic investment and future swaps between Kazakhstan and Uzbekistan's electricity and gas providers, problems continue to reoccur.

More than once Uzbekistan has cut off gas supplies to Kyrgyzstan and Kazakhstan for disputes over prices or payment. Kazakhstan and Kyrgyzstan – which probably have the best bilateral relations of any Central Asian countries – have also periodically sparred over these questions as well. In 1996 Kazakhstan and Kyrgyzstan agreed to exchange coal for water, but when Kazakhstan failed to deliver the coal on time, Kyrgyzstani officials threatened to open the dams to flood their neighbors fields (Bovin, 1998).

Turkmenistan is the one state which has held itself apart and expressed no formal interest in participating in the Central Asian Economic Community. Part of the answer for this isolationist stance seems to be found in the personal rivalries that compound more traditional forms of state competition. President Niyazov probably anticipated that his nation would rapidly ascend to the short list of wealthy, underpopulated energy-rich states. He seems to have believed that the Turkmen future would be much rosier than that of the other Central Asian states, and thus questioned the need to enter unions that would simply drain away Turkmenistan's wealth to more needy neighbors.

For their parts, both Presidents Nazarbaev and Karimov each saw themselves as the region's natural leader, and Nazarbaev in particular held out hopes for a larger CIS and possibly even a global role. Karimov viewed Uzbekistan as the heart of Central Asia, while Nazarbaev saw Kazakhstan as the bridge between Europe and Asia. At the same time, both saw the politics and personality cult developing around Turkmenbashi – "head Turkmen" as Niyazov prefers to be called – as silly and damaging to the image that each was trying to project of himself, his country, and the region. Both men were also smart enough to realize that their states were still too weak and too interdependent to allow their personal and national rivalries to undermine the overarching need for regional cooperation.

President Niyazov is only lately coming to the same conclusion, and has begun to take an increasingly more active role in regional summits (Mikhhailov, 1999). He has become more flexible on questions of importance to other states, such as backing better coordination of efforts to combat narcotics trade, increasing pressure to try to end the Afghanistan conflict, speeding up plans for new transport corridors (including alternative pipeline routings) and backing national sectoral development of the Caspian.

The Central Asian "neighborhood"

In order to consolidate their nations' independence, the Central Asian countries have had to cope not only with internal ethnic and socioeconomic problems and issues of regional interdependence and cooperation, but also with the daunting tasks of foreign policy development and implementation. Even though the Central Asian presidents and their teams had significant government experience, it should not be assumed that the decision-makers appreciated the complexity of the initial decisions that faced them when they found themselves at the helm of newly independent states. None of the present leaders of the region had experience outside the communist world before 1990. Nor did these men have sophisticated assistants or associates. Soviet staffing and promotion practices sharply limited the number of Central Asians who might serve in exactly those fields which the new states required – diplomacy, foreign languages, and advanced technologies – thus making it possible, for example, for Kyrgyzstan to have as its first foreign minister a man who had never been out of the country (Brown, 1992).

Russia has been the dominant player in Central Asia for nearly a century and a half, and although its presence is waning, it is far from ready to disappear from the scene completely. The first five years of Central Asian independence might be viewed as the Russians attempting to resolve the oxymoron of retaining the benefits of the economic and military control which they enjoyed in the Soviet period without having also to pay the social and political costs which had, in large part, driven the Soviet Union to collapse. The net effect of these efforts has been a steady ebb of Russian influence, especially in those states most remote from Russia.

The pace of this ebbing has not been uniform. Russian insistence on military control remains strong, despite the enormous problems manifest in the Russian army. After unsuccessful experiments in relying, first, on a Central Asian joint intervention force under the aegis of the CIS, then on a beefed-up Uzbek army, and finally on Russian "volunteers," to control events in Tajikistan, Russia finally had to move to direct army intervention, both to quell the civil war and to patrol the border with Afghanistan. Possibly unable and certainly unwilling to pay the cost of building a new defense perimeter along its new borders (which are very nearly as long as were those of the entire USSR), and unhappy with the slow growth of military capabilities in the new states (while, paradoxically, also reluctant to permit the development of stronger militaries on its southern flank), Russia has re-assumed direct responsibility for patrolling the former USSR borders everywhere save in Turkmenistan; borders there are patrolled exclusively by Turkmenistan's security forces. After extended negotiations, Russia also regained possession of the nearly 1400 nuclear warheads orphaned in Kazakhstan, and has negotiated a long-term lease of space-launch and missile-launch facilities at Baikonur, Kazakhstan, which essentially makes the facility and its support town a part of Russia (Safronov, 1999).

While Russian military presence has clearly inhibited whatever growth of indigenous Central Asian military capability that might have been possible, it has not otherwise been particularly effective. The Central Asians are obviously aware of the army's failures in Chechnya, and of continuing scandals in the Russian high command and ranks. More pointedly, the Russian army has proof of unclear utility in Tajikistan, unable to seal the border, and although it appeared to be more effective as a power broker in resolving the country's civil war, the timing of Russian intervention could have doomed the peace accords, which were finally reached in June 1997.

Russia began pushing for political settlement of the Tajik civil war because of the social and political costs it was incurring. The war was unpopular with Russians at home, making it difficult to conscript and dispatch youth to what people increasingly regarded as a distant land; perhaps more important, the costs of keeping Tajikistan's economy afloat, to say nothing of repairing the damage done to the country by the civil war, were much more than Russia could bear.

Fear of the destabilization that a Taliban victory in Afghanistan might bring to their own states has been a powerful motivating factor for Uzbekistan, Tajikistan, Kazakhstan and Turkmenistan in their dealings with Russia. Tajikistan's rulers are frightened of a Taliban victory in the Afghan territory that borders on their state, because of the refugee flow of ethnic Tajiks that it might trigger, including armed resistance fighters. For its part Uzbekistan's government fears the flow of ethnic Uzbek refugees from both Tajikistan and Afghanistan, while the Kazakh and Kyrgyz leaders are more concerned with the effects of illegal drugs and arms flowing from Afghanistan through Tajikistan and on into their countries.

In addition to security considerations, the Central Asians have to maintain good relations with Russia for economic reasons. As long as they want to develop their natural resources and boost their foreign trade, they will depend on the courtesy of the Russian government, since Russia currently controls the transit of Central Asian exports to the world markets.

For the fossil-fuel-rich Kazakhstan and Turkmenistan, Russia holds two important levers – its position on the status of the Caspian Sea and the Central Asians' absolute dependence on the Russian pipeline network. Kazakhstan and Turkmenistan have had to offer Russia's major oil and gas firms – LUKoil, Rosneft and Gazprom – equity ownership stakes in some key deposits and refineries in order to mollify the objections of the Russian government to the sectoral division of the Caspian Sea (Greenlee, 1999). However, the unsettled nature of this legal question continues to further complicate the oil and gas transportation issue, in which Russia still largely manages to dictate conditions.

The other, even stronger, Russian lever has been the current lack of alternatives to the transportation of Central Asian oil and gas through the Russian network. Since during the Soviet period Kazakhstan and Turkmenistan were provided with Siberian oil and gas for their internal consumption, each country has only a few pipelines, all of which connect the two newly independent states with Russia. In Kazakhstan the main outward routes are the Atyrau-Samara pipeline, the Transneft pipeline, and an almost complete Tengiz-Novorossiisk pipeline, all of which take Kazakh oil to Russia. Existing Turkmen gas pipelines also take the country's resources to Russia via Kazakhstan and Uzbekistan.

Moscow in effect holds the key to Turkmen and Kazakh exports, which makes the two fledgling states heavily dependent on Russia. Russia has imposed quotas for oil and gas shipments through its territory, which have forced Turkmenistan to "sell" most of its surplus to insolvent partners such as Ukraine, Georgia, and Armenia. Moscow also has denied the Turkmen access to the more lucrative markets in Europe. Similarly, Chevron's development of the Tengiz oil field in Kazakhstan has been seriously hampered by the impossibility to ship "early oil" through the existing pipeline system, which forced the company to ship oil by freighter across the Caspian or by rail through China. Both approaches are cumbersome and costly, leaving no real profit margin for Chevron or for the Kazakhs.

Even if the Central Asian states had unlimited access to Russia's pipeline network, they would still need to construct alternative routes. First, the existing pipeline system could not accommodate the steadfast increase in the volume of fuel, which is expected to flow out of Kazakhstan and Turkmenistan. Secondly, Kazakhstan's main fields (Tengiz and Karachaganak) are situated in the far west, while its main industries, and most of its population, are in the northeast and east. There is an acute need to construct pipelines, which could take Kazakh oil to Kazakh consumers. Until then in spite of its enormous petroleum wealth, Kazakhstan will remain a net importer of oil. The current necessity to purchase oil and petroleum products from Russia has been a major factor in Kazakhstan's burgeoning national debt (Smetanina, 1998).

Bilateral ties to Russia are still the most important foreign relationships that each of these states maintains. Each of the Central Asian states joined the CIS in December 1991, at the time of the Alma Ata meeting of Soviet republic presidents. Two of the Central Asian states, Kazakhstan and Kyrgyzstan have been willing to join the CIS's further economic and military unions. These two states have also signed a four state "deep integration" agreement with Russia and Belarus. Uzbekistan signed the CIS military union agreement, and Tajikistan is part of both the military and economic unions. Consistent with its stated policy of formal neutrality, Turkmenistan is a member of neither the economic nor military union.

While it is still strong, even Russian economic influence has waned in Central Asia. Russia remains a primary trading partner for all the Central Asian states, as well as their most important customer for most commodities, but as time progresses the proliferation of other suppliers and customers, as well as Russia's continued economic difficulties, mean that the Central Asia states, and especially those like Uzbekistan which are not contiguous with Russia, are steadily lessening their economic dependence on the northern giant.

Partnership with Iran in transit of oil would also be beneficial to the Central Asians. The Iranians have initiated an oil swap program, which permits Kazakhstan to ship oil to points on the south Caspian, and then sell oil of Iranian origin from points on the Persian gulf. The Iranian government has also committed to foot 80 percent of the bill for the construction of a pipeline that connected a Turkmen gas deposit in Korpedzhe to the Iranian pipeline network (Levine, 1997).

Strong US opposition to such endeavors has significantly slowed the implementation of proposed plans. It also accounts for the relatively cool attitude of the Uzbek government towards its southern neighbor. Since Uzbekistan's economic success does not depend so much on oil exports, President Karimov seems to have decided to gain a comparative advantage in his country's relations with the US at the expense of Uzbek–Iranian cooperation. All other Central Asian states, however, do maintain good ties with Iran, because they seem to be based on genuine cooperation. While there is a certain amount of proselytizing, the Iranians have recognized that their revolutionary type of Shi'ia Islam is likely to be of little interest to Central Asia's almost exclusively Sunni Muslim populations.

The US would much rather see the Central Asians in close cooperation with Turkey. Turks and Central Asians view themselves as distant ethnic kin. Only the Tajiks are of Persian stock, while all other Central Asians speak Turkic languages as their native tongues. Although Turkey has never ruled Central Asia, Turkey sees itself as the leading *secular* Muslim state in the region, as well as the most important Turkic one, and so saw the granting of independence to the Turkic states of the Soviet Union as serving Turkey's goal of becoming the major regional actor.

Turkish entrepreneurs are very active in Azerbaijan and in Central Asia, probably the most active of any foreign group, measured by the number of investments and jobs created, rather than by the cash value of the investments (Rashid, 1997). Turkey has become a major jumping-off point for international air travel to the four Turkic Central Asian states, and Turkish businessmen often play the role of intermediaries for international businesses seeking to set up operations in the region. Thousands of students from Central Asia are studying in Turkey, many of them on Turkish government scholarships (Hyman, 1995).

Turkey is, however, too far away to have a major impact on Central Asian affairs, though it might have a greater impact in more proximate Azerbaijan. In addition, it does not have the economic might or the political leverage to challenge Russia's role in the region. In fact, the recent signing of a long-term contract on cooperation in the oil sphere between the Russian and the Turkish governments, seems to indicate that Russia might rank higher than the Central Asian states on Turkey's foreign priority list.

Prospects for foreign direct investment

The lack of other sources of funding forced the Central Asian leaders to court foreign investors, which they did with enthusiasm and great energy. Some have been more successful than others, but all have seen some in-flow of funds, while investment in better-favored republics has been huge. In addition to providing their capital-strapped economies with funds, foreign investment reduces economic dependency on Russia.

Foreign investors, who do not have such strong interests in Central Asia as its neighboring states, have predictably been most active in the oil and gas industries, due to the high profits. The Caspian Pipeline

Consortium, consisting of Chevron (which has now been joined by Mobil), the Kazakh, Russian and Omani governments, Shell (as part of the Rosneft share), British Gas, AGIP, and Oryx, owns transport rights to Tengiz, the largest Kazakh oil field. The French company Elf is also vying for deposits in Kazakhstan. The Argentine Bridas participates in a joint venture with the Turkmen Fuel and Energy Ministry, which is authorized to develop the gas deposit in Yashlar. Other companies that have expressed interest in investing in Turkmenistan's oil and gas industry include Unocal, Western Atlas Company and Delta Oil Company (US), Petronage Charigali (Malaysia), and Itochu (Japan), among others.[7] Major US foreign investment in the region has also primarily been in the areas of fossil fuels.

Foreign companies, however, have invested in other spheres of transportation as well. Japanese authorities are committing themselves to a greater foreign aid role in Kazakhstan's transportation sector. In the spring of 1996, the Asian Development Bank and a private Japanese fund pledged to provide $198 million of the $238 million needed to reconstruct the Bishkek-Osh highway in Kyrgyzstan.[8]

The telecommunications industry has also attracted a significant number of foreign partners. The main companies that now operate in Uzbekistan are DAEWOO Telecom, Siemens, Alcatel, Northern Telecom, Motorola, and NEC. Together, they have brought more than $380 million to the country. Turkish, German, and Iranian companies are involved in the Turkmen telecom sector. Deutschetelecom, PLD Inc., Telstra, Indosat, Alcatel, and DAEWOO Telecom have moved into Kazakhstan. Even war-torn Tajikistan has attracted some foreign investors, namely the New Eastern Mobile Cellular Networks, Hughes Network Systems, and Jahon Page.[9]

Exim Bank and OPIC loans are available for US firms that make investments in the region, and the Central Asian American Enterprise Fund has been the most active of any of the US enterprise funds working in Russia or the other newly independent states. In addition, the US has provided technical assistance to these states that has been designed to develop the legal infrastructure necessary to secure and sustain foreign investment.

Unfortunately, the legal guarantees for foreign investment are still largely inadequate. Kazakhstan and Kyrgyzstan, which had begun marketing their major natural resources even before independence, have witnessed a number of brutal political battles about who precisely owns the resources, who may negotiate for their sale and on what terms, and where the generated revenues should go. In Kazakhstan this process has necessitated expensive and embarrassing flip-flops and renegotiations, which among other things have left plans for development of the largest goldfield in the country (Vasil'kovskoye) up in the air.

At the same time though, the states have had quick lessons in the power of international business law. Although large corporations such as Chevron and Cameco were willing to renegotiate already-done deals, apparently to make allowances for the economic and political naïveté shown in the first agreements made by their Central Asian partners, these companies also made unambiguously clear what would happen to the new states if arbitrary, autocratic business practices were to prevail there. Even Uzbekistan, which has generally been much more professional than its neighbors in negotiating deals, still found its international standing dropped quickly when it attempted to deal with internal liquidity problems by sharply limiting convertibility of local currency profits by foreign firms.

The need to rely on foreign investment has also required that the new states follow the needs and interests of foreign capital, which in general favors higher and more rapid return; this has tended to discourage investment in industry, and particularly in the manufacture of the consumer goods for which the region so hungered, since these needs can be better and more cheaply satisfied by imports. Most foreign investment in Central Asia has been directed to resource extraction, preliminary processing, and transport. Although all of the region's presidents seem to be aware of the ensuing danger that their states will become trapped in the classic Third World cycle of selling off non-renewable resources while failing to invest in productive capacity to sustain the economy once the resources are gone, none of the states is fully able to break the cycle.

The successful development of light industry in Central Asia requires attracting small and medium size investors, and this is exactly what Kazakhstan, Kyrgyzstan and Uzbekistan are all aggressively trying to do. However, the absence of secure legal guarantees, the difficulty in currency conversion (a particular problem in Uzbekistan), and the difficulty of moving goods into, out of, and through the region still make attracting such investors extremely difficult.

Conclusion

Until a strong legal infrastructure emerges in each Central Asian state, only the biggest projects with participating foreign investors have a chance to move forward. The Central Asian countries will hardly reap the benefits of their significant natural resources in the near future. Azerbaijan, which has already begun pumping oil from its vast reserves for sale on world energy markets, will soon begin to profit from its resources, though the benefits are unlikely to be spread evenly across Azeri society. Poverty is likely to continue to increase, forcing people to spend even larger portions of their income on the basics of food and shelter, and encouraging some of them to turn to crime. The collapse of education means that the children of the poor will not have the Russian language with which their parents communicated with other Soviets (including those who live in the neighboring Central Asian republics), and will not have the English or Chinese with which their more favored compatriots will be doing business abroad. Instead they will have only their native language; in the case of the rural poor, who still constitute the majority of Central Asia's population, many of these will have difficulty gaining literacy even in their native language. Books will be expensive and, in the native language at least, hard to get, particularly in the technical and social sciences, or in the humanities; the only native language literature which is likely to be easily available will probably be religious tracts.

The continued stagnation of local economies, the lack of public resources which might be applied to regional development schemes, and the increasing dependence for state revenue upon concession of resource extraction rights to foreign investors all seem destined to push the Central Asian states increasingly toward the familiar Third World model of rural unemployment and poverty, urban overcrowding, and extreme imbalances between rich and poor.

This pattern of social transformation in Central Asia is certain to increase political tensions. Even though the Central Asian people have proven to be passive and resigned, there is no way to predict when a straw will break the camel's back. The biggest concerns of the Central Asian leaders will be socio-economical. The region's governments will have to find the answers to mid-term crises of sustainability within their own societies – a challenge which they have not yet proved they can handle.

Notes

1. President Askar Akaev's speech at the Carnegie Endowment for International Peace, Washington, DC, June 1997.

2. Precise figures for ethnic populations in Uzbekistan, Turkmenistan, Tajikistan, Kyrgzstan, and Kazakhstan can be found in Curtis, 1996, pp. 377, 293, 197, 101, 3, respectively.
3. "Uzbek Ethnosocial Problems Viewed," *Sotsiologicheskiye Issledovaniya*, No. 8, August 1992, translated into English in *FBIS-USR-92-012-L*, 6 November 1992, p. 80.
4. "Kazaks Extend Presidential Power," *Energy Intelligence Group*, June 23, 2000.
5. Nazarbaev consolidated his hold on power by holding early presidential elections in January 2000, in which his primary opponent, Akezhan Kazhegeldin, was prevented from running a substantial campaign.
6. "Poverty Situation in Kyrgyzstan Causes Alarm," *The Times of Central Asia*, July 12, 2000, as published on the Internet website of *The Times of Central Asia* (www.times.kg//2000/N10/reg-01.shtml).
7. See "Turkmenistan Emerging as Key Player in Central Asian FSU," *Oil and Gas Journal*, vol. 95, no. 30, July 28, 1997, pp. 26–28.
8. "Central Asia Investment Report," *Moscow Interfax*, February 21, 2000.
9. "Communications and Electronics Report," *Moscow Interfax*, March 9, 2000.

References

Beddoes, Zanny Minton, "A Survey of Central Asia: Fortune's Wheel," *The Economist* February 7, 1998: pp. 18–19.

Bivens, Matt, "Aboard the Gravy Train," *Harper's* August 1, 1997: p. 69.

Bovin, Aleksandre, "Asian Themes," *The Current Digest of the Post-Soviet Press* August 19, 1998: p. 21.

British Petroleum Statistical Reniew of World Energy, Available at http://www.bp.com/centres/energy/index.asp

Brown, Bess, "Central Asia Emerges on the World Stage," *RFE/RL Research Report* January 3, 1992: p. 51.

Curtis, Glen E. (ed). *Kazakstan, Kyrgyzstan, Tajikistan, Turkmenistan, and Uzbekistan: Country Studies* (Washington, DC: Federal Research Division, Library of Congress, 1996).

Dorian, James P., Tojiev Abbasovich Utkus, Mikhail S, Tonkopy, Alaibek Jumabekovich Obozov, and Qiu Daxiong, "Energy in Central Asia and Northwest China: Major Trends and Opportunities for Regional Cooperation," *Energy Policy* vol. 27, no. 5 (May 1999): pp. 281–297.

Fuller, Graham E., "Russia and Central Asia: Federation or Fault Line?" in Mandelbaum (1994): pp. 94–129.

Greenlee, Steven Dale, "Caspian Oil: Gold Mine or Tar Pit?" *The World and I* vol. 14, no. 12 (December 1999): pp. 66–71.

Hunter, Shireen T., *Central Asia Since Independence* (Washington, DC: The Center for Strategic and International Studies, 1996).

Kazhegeldin, Akezhan, "Shattered Image," *Harvard International Review* vol. 22, no. 1 (Winter 1999): pp. 76–80.

Levine, Steve, "Iran Opens Big Gas Pipeline to Neighbor, Defying US," *New York Times* December 30, 1997: p. 10.

Lyaporov, Vlamidic, "Integration: Does Central Asia Need a Union with Russia?," *The Current Digest of the Post-soviet Press* October 16 1998: p. 12.

Mack, Toni, "Chevron: Trying to Get Out of Kazakhstan," *Forbes* November 20, 1995: p. 58.

Mandelbaum, Michael (ed.) *Central Asia and the World: Kazakhstan, Uzbekistan, Tajikistan, Kyrgyzstan, Turkmenistan* (New York: Council on Foreign Relations Press, 1994).

Mikhailov, Vladimic, "Niyazov Supports US," *The current Digest of the Post-soviet Press* June 2, 1999: pp. 15–16.

Neshrumai, Vadin, "Central Asian Economic Community Issues Statement," *ITAR-TASS*, 28 June 1999.

Olcott, Martha, Anders Aslund, and Sherman Garnett. *Getting it Wrong: Regional Cooperation and the Commonwealth of Independent States* (Washington, DC: Carnegie Endowment for International Peace, 1999).

Rashid, Ahmed, "Power Play," *Far Eastern Economic Review* April 10, 1997: pp. 22–24.

Rubin, Barnett R., "Tajikistan: From Soviet Republic to Russian-Uzbek Protectorate," in Mandelbaum (1994): pp. 207–24.

Safronov, Ivan, "Baikonur Reopens," *The Current Digest of the Post-Soviet Press* December 22, 1999: p. 23.

Sagers, Mathew J., "Gold Production in Central Asia," *Post-Soviet Geography and Economics* vol. 39, no. 3 (March 1998): pp. 125–33.

Smetanina, Svetlana, "Nazarbayer Confronts 'Russia Question'," *The Current Digest of the Post-Soviet Press* August 5, 1998: p. 16.

Vitrovskaya, Galina, "Emigration of the Non-Titular Population From Kazakhstan, Kyrgyzstan, and Uzbekistan," unpublished manuscript.

3
Economies and Energy

Yelena Kalyuzhnova

Introduction

With the dissolution of the former Soviet Union in 1991, the Caspian Sea region republics began the transition to market driven economies. Gradually the Caspian region is developing into a significant oil and gas exporting area, and a potentially major world oil transit centre. Proven oil reserves for the entire Caspian Sea region are assessed at 18–35 billion barrels, and natural gas reserves are even larger, accounting for almost two-third of the hydrocarbon reserves (proved plus possible) in the Caspian Sea region. Getting this oil and gas out of the region to world markets, however, is complicated by several factors (both political and economic), including high transaction costs and the macroeconomic environment.

This chapter is devoted to the Caspian Sea region's economies (CSRE), mainly Kazakhstan, Uzbekistan, Turkmenistan and Azerbaijan. The Russian economy is touched upon only in comparison with and in terms of its links to the other economies of the Caspian region. It is a commonly accepted fact that the development of the Caspian region's oil and gas resources requires substantial investments, both by the governments and private companies, on the basis of an objective assessment of where their money will generate the best and safest returns. Of practical importance here will be governmental help in reducing the level of political and economic risks associated with energy investments.

Prospects for economic growth will be important for the future development of the Caspian nations. The links between energy efficiency and economy are crucial in evaluating the role of energy in the economy. Energy is essentially important as a means of production as well as through its contribution to quality of life. In order to establish an effective market structure, governments of the CSRE have to establish real-cost pricing as well as eliminate soft-budget constraints (in the form of subsidies), using taxes and establishing the clear rights of property ownership. We maintain that there are some transitional cases where the full-costs pricing and removal of subsidies could cause socioeconomic difficulties. In these cases it would be important to give market players time to adjust.

In order to build a picture of past changes and future potential for energy efficiency in the CSRE, it is beneficial to examine the specific economic sub-sectors, as well as energy intensity – energy use per unit of activity. Intensity is related to efficiency, but is not exactly the same. Improving efficiency reduces the amount of energy required to provide a given output, that is an output of the same quality and quantity.

The notable structural changes which have taken place in some sectors since 1990 have had a significant impact on the aggregate energy use per unit of total value-added in manufacturing. Structural information in the CSRE may be the key to interpreting the evolution of sectoral energy use and efficiency.

Industry has accounted for a large portion of total energy demand in the CSRE. The effect of economic restructuring on the industrial sectors in the CSRE was dramatic. Between 1990 and 1997, energy consumption declined by 30 percent in the CSRE. In order to understand how energy efficiency developed in industry, it is necessary to consider how energy efficiency changed at the same time. The drop in energy use may have been in large measure related to the decline in industrial output rather than any increase in efficiency. Consumer energy use may have been constant as it was subsidized by government. People may still be overheating their homes and leaving lights on 24 hours a day because they do not face real costs but industry may have cut back operations for recessionary reasons, leaving less energy use while the household sector is still very inefficient. However due to the rapid changes in the development of the CSRE, however, it is difficult to measure. Instead, in order to detect the presence of a relationship between energy consumption and GDP, the Granger causality test has been used. Finally, we drew some conclusions regarding the management of oil and gas wealth.

Economic outlook: disintegration and interdependence

Prior to transition (1991) the CSRE were part of the single economic system – the Soviet economy – where they were responsible for "particular tasks" in the Soviet labour specialization, mainly production of raw materials and agricultural production.

Nevertheless, there are several economic concerns regarding this regional cooperation that should be highlighted. First, the continuation of control over foreign exchange in Uzbekistan and the non-convertibility of its currency have encouraged the existence of parallel markets in foreign exchange, which could be a real obstacle in regional economic integration. Second, the CSRE are major natural resource exporters, who suffer from fiscal constraints. This provides a strong incentive for these governments to monetize the revenues from exports of oil and other natural resources.

The potential danger is *Dutch disease* – "the negative effects of an inadequately managed natural resource boom" (Rosenberg and Saavalainen, 1998, p. 4), which could make the gains from regional cooperation and trade with the rest of the world minimal. Dutch oil disease tends to operate as follows: an inflow of oil money creates inflationary pressure, which tends to foster particular patterns of consumption and investment, and finally affects other industries, eventually weakening the diversification of the economy.

This phenomenon may happen in the CSRE, as a consequence of a lack of diversity of the industrial structure and the strong orientation towards mineral sectors of the economy in the composition of export. The specific dangers to the CSRE are that the countries have the lack of abilities (from the policy point of view) to develop diversified economies, or other exports, besides raw materials. The CSRE are very dependent on imports for a wide variety of consumer, intermediate and capital goods. In this case, imports can increase so as to offset the effect of oil exports on the foreign exchange rate. Similarly, capital outflows (legal or illegal) will have the same effect.

The main mistake of the Kazakhstani government was in focusing on speed as the priority for reform rather than implementing privatization and other reforms as part of a strategic plan incorporating the building of background institutions to support the reforms. The policy route which Kazakhstan pursued was an *incentive-conscious rent-seeking* approach (Kalyuzhnova, 2000).

Among the CSRE, Uzbekistan, which rejected IMF policy advice, has suffered the lowest cumulative fall in GDP since 1991. There are some downsides to this, though, namely the administrative double exchange rate, which reflects strong inflationary tendencies in the economy. In addition, prior to transition, Uzbekistan had a low level of industrialization compared to Kazakhstan or Russia, near energy self-sufficiency, and the availability of cotton, which could be defined as a hard currency earner, to support the exchange rate.

During the first decade of transition, several developments have affected the CSRE economic patterns: new national currencies have been launched, the partner-composition of trade has been diversified and, in a few cases, economic policies have changed. As a consequence, few CSRE countries experienced a profound economic decline: between 1989 and 1995 the GDP fell by 37, 60.8, 64.2 and 80.5 percent in Azerbaijan, Kazakhstan, Turkmenistan and Uzbekistan respectively (see Figure 3.1).

In all the CSRE, production dropped throughout the early 1990s (see Table 3.1) because the adjustments required for the post-Soviet system (and in Azerbaijan's case because of the Nagorno–Karabakh conflict) eroded consumer buying power, and also because of the retention of the rouble alongside the national currency. A major factor explaining the CSRE decline was also the deterioration of trade relations with the other former Soviet republics. In the early 1990s the CSRE remained heavily dependent on the other former republics of the Soviet Union, especially Russia.

For instance, in the late 1980s, Azerbaijan's exports to other Soviet republics averaged 46 percent of GDP and over 90 percent of total

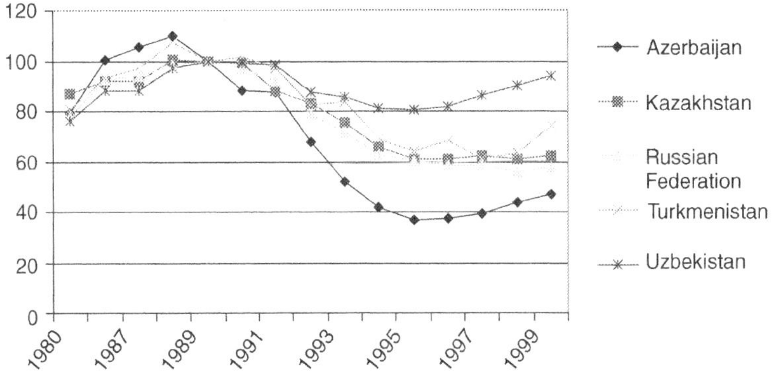

Figure 3.1 Real GDP/ NMP in the CSRE, 1980, 1986–99 (%).

Source: UN/Economic Commission For Europe Common Database, derived from national and CIS Stastic.

Note: NMP data for 1980–1990 were chain-linked to GDP data from 1990. Country indices were aggregated with previous year Purchasing Power Parity-based weight obtained from the European Comparison Programme for 1996.

Table 3.1 Real gross industrial output in the CSRE , 1980, 1986–99

(Indices, 1989=100)

	1980	1986	1987	1988	1989	1990	1991	1992	1993	1994	1995	1996	1997	1998	1999
CIS*	73.4	91.2	94.5	98.2	100.0	99.9	93.1	78.2	68.4	53.6	50.7	49.0	50.2	48.7	52.2
Azerbaijan	76.1	92.7	96.1	99.4	100.0	93.7	85.4	59.4	47.7	35.9	28.2	26.3	26.4	27.0	28.0
Kazakhstan	72.4	90.2	94.1	97.6	100.0	99.2	98.3	84.7	72.2	51.9	47.7	47.8	49.7	48.5	49.8
Russian Federation	74.4	91.8	95.0	98.6	100.0	99.9	91.9	75.4	64.7	51.2	49.5	47.5	48.5	46.0	49.7
Turkmenistan	75.4	90.1	92.9	96.9	100.0	103.2	108.2	92.0	95.7	72.1	67.5	79.5	53.8	54.0	62.0
Uzbekistan	68.5	91.2	93.4	96.5	100.0	101.8	103.3	96.4	99.9	101.5	101.6	104.2	108.5	112.4	119.2

Notes: Data for 1980–90 were chain-linked to national or CIS data from 1990. Country indices were aggregated with previous year PPP-based weights on the basis of data obtained from the European Comparison Programme for 1996.
*Generated from components.
Source: UN/ECE Common Database, derived from national and CIS statistics.

exports; its imports from those republics averaged 37 percent of GDP and nearly 80 per cent of total imports. At the same time, the main trade partners for Kazakhstan from the CSRE included Russia (52 percent), Uzbekistan (6.4 percent) and Azerbaijan (2 percent) (Daviddi and Spa, 1995).

All the CSRE tried to decrease the predominant role of Russia in their economies. Although it was steadily declining, Russia remained the main trading partner for CIS countries, accounting for 76 percent of total CIS exports and 70 percent of total CIS imports (1999). A key measure of vulnerability has been a country's share of total trade represented by trade with Russia.

The CSRE have been affected by several factors over the past three years, including the Asian economic crisis, the Russian financial crisis, and fluctuations in prices for export commodities such as energy and metals. The 1997–98 Asian crisis hurt investor confidence in developing markets such as Kazakhstan and Azerbaijan. The re-emergence of developing markets as this crisis has eased renewed investor interest in the CSRE. The 1998 Russian monetary crisis had a greater effect because Russia is for most CSRE, particularly Kazakhstan (28.9 percent of export and 39.4 import relations), their largest trading partner, and Russia's devalued rouble discouraged exports *to* Russia and encouraged imports *from* Russia.

Turkmenistan depends heavily on energy (particularly gas) exports to Russia, since, until very recently, all of the country's gas export pipelines ran northwards to Russia. Turkmenistan's gas production fell steeply during the first half of the 1990s, as other former-Soviet republics were unable to pay for supplies. The country's gas exports virtually ceased in 1997 when Russia's Gazprom refused to allow Turkmenistan's gas access to its pipeline network after a dispute over pricing. For a detailed analysis of the existing and planned oil and gas export infrastructure of the Caspian region see CGES (1998). In 1998, Turkmen exports to Russia accounted for only 4.7 percent of its total exports, while imports from Russia were 11.6 percent of total imports over the same period. Turkmenistan's gas production began to increase again in late 1998 and early 1999 as a result of a new gas supply deal with Ukraine (which collapsed again in May 1999) and a resumption of gas exports to Russia, *albeit* under less favourable terms to Turkmenistan.

Azerbaijan and Uzbekistan were less dependent on trade with Russia. Azeri exports to Russia accounted for 23 percent of the total in 1998, equivalent to 6 percent of Azerbaijan's GDP. As a result of the Russian crisis, budget revenues were reduced by around 155 million dollars, and the budget deficit exceeded the limit set by parliament of 4 percent of GDP. In 1998, Russia remained the leading supplier for Uzbek markets, with a share of 14.9 percent of export and 16.0 percent of import.

As a consequence of the economic turmoil in Russia, the CSRE rushed to reconsider the option of "economic integration" within the CIS. This process was accelerated in early 1999, as the collapse of the Russian rouble cut off these countries' exports to Russia and to one another.

The economic growth that was expected in the Caspian region slowed down and economies like Kazakhstan's went into recession. In 1998 only Azerbaijan and Uzbekistan reported GDP growth. Oil production and oil-related projects picked up in Azerbaijan. Uzbek exporters have been able to redirect sales away from CIS markets hit by the Russian crisis and towards the EU. In 1998, 26.0 percent of Uzbek exports went to members of the CIS and 23.3 percent to the EU, compared with 34.4 percent and 18.2 percent, respectively in 1997.

Besides the slowing down in exports and growth results, the Russian crisis negatively influenced the CSRE currencies. Kazakhstan's Tenge and Azerbaijan's Manat were devaluated steeply. In 1999, these economic problems were exacerbated by the Kazakhstani government's efforts to protect the value of the Tenge. This harmed exports and reduced hard-currency reserves. In April 1999, the decision to allow the Tenge to float, partly to boost industry, was finally made. Nevertheless, it did not immediately stop a decline of the real sector, nor did it boost exports, as Kazakhstani products remained non-competitive in foreign markets. By August, however, the devaluation had a favourable impact on tax collection, which was 2.1 billion Tenge higher in the second quarter of 1999 than in the first quarter. This became possible due to industrial recovery and the increased ability to pay taxes by Kazakhstani enterprises. However, the tax burden was distributed unevenly across the economy. According to the National Statistical Office, the Kazakhstani economy has a substantial shadow sector, amounting to 30 percent of GDP.

Through administrative controls and a rapid increase in gas exports Turkmenistan has avoided devaluation. The rate of inflation in the above-mentioned countries was relatively low in contrast to Russia and Uzbekistan. In Uzbekistan fiscal and monetary policies placed even greater pressures on prices and exchange rates.

Despite some common features, the CSRE present contrasts. All CSRE are at low levels of economic development, which is demonstrated in annual per capita income levels. However, real per capita income data, which range from $1230 to $550, add to the picture of divergent development(see Table 3.2). Kazakhstan has the highest per capita income ($ 1230), Uzbekistan at $720, Turkmenistan at $660 and Azerbaijan at $550 each (World Bank Development Report 2000/2001).

In addition, size and distance influence the potential for economic growth in the Caspian region. The Caspian region is a large, landlocked area with low population density and low GDP per capita. All these factors limit the size of domestic markets and make economic development in the region difficult. Economic cooperation can help to eliminate these obstacles by providing expansion of the domestic markets for local producers as well as opportunities for increasing economies of scale in production, more effective use of resources and increasing trade opportunities.

The role of energy in the Caspian economies

The energy sector is one in which the needs and opportunities for economic cooperations are well understood by the CSRE. For example, Kazakhstan seeks market diversification for its oil, Uzbekistan's and Turkmenistan's gas have a natural market in Kazakhstan and Russia. The most important public objectives for the CSRE are to overcome periodic energy shortages and dependence on unreliable energy sources as well as to develop new international markets for their energy, which would be able to provide a stable source of foreign exchange.

Throughout the last decade, the hydrocarbon sector contributed strongly to the economies of the Caspian Sea region. In Kazakhstan, in 2000, production of oil and gas condensate reached its highest level 35.191 – million tonnes (706 650 b/d) as did exports of these commodities. According to preliminary results for 2000, oil accounted for 45.5 percent of all Kazakhstani industrial production. In Azerbaijan, in 2000, oil production totalled 14.14 million tonnes (284 000 b/d), which is over 50 percent of Azeri industrial production. In Turkmenistan, natural gas production reached 47 billion cubic metres/(bcm) in 2000, which is around 17 percent of GDP. In Uzbekistan, oil and gas production is slowing down: production of oil and gas condensate in 2000 is estimated at 8.72 m tonnes

Table 3.2 Per capita energy use and carbon dioxide emissions

Indicator	Population (millions)		Carbon dioxide emissions per capita (metric tons)		Commercial energy use per capita (kg of oil equivalent)		Value added as % of GDP – manufacturing	GNP per capita in US dollars
Years	1990	1999	1990	1996	1990	1997	1999	1999
Kazakhstan	16.7	15.4	17.7	10.9	6 486	2 439	23	1 230
Russia	147.9	146.5	13.1	10.7	6 112	4 019	-	2 270
Turkmenistan	3.67	4.8	8.5	7.4	5 159	2 615	29	660
Uzbekistan	20.32	24.5	5.0	4.1	2 130	1 798	13	720
Azerbaijan	7.16	8.0	6.4	3.9	3 191	1 529	6	550

Source: World Bank Development Report, 2000/2001, Statistical yearbook of Kazakhstan, 1991; UN statistic division; Monthly bulletin of statistic online, 2000. TASIS; Russia and the EU member states, statistical comparison 1990–96.

(a 6 percent decrease compared with the previous year), however, the figures might be under-reported by Uzbekneftegaz and local refineries, due to the incentive gained by illegally exporting excess production, because of the existence of low domestic prices of crude oil and refined products (see Figure 3.2).

Therefore the fundamental impediments to economic development lay with the set of structural distortions inherited by the CSRE from the centrally planned system. The problem of structural changes has been discussed in depth in the academic literature (Kalyuzhnova, 1998, 2000; Rumer and Zhukov, 1998).

There are some difficulties in interpreting the official macroeconomic data due to the fact that the CSRE possess significant informal sectors. In addition, the accuracy of measurement of the formal sector of the economy, for example some official data of GDP dynamics, give reason to distrust the picture of economic recovery (Kalyuzhnova, 1998, pp. 100–4).

The apparent failure of a number of early attempts at reform led to reformers being accused of adopting strategies that came from economic textbooks rather than the actual conditions obtaining in the late period socialist systems.

The economic policies adopted by the CSRE varied from country to country. All of the countries except Turkmenistan initially accepted IMF policy recommendations conditionally in return for financial and technical assistance. The IMF package of reforms was accepted straightaway by Azerbaijan and Kazakhstan, and later a cool acceptance of the

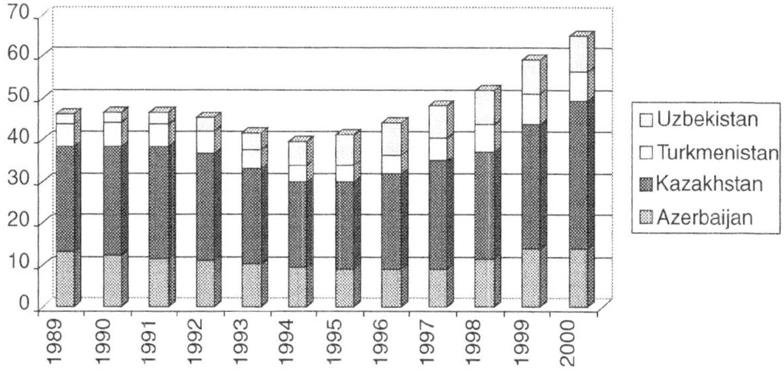

Figure 3.2 Oil production, 1989–2000, million tonnes

Source: BPAmocoalive (2000) and Centre for Global Energy Studies, 2001.

IMF's initiative was given by Uzbekistan, which applied a gradualist policy (Kaser, 1997; Kalyuzhnova 2000). Turkmenistan, however, rejected the help and advice of the IMF on the basis that its growth prospects were dependent on natural gas production, and on the sector's ability to find appropriate export markets.

In addition, mineral-related investment, trade and service activities have made significant contributions to GDP, particularly in Azerbaijan and Kazakhstan. These two countries have been able to attract large inflows of foreign investment. In Azerbaijan, "foreign investment in the form of equity and debt inflows, accounted for 47.7% of total investment in the first three quarters of 2000 – 10.6% of GDP" (EIU, Azerbaijan Country Report, 2001, p. 21). In Kazakhstan during the same period extractive industries received investment equivalent to 8.6 percent of GDP.

On the other hand, these economies have become increasingly linked to international energy and metals markets, and are therefore vulnerable to sharp swings in energy and metals prices.

Energy prices changes

Due to the fact that energy is a world market commodity, prices are highly competitive and variable. In most CSRE, energy prices still remain below cost-recovery level. As a consequence, such a distortion induces demand, and creates little incentive for energy efficiency. This could lead energy companies to invest in non-necessary capacity (*supply-side focus* of investment). The paradox here is that governments are in a better position to provide budgetary support for capacity extension rather than to implement measures that improve efficiency. Another explanation of focusing on the supply side lies in the preferences of governments and industries for large-scale investments for which they can more easily receive support from international financial institutions.

After the critical period of 1998 when oil prices declined rapidly, 1999 and 2000 may be characterized as years of recovery for CSRE, more than offsetting the weakness of the previous year. In 1999, the annual average price of Brent crude rose to \$18.25 a barrel, up 39 percent compared with 1998, and it rose by a further 55 percent to \$28.39 a barrel on average in 2000 (Figure 3.3). Oil prices were rescued in 1999 through output cuts by the world's main oil producers. OPEC countries were joined by others such as Mexico and Norway (who cut output in 1999 by 4.8 percent and 0.6 percent respectively), and oil

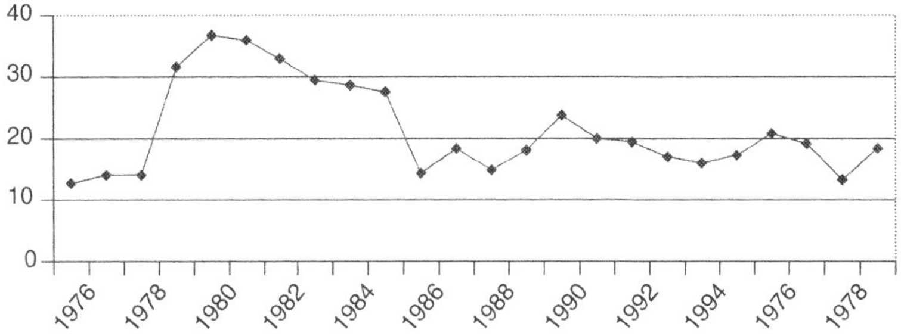

Figure 3.3 Spot crude prices, Brent, $, 1976–99

Source: BPAmocoalive (2000) For information: Price for Tengiz crude, on average, equals Brent price + (US$ 0.5-1.0/barrel), while Azeri Light equals Brent price + (US$ 1.0-1.5/barrel).

output also fell sharply in the USA in 1999 (dropping by 3.8 percent) as low prices the previous year reduced investment in the industry. The exception to these statistics was the UK, where output rose by 3.4 percent as production increased from fields brought into production in late-1998. Some newer producers, including the Caspian, Vietnam, West Africa and Brazil also increased output in 1999. The year 2000 saw oil output rise again as OPEC and others increased output in response to very high prices.

In 1999, world oil consumption rose by 1.6 percent, slightly faster than the 1989–99 average, however at the same time the CSRE showed a constant average decline in consumption (Table 3.3). This oil consumption trend illustrates the links between the general economy, individuals and companies: a continuing decline in NMP/GDP (Table 3.2), drastic reduction in the output of the local refineries (Kalyuzhnov and Nanay, 2000, p.62), high inequalities in income distribution and high (unaffordable by the majority of agents) domestic prices for oil products. Generally speaking, for the CSRE, demand for some end-users was suppressed during the first decade of transition.

As shown in Tables 3.3 and 3.4, energy use in Kazakhstan has constantly declined since 1991. In Uzbekistan, the drastic decline continued until 1995 (6.7 million tonnes) compared to 1989 (13.1 million tonnes). In total, CSRE energy use has steadily declined since 1990, falling to 52 percent of the 1990 level in 1999.

In 1999, world natural gas consumption rose by 2.4 percent the fastest rate since 1996, and significantly higher than the 1.7 percent

Table 3.3 Oil consumption* in the CSRE, 1989–99, million tonnes

Country	1989	1990	1991	1992	1993	1994	1995	1996	1997	1998	1999
Azerbaijan	8.1	8.5	8.2	8.1	8.2	8.1	8.5	7	6	5.9	6.3
Kazakhstan	18.6	21.5	21.7	20.3	15.7	12.3	12	10.2	10.3	8.5	6.4
Turkmenistan	3.5	4.4	5	4.9	3.2	3.7	3.9	3	3	4.3	4.5
Uzbekistan	13.1	12.6	11	9.1	8.1	7.2	6.7	7.4	6.7	7	7.1
Total	43.3	47	45.9	42.4	35.2	31.3	31.1	27.6	26	25.7	24.3

* Inland demand plus international aviation and marine bunkers and refinery fuel and loss.
Source: BPAmocoalive (2000).

average of the past 10 years. In 1999, Uzbekistan gas consumption increased by 33 percent compared with 1990. Total natural gas consumption for CSRE declined from 1989 (69.7 million tonnes oil equivalent) to 1997 (61.4 million tonnes oil equivalent) and from 1998 this indicator increased (Table 3.4).

Total gas production in the CSRE declined by 45 percent in 1998 compared to 1989, with a significant drop in Turkmenistan from 83.9 million tonnes oil equivalent in 1989 to 12.4 million tonnes oil equivalent in 1998 (Figure 3.4).

In order to understand the role of energy in the economy it is possible to use an aggregation of different energy flows. Below we examine the relations between energy use and GDP. The form of aggregation used for the analysis was the summing up of individual variables according to their oil equivale namely

$$E_t = \sum_{i=1}^{N} E_{it}$$

where E is the oil equivalent of fuel i (N types) at time t. This approach provides an advantage over simply counting the main resources of primary energy in the CSRE. There are other possible ways to approach the aggregation, such as basic heat equivalent approach, economic approach based on the aggregation of prices or marginal product (Cleveland *et. al.*, 2000).

Table 3.2 provided data for per capita energy use and carbon dioxide emissions for the CSRE. Energy use per capita was highest for Turkmenistan in 1999 with 2615 kg, followed by Kazakhstan with 2439 kg. Azerbaijan had the lowest per capita energy use with 1529 kg. Carbon dioxide emissions per capita are relatively high, ranging from 10.9 metric tons for Kazakhstan to 3.9 for Azerbaijan.

The decline in energy use in the CSRE has alleviated some environmental problems, such as air pollution. Due to the industrial decline, the demand for coal also decreased from 45.9 million tonnes oil equivalent in 1989 to 21.6 million tonnes oil equivalent in 1999. (Table 3.5) In the CSRE, between 1989 and 1999, oil's share of primary energy supply went up at the expense of natural gas and coal.

Link between energy consumption and GDP in the CSRE

The modelling strategy which we applied here in order to detect the presence of a causal relationship between energy consumption and GDP variables is based upon the Granger causality test. Similar analysis has been carried out in the case of Asian developing countries by

Table 3.4 Natural gas consumption in the CSRE, 1989–99, million tonnes oil equivalent

Country	1989	1990	1991	1992	1993	1994	1995	1996	1997	1998	1999
Azerbaijan	13.9	14.2	13.6	10.6	7.8	7.3	7.2	5.3	5.0	4.7	5.0
Kazakhstan	10.6	11.3	11.8	12.2	11.7	9.2	9.7	8.1	6.4	6.5	7.1
Turkmenistan	13.1	8.8	8.6	8.4	8.4	9.2	7.2	9.0	9.1	9.2	10.2
Uzbekistan	31.1	33.2	33.4	33.6	36.6	37.2	38.1	39.0	40.9	42.3	44.3
Total	68.7	67.5	67.4	64.8	64.5	62.9	62.2	61.4	61.4	62.7	66.6

Source: BPAmocoalive (2000).

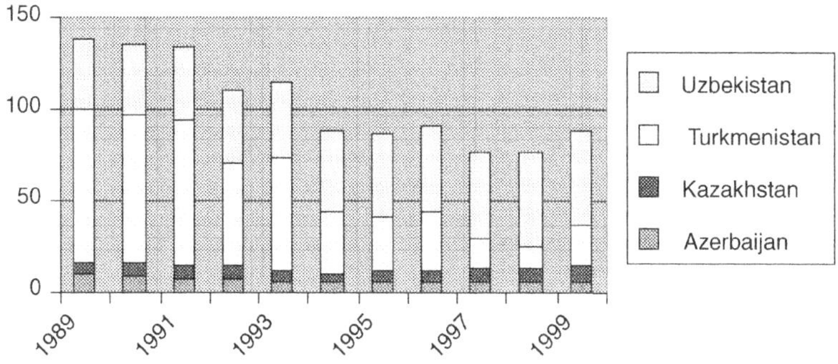

Figure 3.4 Natural gas production, 1989–99, million tonnes oil equivalent

Source: BPAmocoalive (2000)

Asafu-Adjaye (2000), Yang, (2000) and Cleveland, *et al.* (2000). The standard Granger causality test is determined as follows:

$$\Delta Y_t = \gamma_{12} + \sum_{i=1}^{T_{11}} \lambda_{11i} \Delta Y_{t-i} + \sum_{j=1}^{T_{12}} \lambda_{12j} \Delta X_{t-j} + \upsilon_{12t} \quad (3.1)$$

$$\Delta X_t = \gamma_{22} + \sum_{i=1}^{T_{21}} \lambda_{21i} \Delta X_{t-i} + \sum \lambda_{22} \Delta Y_{t-j} + \upsilon_{22t} \quad (3.2)$$

where Δ is the difference operator; Y_t is GDP; X_t-is primary energy consumption; T is the number of lags; γ and λ are parameters, which should be estimated; and υ_t is the error. Equations (3.1) and (3.2) are made to detect whether the coefficients of the past lag of primary energy consumption and GDP respectively can be zero as a whole. According to the Granger methodology, changes in primary energy consumption are deemed to cause changes in GDP if the estimated coefficients on the lagged values of primary energy consumption or the estimated coefficient on the lagged value of the error term is statistically significant.

Data and empirical interpretation of results

In order to investigate the causal relationship between GDP and energy consumption in the CSRE, we have used data series (which was available – observations during the first decade of transition) for the period of 1990–99. The GDP index (*GDP*), with 1990 = 100, was used to model changes in GDP in each country, while primary energy consumption

Table 3.5 Supply and final consumption fuel shares in CSRE

	1989						1999					
	Oil	Natural Gas	Coal	Nuclear Energy	Hydro electricity	Total	Oil	Natural Gas	Coal	Nuclear Energy	Hydro electricity	Total
Final Consumption million tonnes oil equivalent												
Azerbaijan	8.1	13.9	0.1		0.1	22.2	6.3	5			0.1	11.4
Kazakhstan	18.6	10.6	41.4	0.04	0.6	71.24	6.4	7.1	19.8		0.6	33.9
Turkmeinistan	3.5	13.1	0.3		0.04	16.94	4.5	10.27				14.7
Uzbekistan	13.1	31.1	4.1		0.5	48.8	7.1	44.3	1.8		0.6	53.8
Primary Supply million tonnes oil equivaient												
Azerbaijan	13.2	9.3				22.5	13.8	5				18.8
Kazakhstan	25.4	5.6	71.4			102.4	30	8.3	29.9			68.2
Turkmenistan	5.08	75.5			80.58	7.4	19.1					26.5
Uzbekistan	2.7	34.5				37.2	8.1	46.7				54.8

Source :BPAmocoalive (2000).

Table 3.6 Granger's causality tests between GDP and PEC

Regressions	*F*-value
Azerbaijan	
$\Delta GDP_t = \gamma_{12} + \sum_{i=1}^{5} \lambda_{11i} \Delta GDP_{t-i} + \sum_{j=1}^{5} \lambda_{12j} \Delta PEC_{t-j} + \upsilon_{12t}$	F(2, 6) = 0.70785 [0.5297]
$\Delta PEC = \gamma_{22} + \sum_{i=1}^{5} \lambda_{21i} \Delta PEC_{t-i} + \sum \lambda_{22} \Delta GDP_{t-j} + v_{22t}$	F(2, 6) = 1.7688 [0.2490]
Kazakhstan	
$\Delta GDP_t = \gamma_{12} + \sum_{i=i}^{5} \lambda_{11i} \Delta GDP_{t-1} + \sum_{j=1}^{5} \lambda_{12j} \Delta PEC_{t-j} + \upsilon_{12t}$	F(2, 6) = 3.2311 [0.1116]
$\Delta PEC = \gamma_{22} + \sum_{i=i}^{5} \lambda_{21i} \Delta PEC_{t-1} + \sum \lambda_{22} \Delta GDP_{t-j} + v_{22t}$	F(2, 6) = 8.7356 [0.0167]*
Turkmenistan	
$\Delta GDP_t = \gamma_{12} + \sum_{i=1}^{5} \lambda_{11i} \Delta GDP_{t-i} + \sum_{j=1}^{5} \lambda_{12j} \Delta PEC_{t-j} + \upsilon_{12t}$	F(2, 6) = 2.8792 [0.1329]
$\Delta PEC = \gamma_{22} + \sum_{i=1}^{5} \lambda_{21i} \Delta PEC_{t-i} + \sum \lambda_{22} \Delta GDP_{t-j} + v_{22t}$	F(2, 6) = 0.29342 [0.7558]
Uzbekistan	
$\Delta GDP_t = \gamma_{12} + \sum_{i=1}^{5} \lambda_{11i} \Delta GDP_{t-1} + \sum_{j=1}^{5} \lambda_{12j} \Delta PEC_{t-j} + \upsilon_{12t}$	F(2, 6) = 11.794 [0.0083]**
$\Delta PEC = \gamma_{22t} + \sum_{i=1}^{5} \lambda_{21i} \Delta PEC_{t-i} + \sum \lambda_{22} \Delta GDP_{t-j} + v_{22t}$	F(2, 6) = 8.93 [0.0159]*

* Significance at the 5% level.
** Significance at the 1% level.

(*PEC*), in million tonnes oil equivalent, was used to model energy consumption.

The results of Granger's causality test between *GDP* and *PEC* are presented in Table 3.6. The application of the standard Granger causality test requires that the series of variables be stationary. Since non-stationarity can be rejected for the series of all the variables using first differences, we then apply the standard Granger's causality test, specified in Table 3.6. Therefore, *F* statistics are calculated to test whether the coefficients on the lagged variables are jointly equal to zero. We found different results depending on the country under consideration. In the cases of Azerbaijan and Turkmenistan, no causality was found. In the case of Kazakhstan, there was a unidirectional causality from *PEC* to

GDP. Uzbekistan's case showed bi-directional causality; that is, causality in both directions (*GDP–PEC* and *PEC–GDP*).

Table 3.6 reveals that for the GDP equation we may accept the hypothesis that change in energy consumption Granger causes a change in GDP. In economic terms, this means that the inclusion of past values of energy consumption in the GDP equation provides a better explanation of current values of GDP than when excluded. Conversely, the inclusion of GDP into the PEC equation provides a better explanation of the energy results rather than if excluded.

The CSRE national currencies are stabilizing (excluding perhaps Uzbekistan), but the mixed (state and private) industry makes it difficult to value outcome in monetary terms. The decline in value-added share seen in Kazakhstan after 1990 is in part an effect of the structural changes in the economy. The development of manufacturing activity in the CSRE varies – in Turkmenistan the share of industry was 59 percent of GDP in 1992, which shrunk to 29.2 percent in 1998; reciprocally Kazakhstan's industry was 30.1 percent in 1992, the substantial decline of which was in 1998. In all CSRE, the manufacturing sector's share of GDP declined significantly following the first wave of reform of 1992–97. However, from 1999 onwards the decline seems to have stopped (Figure 3.5).

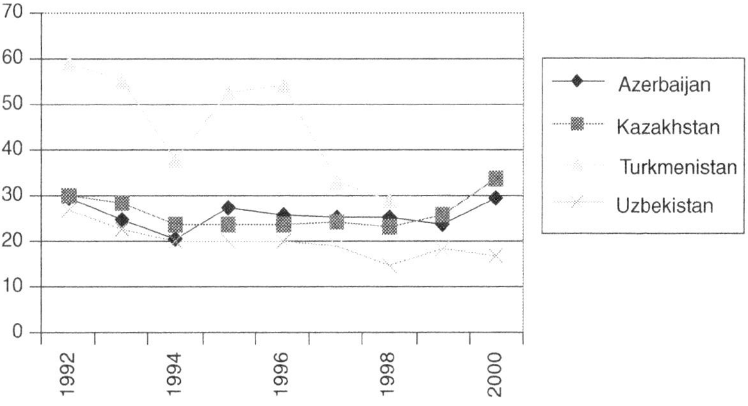

Figure 3.5 Share of industry in GDP (in percent), 1992–99
Source: Transition Report 2000. Azerbaijan 2000: Economic Trends, Azerbaijan (April–June 2000), TACIS. European Bank For Reconstruction and Development. Kazakhstan 1999–2000: Economic Trends, Kazakhstan (April–June 2000), TACIS Uzbekistan 1999: Economic Trends, Uzbekistan (July–December1999), TACIS. Uzbekistan 1999–2000: Economic Trends, Uzbekistan (April–June 2000), TACIS.

It is difficult, however, to draw conclusions on changes in energy efficiency based on this information. For the CEE/CIS economies, there are problems in calculating comparable value-added figures. Also, comparisons are complicated because there are differences in the structure of the manufacturing sector, both between countries and over time within a country. A country that produces a major share of its value-added from energy-intensive raw materials will not have a higher aggregate energy intensity than a country that produces less energy-intensive products. Similarly, a country's aggregate manufacturing energy intensity may decline over time as the share of heavy industry is reduced and replaced by less energy-intensive manufacturing. In both cases, the aggregate intensity does not necessarily tell how efficient a country is compared to others, nor does it tell whether the efficiency is improving over time. To get a clearer picture, information on the development of the structure of manufacturing is needed. However countries' value-data in real terms are not available for the CSRE; as a result, the ratio of primary energy consumption to GDP was used for the CSRE (Figure 3.6).

As Figure 3.6 shows, in 1990–96 (the most depressed period for the CSRE), the ratio of primary energy consumption to GDP steadily increased year by year (up to 1996 – the highest in the period of 1989–99). This illustrates the structural changes which were taking place during the first decade of transition, namely: while most output was declining, the industrial units still used a similar (in proportion to GDP higher) amount of energy. However, the production of these

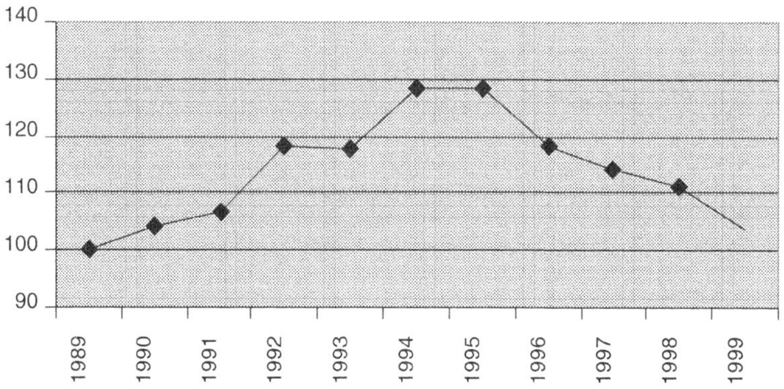

Figure 3.6 CSRE Ratio: PEC/GDP (percent), 1989–99

Source: Author's calculations on the basis of data from BPAmocolive (2000).

enterprises contracted at a faster rate than the reduction in the PEC. In other words, the decline in GDP, as well as in industrial output, was more rapid than the decline in the PEC. Structural changes play an important role in the reduction of energy use and, as practice shows, at that time (1990–96) there was a lack of structural change in the transformation process of the CSRE, which gave a high (inefficient) use of prime energy.

One of the most energy-intensive activities in many CIS economies has been in the metallurgical industry. Trends in steel production for Kazakhstan are displayed in Figure 3.7. The production levelled out at about 60 percent of 1990 levels. Similar trends can be seen in the production of other energy-intensive products, such as cement (Figure 3.7).

At the present time, there is a large potential for energy efficiency gains in the manufacturing sector in the CSRE, which very much depends on the governmental commitments to pursue further the process of restructuring.

Management of oil and gas wealth

The governments of the resource rich countries are facing two major issues: "The first-related to the finite nature of these resources – is how much oil income to spend on the present generation and how much to save for future generations. The second is how to adjust government spending and cushion the domestic economy from the sharp and unpredictable variations in oil prices and revenue" (Fasano, 200, p. 3).

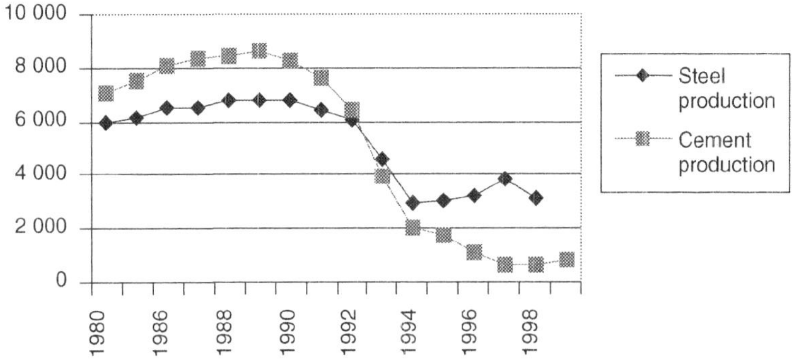

Figure 3.7 Kazakhstan: steel and cement production, 1980, 1985–2000 (thousand tonnes)

Source: Stastical yearbook of Kazakhstan, various years, 1991–2000.

As demonstrated above, the importance of the oil and gas sector in the CSRE has grown substantially during the last decade. In this respect, an appropriate macroeconomic policy is essential. The main components of such a policy include increasing the direct income transfers to governments and inflow of foreign exchange from foreign investments. Adjustment by monetary and fiscal policies should provide an escape from excessive real exchange rate appreciation. Resource-rich transition economies run the risk that high rates of inflation will make non-mineral industries non-competitive. This effect is linked to the Dutch disease effect, which "will only be apparent (as a *disease*) if the real appreciation overshoots the equilibrium" (IMF, 2000c, p. 44). In such a situation, the easing of monetary policy could prevent further problems. For example in Kazakhstan, continued high inflows could hinder the National Bank of Kazakhstan's efforts to avoid currency appreciation and increase the probability of Dutch disease. Increased income from an oil industry windfall leads to increased demand, exchange rate appreciation and loss of competitiveness in the Kazakhstani economy as a whole.

The Dutch disease problem is potentially serious where governmental policy attempts to constrain imports, either as a protectionist subsidy to the domestic development of import competing goods, as a means to hold down consumption, or in an attempt to prevent capital outflows. Of course, large inflows of foreign investment could make matters worse (in terms of its effects on the exchange rate) but this suggests that policy be directed towards promoting the domestic financing of investment rather than importing capital.

Oil trust funds could be an effective instrument for oil revenue management. Azerbaijan and Kazakhstan have already established such funds. The oil revenue paid into these funds can be used for different investment projects. In Kazakhstan, for example, one such project is the pension funds project, where the oil revenue is partially implemented as initial capital endowment of the Kazakhstani funded pension scheme. In other words, the Kazakhstani government has made an attempt to use this fund as an institutional investor in the capital market. According to Prime Minister Kasymzhomart Tokayev, the $450 million raised by the sale of a 5 percent stake in the Tengizchevroil consortium to Chevron of the United States, was the first contribution to this so-called "generation fund".

The data regarding oil revenue (1995–99) in Azerbaijan shows that the biggest contribution came from the state oil company, /SOCAR/ (Figure 3.8). The budgeted government capital expenditures have been

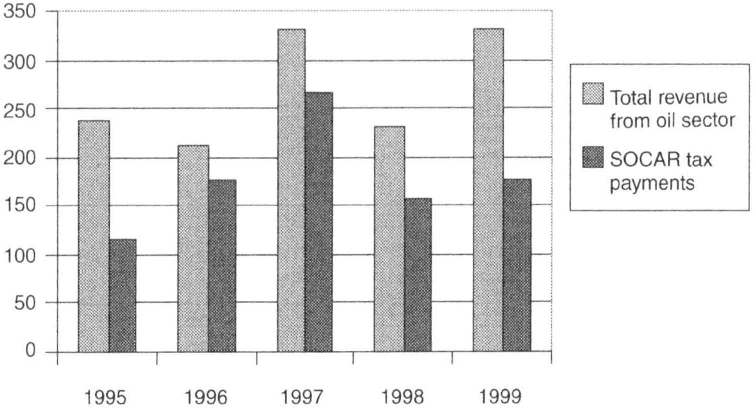

Figure 3.8 Azeri oil revenue, 1995–99 (US$ millions)
Source: Azerbaijan State Committee on Statistics, and State Oil Company of the Azerbaijan Republic.

very low, and the oil revenue has been used to fund current expenditures, which averaged more than 7 percent of GDP in 1995–2000.

In general, the Kazakhstani and Azeri funds appear to be similar. The provision of both funds will be supported by taxes from the oil companies, oil royalties and signing bonuses.

The supervision of both will be done through a special governmental body and held in a special government account. At the moment, the audit mechanism is unclear along with the lack of clarity in duties of the supervisory committee. Also, the mechanism for allocating and spending money remains to be seen. One of the critical questions is the interaction of the fund and cooperation with the government budget, otherwise, there is a danger of injecting too much cash into the economy. Therefore, an appropriate macroeconomic framework is essential for defining the role of the oil fund in both Kazakhstani and Azeri economies.

All Caspian Sea region's governments need to establish clear rules and guidelines that will determine the use of the natural resource revenue in the economies: they are only at the beginning of this process. The statistical data regarding consumption from oil wealth lacks transparency and consistency. It is unclear how much is invested in foreign financial assets and how much into fixed capital. The governments need to strengthen governance in order to eliminate the possibilities of rent-seeking behaviour of some government bureaucracy associated with resource wealth (Sachs and Warner, 1995). Another important indicator of the welfare of the CSRE related to oil and gas is the question of foreign markets for energy products. Chapter 5 provides an extensive overview of the pipeline and gas line routes. Therefore, our attention is concentrated only on the actual contribution of the energy trade to the CSRE.

The boom in oil and gas prices after the 1998 world commodity crisis gave these states the chance to recover their trade positions. In Kazakhstan, oil and oil products exports, which represent more than one-quarter of all exports of goods, were 23.331 m tonnes (562 000 barrels/day) in January–October 2000. "Oil and gas condensate accounted for 48.2% of export earnings on custom basis in the first 10 months of 2000, compared with 36.2% in the same period of 1999" (EIU, 2001b, p. 30).

A similar situation exists in Turkmenistan, where the country has substantially improved its own trade balance by the resumption of gas sales to Russia as well as booming energy prices. During the first nine months of 2000, the export revenue increased by 99 percent (in US dollar terms) compared with the same period of 1999, giving the country US$1.7 billion. The trade surplus during this period was US$354 million. The last five years have demonstrated that Turkmen energy exports very much depend on Russia, since Russia accounted for more than 45 percent of its export revenue in 2000. In the light of recent difficulties (including the 1998 Russian financial crisis), in 1999 Turkmenistan focused on boosting its oil output. There is direct export of crude oil abroad and Turkmen oil also provides crude supply for local refineries (see Chapter 6). A large share of the refined oil is exported.

A similar picture emerged in Azerbaijan, where high oil prices, together with a growing volume of oil exports, produced a trade surplus in 2000. In 2000, "crude oil export volumes rose by 140% year on year. Most oil exports came from the Azerbaijan International Operating Company" (EIU, 2001a, p. 30). In 1999, oil and oil products accounted for 75.9 percent of the country's total exports. Total revenue from the oil sector rose from US$239 million in 1995 to US$331 million in 1997, declined to US$232 million in 1998 and then recovered in 1999 (US$331 million).

In contrast with the rest of the CSRE, Uzbekistan does not have a big share of energy products in their export mix. Statistics are limited due to the under-reporting of production by officials: in 1998 energy products were 22.7 percent of the total exports, worth US$87.3 million, compared with imports costing US$4.7 million.

As demonstrated above, the CSRE (with the exception of Uzbekistan) depend heavily on their hydrocarbon sectors. This lack of industry diversification can be considered as one of the main weaknesses of the economic structure of these countries. Structural shifts as a result of the Russian crisis make the economies even more vulnerable to external shocks than before. The diversification of industry decreased significantly, and the perception of reliance on commodities has been strengthened.

Conclusion

The last decade has been turbulent for the CSRE. The early years of independence saw a sharp decline in most sectors of these economies and increasing disintegration of the economic links between them, which, conversely, highlighted their interdependence. The states are still trying to disengage their economies: "In early 1999, the states of Central Asia began to impose severe restrictions and customs duties on imports" (Rumer, 2000, p. 11). However, as was shown in the chapter, the CSRE are still closely tied to each other, which is a legacy of the Soviet economic system.

"Confidence" in their independence from neighbouring countries comes from the start of the development of the hydrocarbon sector. Control over energy resources is connected to the desire for power in the region. However, all the CSRE are still attempting to establish themselves as major energy producers and exporters. Their success will be highly dependent on the policies adopted by the governments, as well as external factors, including the fluctuation of world oil prices.

As argued throughout the chapter, economic development in the Caspian region has been affected by several external factors where, besides the Asian economic crisis, and the Russian financial crisis fluctuations in prices for export commodities have played a significant role.

Although all CSRE have reduced to some extent the predominant role of Russia in their economies, the Russian financial crisis demonstrated the vulnerability of the CSRE and the prevailing importance of Russia in their economic structures.

Only after the recovery of world oil prices did the CSRE gain some confidence and the first signs of the economic growth appear. Provided world market prices for oil and other commodities remain at a suitable level, GDP will continue to grow in the coming years (especially in Azerbaijan and Kazakhstan). However, a much higher level of industrial diversification is necessary in order to make growth sustainable. At the present time, the natural resource boom has defined the economic development of the region. For instance, Turkmenistan is likely to have the most volatile growth in the region as GDP continues to be based on natural gas. The key challenge for Turkmenistan is to find stable, solvent export markets for its gas. Due to geographical and political circumstances, this will be problematic. In contrast, Kazakhstan has a more diverse economic structure in the region, although it is faced with a lot of structural challenges in its economy.

The crucial question here is the role that energy could play in the CSRE. The development of the hydrocarbon sector in the CSRE is complicated by the structural changes that are ongoing in these economies. It is important to take into account transition specific factors, including privatization and restructuring. The latter can distort the picture of energy consumption and lead to misleading conclusions regarding energy use as highlighted in the chapter. Therefore, in order to identify the presence of a relationship between energy consumption and GDP, data for GDP and PEC for the CSRE have been used, and the causal relationship between GDP and PEC has been investigated using Granger's technique. The result of this econometric exercise was the establishment of bidirectional causality between GDP and PEC in Kazakhstan and Uzbekistan.

In addressing the significance of the hydrocarbon sector for the CSRE, it is important to assess the management problem of oil and gas wealth. Kazakhstan and Azerbaijan are poised to participate in the oil boom and will face the challenges of managing this new-found wealth. International experience provides many examples of the negative consequences of income booms for oil-rich countries. "Dutch disease", for instance, refers to the negative effects of real exchange rate appreciation due to strong oil and/or gas exports on other sectors of the economy. In 2000, the Kazakhstani government started to promote an import substitution policy, imposing on foreign investors the principle of placing more of their spending in Kazakhstan. However, this policy needs to be based on firmer ground, with efficient Kazakhstani firms, products, and competitive prices.

Constraining imports as a response to the effects of the Dutch disease would make matters worse, since that would mean a forced reduction of demand for foreign products (and currency) and a forced increase in demand for domestic products, leading to a further real exchange rate appreciation. More rapid money growth does not help combat

Dutch disease, either, since it does not help to improve the competitive position of non-oil and gas products.

However, the transition challenges might mislead and give similar symptoms to the Dutch disease. For example, in Azerbaijan and Kazakhstan, much of the non-oil and gas industry that existed at the time of the break-up of the USSR had already disappeared by the time oil exports started picking up, so this cannot be contributed to a "Dutch disease". Also, in 2000, various non-oil and gas sectors in these countries showed strong performances, indicating that the Dutch disease is not a significant problem at present. However, if oil and gas exports start picking up significantly in a few years time, Dutch disease-type effects might hamper the ability of other sectors to develop.

The introduction of oil funds can make a contribution to combating Dutch disease-type effects if the money accumulated in the funds is invested in foreign currency denominated assets. This would increase the demand for foreign currency, driving down the real exchange rate. Foreign direct investment flows are expected to be relatively large in most of the CSRE. However, in order to generate higher growth rates, governments will have to focus on developing the CSRE's significant non-oil sectors, such as agriculture, food processing, manufacturing and so on. This will require continuing the difficult structural reforms in the region.

Acknowledgement

I am grateful to Julian Lee and Maria Vagliasindi for the help and support which they provided while writing this chapter. My thanks go to Ron Soligo for his useful comments. Andrei Kalyuzhnov provided much encouragement throughout the research.

References

Asafu-Adjaye, John (2000) "The Relationship Between Energy Consumption, Energy Prices and Economic Growth: Time Series Evidence from Asian Developing Countries". *Energy Economics*, 22, pp. 615–25.

BPAmocoalive (2000) *Statistical Review of World Energy*, June.

CGES (Centre for Global Energy Studies) (1998) "Breaking the Stranglehold".

Clark, Jennifer Cook, Clark, Allen L. and Naito, Koh (1998) "Emerging Mineral Policy and Legislation in the Economic Development of the Central Asian Republics", *Resources Policy*, 24 (2) 115–23.

Cleveland, Cutler J., Kaufmann, Robert K. and Stern David I. (2000) "Aggregation and Role of Energy in the Economy", *Ecological Economics,* 32, pp. 301–17.

Chevron Corporation (2000) "The Energy to Grow" *1999 Annual Report.*

Daviddi, R. and Spa, E. (1995) "Regional Trade and Foreign Currency Regimes, Among the Former Soviet Republics", *Economics Planning,* 28, pp. 29–57.

EIU/(Economist Intelligence Unit) (2001a) *Azerbaijan, Country Report,* January: EIU(Economist Intelligence Unit)(2001b)Kazakhstan Country Report, January.

Fasano, Ugo (2000) "Review of the Experience with Oil Stabilization and Savings Funds in Selected Countries" *IMF Working Paper* WP/00/112.

IMF, (1999) *Turkmenistan: Recent Economic Developments,* Staff Country Report No. 99/140, December. (Washington, DC: International Monetary Fund).

IMF, (2000) *Republic of Kazakhstan: Selected Issues and Statistical Appendix,* Staff Country Report No 00/29, March. (Washington, DC: International Monetary Fund).

IMF, (2000) *Republic of Uzbekistan: Recent Economic Developments.* Staff Country Report No 00/36, March. (Washington, DC: International Monetary Fund).

IMF, (2000) *Azerbaijan Republic: Recent Economic Developments and Selected Issues,* Staff Country Report No 00/121, September (Washington, DC: International Monetary Fund).

Kalyuzhnov, Andrei and Nanay, Julia (2000) "Caspian area Refineries Struggle to Overcome Soviet Legacy", *Oil and Gas Journal,* August 21, pp. 62–6.

Kalyuzhnova, Yelena (1998) *The Kazakhstani Economy,* (London: Macmillan Press, now Palgrave)

Kalyuzhnova, Yelena (1999) "An Assessment of Industrial Policy and Employment Prospects in Central Asia" *The Central Asia 2010: Prospects of Human Development,* New York: UNDP publication.

Kalyuzhnova, Yelena (2000) "The Economic Transition in Kazakhstan and Uzbekistan' in Y. Kalyuzhnova and D. Lynch (eds), *(The Euro-Asian World)* (London: Macmillan press now Palgrave)

Kaser, Michael (1997) *The Economies of Kazakstan and Uzbekistan* (London: The Royal Institute of International Affairs).

Rosenberg, Christoph and Saavalainen, Tapio (1998) "How to Deal with Azerbaijan's Oil Boom? Policy Strategies in a Resource-Rich Transition Economy", *IMF Working Paper,* WP/98/6.

Rumer, Boris, Zhukov and Stanislav (eds), (1998) *Central Asia and The Challenge of Independence:* M.E.Sharpe Armonk (New York and London: England,)

Rumer Boris, Zhukov and Stanislav (eds), (2000) *Central Asia and the New Global Economy* M.E. Sharpe (Armonk, New York and London: England,)

Sachs, Jeffrey D. and Warner, Andrew M. (1995) "Natural Resource Abundance and Economic Growth", *NBER Working Paper 5398* (Cambridge, MA: National Bureau of Economic Research).

World Bank Development Report (2000/2001) Washington D C: World Bank.

Yang, Hao-Yen (2000) "A note on the Causal Relationship between Energy and GDP in Taiwan", *Energy Economics,* 22(3), pp. 309–17.

4

Islam and Energy Security

Mehrdad Haghayeghi and Fred R. von der Mehden

Introduction

The collapse of the Soviet Union in 1991 brought into our foreign policy discourse several new concerns, of which Islamic resurgence in Central Asia was considered to be a potentially serious threat. The region's close proximity to revolutionary Iran, fragmented Afghanistan, and the civil strife in Tajikistan – with its religious underpinnings – shaped our initial understanding of this issue and thus prompted an early visit to the region by the former Secretary of State, James Baker in 1992. On Secretary Baker's agenda was an unequivocal message to the republican leaders that called for vigilance to curb the spread of Islamic fundamentalism into the region.

Later observations, however, revealed several ethno-religious patterns that did not lend themselves to the alarmist interpretations of an impending Islamic ideological takeover from the south. To the contrary, inter and intra-republican diversity in Islamic belief, the largely liberal and tolerant nature of the prevailing Islamic doctrine, the weak financial and mobilization capabilities of politically active Muslim groups, and ethnic and sub-ethnic allegiances, provided powerful evidence as to the moderate character of Islamic revival.

However, the Tashkent bombings in the winter of 1999 and the militant Islamic incursions from Tajikistan and Afghanistan into Kyrgyzstan and Uzbekistan in the summer and fall of 2000 have once again drawn our attention to Islamic politics in Central Asia. These alarming incidents were interpreted by some observers as early tremors of a much larger political earthquake that could destabilize much of the region.[1] This study is designed to assess the impact of Islam on energy security in Central Asia. It will be argued that while in the short-term the growth of Islamic radicalism poses a limited and largely manageable threat to energy production and distribution in Central Asia, in the long-term it may pose a far more serious threat to regional stability and thus energy security.

The religious environment

The majority of an estimated 45 million Central Asian Muslims adhere to the Hanafi school of Sunni Islam that rose to prominence during the Abbasid (750–1258) dynasty in Kufa and later spread eastward into Khorasan and Transoxania. A branch of the Hanafi School was established in Bukhara in the early ninth century. It quickly grew in popularity, attracting a sizable following. It also produced famous scholars, of whom Abu Hafs (d. 832) was referred to as the "teacher of scholars of Mawarannahr." The Hanafi school wielded considerable influence, both religious and political, particularly since the 11th century AD and in subsequent decades was adopted by the Seljuk and Ottoman dynasties that ruled over much of the region. Central Asia is also home to a small Shi'i population – the twelver Shi'is of Samarkand and Bukhara and the Ismaeli Shi'is of the Badakhshon region of Tajikistan.

Three aspects of the Hanafi Islam were critical in generating widespread popularity in Central Asia. First, its founder, Abu Hanifah, was a Persian. His non-Arab heritage was highly valued by the Central Asian population most of whom had lived under the umbrella of Persian culture and civilization for centuries. Second, the liberal orientation of the Hanafi doctrine allowed for the incorporation of the pre-Islamic traditions of Central Asia, many of which have been preserved until now. Lastly, it allowed for a more lax practice of Islamic precepts. Furthermore, such liberal tendencies were incorporated into the belief system of a number of Sufi orders in the region, the most popular of which, the Naqshbandiya, share many of the Hanafi doctrinal underpinnings.[2]

The available literature on pre-Soviet Central Asia offers a sketchy view of the level of adherence to Islam among the population. Broadly, however, there seems to have existed a clear regional divide between the *sedentary* Uzbeks and Tajiks who were more thoroughly converted to Islam, and the *tribal* Kazakh, Turkmen, and Kyrgyz who were generally less exposed to the teachings of Islam.[3] Yet as undifferentiated traditional societies, in the Uzbek principalities of Bukhara, Kokand, and Khiva, government and religion enjoyed qualitative overlaps in administration of laws (Shari'a), the economy (land tenure), and education of the public (maktab and madrasah). As such, the notion of secularism as strictly advocated by the current regimes may not be entirely applicable to Central Asia. Nevertheless, the clergy did not possess political power – an element that is playing an increasingly critical role in defining the contemporary Islamic fundamentalist notion.

With the Soviet takeover of the region, and the ensuing anti-religious campaign for nearly 70 years, Islam's institutional network and its public manifestations were somewhat weakened but communism failed to eradicate Islamic belief in Central Asia. It should be indicated, however, that the secular orientation of the Soviet polity led to the development of a class of intelligentsia in each Central Asian republic, whose modern outlook stood in contrast to the traditional world view prevalent in pre-communist Central Asia. Though culturally and historically sensitive to its heritage, the intelligentsia continues to favor largely a secular and parliamentary alternative rather than a return to strict traditional ways of life.

Despite the apparent continuity with the pre-communist past, the Islamic revival in post-independence Central Asia included several new dimensions that have been inspired by the contemporary Islamic trends elsewhere in the Middle East. The most notable trends were the formation of Islamic parties and organizations that aimed at gaining access to the political process, and the introduction of Islamic fundamentalist ideology that called for a strict adherence to Islam and largely rejected secular belief. A discussion of the former will be presented later. As for the latter, the ultimate objective continues to be the establishment of an Islamic state in the region. What distinguished the Central Asian brand of fundamentalism from its Middle Eastern variants, was that it largely lacked an anti-Western ideological orientation, and at least in principle ruled out violence as a method of achieving statehood.

Two manifestations of Islamic fundamentalism was identified early on although both shared common characteristics, including demands for the implementation of Shari'a and mandated Islamic rituals. Wahhabi movement, inspired and funded by Saudi Arabia, advocates a strict religious adherence to Islamic precepts, as stated in the Koran and Hadith (the sayings of the Prophet Muhammad).[4] However, it does not sanctify clerical political involvement. Nor does it support a change in the political rule, so long as the Shari'a law is reinstated. It should be indicated, however, that the Saudi backing for the expansion of Wahhabism in Central Asia appears to be non-governmental, although it is difficult to envisage that the Saudi ruling elite is unaware of such financial and logistical contributions by its private citizens.[5] Wahhabi tradition is opposed to any ritual that had not been followed by the Prophet Muhammad himself.

The second manifestation that may be referred to as political Islam aimed at competing for power through parliamentary means in order to establish an Islamic state.[6] The republican governments hoped to stave off the growing popularity of Islamic fundamentalism with the introduction of legislation that banned religious parties and called for the separation of church and state. With this ban the parliamentary path to gaining or sharing political power was effectively removed, paving the way for more radical expressions of Islamic activism, the manifestations of which are becoming more apparent in Uzbekistan. The most significant of these expressions, the Jihadi movement, has been gathering strength since 1995, though early manifestations of the movement existed in Uzbekistan and Tajikistan as far back as 1991–92.[7] The Jihadi movement in essence considers the current regimes in the region illegitimate and sanctifies an arms struggle to remove them, in order to establish an Islamic state. Seen in this light, the Jihad or holy war against the regimes is considered an obligation to be fulfilled by all capable Muslim men.

Several factors account for the increasing popularity of the Jihadi movement. First, as indicated above, the newly emerging Muslim forces have been denied access to the political process through parliamentary means and electoral competition. In addition to banning religious parties, and in gross violation of the principle of separation of church and state, the Central Asian governments have quickly monopolized the so-called official Islam and its institutional network, thus denying yet another avenue of expression by the independent Islamic leaders.[8] In 1993–94, the Uzbek government went so far as to limit the activities of those organizations that did not have an apparent political motive.[9] Such exclusionary tactics have added to the frustration of Muslim groups and have affected adversely the legitimacy of the regimes in Central Asia.

Second, and equally significant, has been the failure of official Islam to teach adequately and effectively the liberal principles of Hanafi Islam.[10] Moreover, from both qualitative and quantitative point of views, the official Islamic schools in Uzbekistan, Kyrgyzstan, Kazakhstan and Turkmenistan have failed to satisfy the enthusiasm generated for Islamic learning and rituals after independence. This in turn helped the growth of autonomous schools taught by the so-called unofficial clergy, many of whom subscribe to a largely politicized reading of Islam, and lack adequate knowledge of Islamic principles. Although almost invariably all Central Asian governments have been engaged in promoting Islamic culture, their efforts have been perceived as insincere and inadequate.

Third, corruption and nepotism have been critical elements in radicalizing Islam and at the same time gradually deepening the crisis of legitimacy facing the regimes. While the scope of the problem varies from republic to republic, corruption has been a major problem in limiting the scope and speed of economic recovery that has so far yielded very little tangible results at the household level. Consequently, the merits of the establishment of a Western-style capitalist market economy in these societies have come under serious question.[11]

Finally, increasing repression has gradually strengthened the drive of the political Islam, as an ever greater number of its members has been arbitrarily detained, or murdered, and as penalties for advocating Islamic ideas have been stiffened.[12]

Orientation of Islamic organizations

Two types of Islamic organizations with overlapping objectives emerged shortly after the Central Asian republics achieved independence. The first were the republican parties that commanded a relatively small following and lacked republic-wide networks.[13] The most radical of these organizations were established in the Fergana Valley of Uzbekistan, and were forced to go underground by 1994 as their members and sympathizers were subjected to coercion and imprisonment. Mostly militant, these organizations refused to follow a parliamentary strategy that was recommended by the more moderate Muslim organizations such as the all-Union Islamic Revival Party (IRP), *Partiya Islamskovo Vozrozhdeniya.* Constituting the second type of Islamic organizations that took root in the region, the IRP enjoyed greater popular support than the other republican organizations. It also succeeded in establishing branches in Tajikistan and Uzbekistan. Though short-lived, these branches developed successful working networks that were maintained through mosques and prayer houses prior to the government ban on their activities.[14] But the negative publicity surrounding the activities of the IRP tarnished its reputation throughout the former Soviet Union, leading to a decision to disband the main branch in 1996. The Central Asian branches, however, continued their underground activities in Uzbekistan and guerrilla war in Tajikistan. Although the status of the Uzbek IRP remains illegal, the Tajik IRP may be reinstated as part of the peace agreement that was signed on June 27, 1997 between the government and the Islamic opposition (UTO).[15]

Nowhere is the support for militant Muslim organizations stronger than in Uzbekistan, where government crackdown has been most severe. Legally banned to compete for power through parliamentary means, many of the Uzbek IRP members and sympathizers have joined the ranks of the so-called Jihadi organizations that struggle to topple the regime through open confrontation. Several violent incidents have taken place since 1995, casting serious doubt as to the ability of the Uzbek government to maintain long-term stability despite greater reliance on repression of Muslim forces.[16] So far, it appears that the government efforts to neutralize these groups have failed, and several have continued to recruit new members, the majority of whom are young angry men with little secular or religious education. Largely unemployed, these men have lost trust in governments' ability or willingness to improve socioeconomic conditions or to lead a genuine Islamic revival.

The Adolat organization that was established in 1991 by Hakim Sotimov was the precursor to several other militant organizations whose emergence coincided with the ban on the activities of the IRP. Adolat began to organize self-appointed neighborhood committees, the members of which began to patrol the streets of Namangan in order to combat crime and oversee the implementation of Islamic codes of conduct. In December 1991, Adolat organized a public rally to form a Muslim self-government in Namangan. A government crackdown later that year led to the arrest of 71 members, many of whom still remain in prison.[17] Tohir Yoldash, one of the masterminds of the December 1991 event later split from Adolat and created the Islam Lashkarlari (Armies of Islam), a militant organization that aimed at a violent overthrow of the Uzbek regime. In early 1992, Yoldash and Jumabay Namangani fled Uzbekistan and took refuge in Tavildara of the neighboring Tajikistan, where they undertook training of estimated 200–400 Islamic militants to engage in a holy war against the Uzbek government. Two smaller organizations, Towba led by Abduvali Yoldash and Tolib Mamadjonov, and Amirlar have also been connected to the Islam Laskarlari. Some of their members were among those arrested in connection with the murder of the police chief in 1997 in Namangan.[18]

Apart from Uzbekistan, the other Central Asian republics lack militant organizations, though Kyrgyz and Uzbek citizens of Osh and Jalalabad and Uzbeks of Shimkent have been cooperating with the Uzbek groups by providing safe haven and logistical support. Recent reports also indicate the possible entry into Central Asia of the Hizb-i Tahrir Islamiya through Pakistan.[19] Founded by Sheikh Taqi Al-Din Al-Nabhani in Jordan, the party calls for the creation of a Khilafah that would eventually encompass the whole of the Muslim world.[20] The Hizb-i Tahrir is known to favor a dual strategy of consciousness raising at the grassroots level to bring about a revolution, and/or tap into the power structure to seek sympathetic individuals willing to stage a coup against the current leaders.

Despite the fragmented nature of the militant Muslim organizations in Uzbekistan and their differences in the method of struggle, almost all share the objective of removing the current regime that has been declared illegitimate. With the porous borders and greater opportunity for training and logistical support in Afghanistan and Pakistan, the arms struggle is slowly becoming a viable alternative, particularly in light of the success of the Islamic opposition in Tajikistan. The second long-term objective of these organizations is to establish an Islamic state. But there does not seem to be a consensus as to the geographical scope of such a state. While some groups advocate republican based states, new emerging trends speak of larger transnational arrangements. For instance, Islam Lashkarlari calls for the establishment of an Islamic state over the former territory of Kokand that includes the Uzbek Fergana, Tajik Isfara, and Kyrgyz Osh regions.[21] The Hizb-i Tahrir, on the other hand calls for the establishment of a Khilafah that would initially encompass the former Turkistan.

Based on preliminary evidence available, several factors make these organizations potentially more successful in achieving their objective. First, an ever greater number of their members have been receiving military and explosives training in camps in Afghanistan and elsewhere, which make them a more formidable force in future military confrontations. Furthermore, some Uzbek Muslim activists have been battle hardened because of their participation in the Tajik civil war.[22] Second, it appears that the logistical capabilities of these organizations have increased, as the magnitude of Tashkent bombings clearly demonstrates. Third, the continuing crackdown has increased the level of support and sympathy for the organizations, thus expanding the pool of potential members who are willing to fight for what they perceive to be a legitimate cause. Finally, these radical organizations have managed to develop an efficient cross-the-border network that has offered the leaders, as well as the rank and file members, increased mobility – a critical ingredient for a successful expansion of their operational capabilities.

Islam as an energy security issue

Short-term threats

Given the nature of oil the industry from the point of view of exploration, extraction, processing, and transportation, Central Asia will continue to face security threats similar to those in other oil-rich regions of the world. These threats may be identified as follows:

- terrorist attacks that could disrupt oil extraction and transportation through existing pipelines;
- violent attacks or the threat of such action by Muslim groups targeting Western oil personnel;
- the weakening or overthrow of governments friendly to Western interests by Islamic or nationalist organizations.

While the growing radicalization of Islam in Central Asia, at this juncture, does not pose an unmanageable threat to energy production and distribution in Central Asia, in the long term it may pose a far more serious threat to regional stability and thus energy security.

In Central Asia most of these threats are not present today, but could develop in the future. There are no unfriendly Islamic governments in the region since no republic is presently led by an Islamic elite and is not likely to be in the near future. With regard to other possible dangers, the impact of Islam on energy can be viewed as severely limited at this time, but potentially dangerous. Several factors will continue to minimize short-term threats to energy security in region. First, the current republican leaders will manage to contain the Islamic threat through severe repression. Although generally successful in the short-term, repression cannot be relied upon as a long-term solution. Second, the major oil-producing regions with significant concentration of foreign investment in Central Asia are located outside the so-called areas with heightened Islamic activity. Both Kazakhstan's and Turkmenistan's oil-producing regions are conveniently away from Uzbekistan and Tajikistan, where Islamic radicals traditionally have maintained strongholds. Third, the geographic distance is further reinforced by the fact that Islamic proclivity in Kazakhstan and

Turkmenistan is much weaker than in the other Central Asian republics. Finally, the Islamic forces lack adequate nation-wide support to be able to overthrow the current regimes at present.

We now turn to a state-by-state analysis of the role of Islam in the political life of the republics and attempts by Muslim activists to organize and assert political power. Islam in the Kyrgyz Republic had traditionally been weak, except in the southern region.[23] There has been some recent growth in interest in Islam and some Muslim leaders have called for "a mosque in every village."[24] There still remains a major difference between rural and urban elites. The founding of the Islamic Renaissance (or Revival) Party brought very few adherents. The moderate Kyrgyz Democratic Wing has supported the government while calling for the renovation of mosques and religious schools. The civil violence in Tajikistan in the early 1990s did bring some armed Muslim forces into the more religious Fergana Valley, raising fears of an Islamic threat.

However, Kyrgyz authorities have rather effectively dealt with the possibility of religious opposition. In part, this has been due to the government's desire to assuage the fears of the country's sizable Russian minority. In the process, there has been an effort to maintain a division between the state and religion, although some Muslim feast days and Christmas are state holidays. Religiously based political parties were banned, and the government obtained the agreement of a parliamentary commission to drop a reference in the constitution's preamble to spiritual rebirth based upon Islamic values.[25] In 1996, the government created a new State Commission of Religious Affairs ostensibly to promote tolerance and freedom of conscience and to oversee laws dealing with religious matters. Both Muslim and Christian groups have been suspicious of state efforts dealing with religion, particularly requirements for the regulation of all religious organizations and the use of the phrase "national security" in Commission statements. Christians and Muslims with foreign support have apparently been especially targeted.[26]

As indicated earlier, Islam has also traditionally been comparatively weak in Kazakhstan. Religious knowledge was relatively undeveloped, although traditional Muslim customs and ceremonies continued to be important during the Soviet period within sections of the population. However, those years saw major efforts to control official Islam and only some 30 mosques remained at the end of the Stalin era, with the capitol having but one where there had once been over 60. A Muslim Religious Board acted to assure a compliant Islamic order controlled official Islam, even after Stalin. This began to change in 1990–91 when, under a new more independent Mufti, Muslims sought to open new mosques and the first madrasah of the modern era was founded. This period also saw the inauguration of the Alash Party, founded by those who wished to unite the idea of Turkism with Islamic "fundamentalism." Although relatively small and with a quite young membership, it became very active in the republic. Its dual Turkic–slamic ideology attracted many ethnic minorities. Authorities had long feared the development of a political Islam and the party was soon declared illegal. Special efforts have been made to control foreign involvement in religious affairs, which must be coordinated with the government. However, these moves appear to be directed more at Christian missionary activities. As with other governments in the region, the conflict in Tajikistan was viewed as their possible future if Muslim activists were allowed to freely speak and organize.

Kazakhstan has emphasized its secular foundations. The first article of the Principles of Constitutional Structure" reads "The Republic Kazakhstan is a democratic, secular and unitary state" and the country's President, a self-proclaimed atheist, has stated "We want to build a normal democratic state with an open economy, which is completely incompatible with any religious fundamentalism... One must take into account that in our republic there are various faiths... But none of them can become [a] state] religion].[27]

While there had been an active Muslim movement in nineteenth century Turkmenistan, Czarist and Soviet efforts had sharply diminished the public role of Islam by the end of the Soviet era. From 481 mosques in 1911 there were but five in 1941.[28] Although Muslims in the republic tended to maintain traditional religious practices, political Islam was repressed. The Islamic Revolution in Iran began to influence local Muslims after 1979 and small clandestine Islamic groups appeared. Since independence, those in authority have sought to display their symbolic support of Islam through membership in the Islamic Conference Organization and presidential state visits to Saudi Arabia and Iran. Religious organizations are required to register with the authorities, but this has not appeared to be a major obstacle. There appears to be no efforts to block religious literature, although permission is needed for mass meetings for the purpose of proselytizing.[29] Political opposition is systematically repressed in the republic, however and religious organizations are tightly scrutinized. Islamic political activism thus remains weak, disorganized, and generally underground.

The last years of Soviet rule in Uzbekistan saw growth in interest in Islam both within the Communist Party and the general public. The

Fergana Valley, with some quarter of the country's population, has long been a center of Islamic activities. Party officials expressed concern over this organizational and public support of Islam and the mid-1980s saw the expulsion of party members for participating in religious rituals. In the post-independence era the government has followed a policy of supporting Islamic personal values while attempting to control any Islamic involvement at the political level.

Uzbekistan's post-independence leader, Islam Karimov, declared "Consideration for religion and Islam plays an important part within our internal and international politics and conduct... It manifests itself in the way of life of the people, their psychology and in the building of spiritual and moral vales, and in enabling us to feel rapport with those who practice the same religion."[30]

As pointed out at the outset, however, growing repression of Islamic forces in Uzbekistan has brought about a growing militant reaction organized and led by Jumabay Namangani and Tohir Yuldah.[31] As with other states, the official clergy has not supported the Islamists, and there remain wide religious divisions including differences between orthodox Sunni elements and Sufi and Wahhabi groups. The official religious establishment has vigorously attacked the Wahhabi, accusing them of extreme fanaticism. The Wahhabi have been very active in the Fergana Valley where economic problems have exacerbated living conditions and been a factor in increasing Islamic identity. According to one observer, "It is the Wahhabi movement in the Fergana valley that is the most determined and best-organized of all the fundamentalist movements seeking the overthrow of the government."[32]

By far the greatest threat from Islamic elements to a post-independence regime in Central Asia was in Tajikistan. The conflict there has been presented as an example of the dangers of political Islam by those in power elsewhere in the region. It is not the intention here to go into detail regarding the civil war that raged in the republic in the early 1990s.[33] However, several points need to be made that elucidate the issue of instability involving political Islam. First, the Islamists ultimately were unable to permanently capture political power and eventually accepted a brokered peace settlement that called for a power-sharing formula thereby 30 percent of government portfolios were to be offered to the opposition. There is no question that organized Islamic military and political elements have played very important roles in Tajikistan, and there remains considerable sympathy for and belief in the Muslim cause. However, it would be inaccurate to present the disunity in the republic as purely religious in nature.

Tajikistan was the poorest state in the Soviet Union. A relatively low level of economic development and the serious problems with living conditions were important catalysts in generating antagonism towards those in authority. In addition, it had the weakest sense of national identity with ill-defined nationhood upon obtaining independence. Not only did religious divisions exist, but there were major ethnic and regional tensions at work as well and these played out in the civil disturbances that developed.

In Central Asia, and particularly Tajikistan, external events and powers were essential elements in defining the role of Islam in domestic developments. The growth of Islamic identity was aided by the Soviet conflict in Afghanistan. Tajik military sent into Afghanistan with other Soviet troops came in contact with Muslim-oriented Afghan forces, and the war spilled over into Tajikistan. Iran also contributed to the Islamic movement with funds and supplies and allegedly with weapons to Islamic militia forces. In general, however, Iran has not played a major political or military role in the Central Asian republics. What brought about the eventual peace agreement to Tajikistan were the military involvement of both Russia and Uzbekistan, and the strong resolve of the moderate elements within the Tajik opposition to end the violence.

Azerbaijan has many similarities with the Central Asian republics and one significant difference. Like the others, Azerbaijan continues to be ruled by an undemocratic regime under a constitution that guarantees human rights, but does not always follow its strictures. Its economy has suffered since obtaining independence and there are major differentials in wealth. In part the country's plight is because of the long conflict over Nagorno Karabakh, an Azerbaijanian territory conquered by the Armenians with Russian help.

Azerbaijan is also constitutionally a secular state that supposedly allows all religions the right to practice their religions freely. Christians have reportedly not received equal treatment because of the Armenian controversy. Like its Central Asian counterparts, there has been an effort to assure that political Islam is contained. Islamic religious organizations are under an umbrella bureaucratic institution, the Directorate of Caucasus Muslims. Parliament has also decreed that the production, importation, and dissemination of religious literature must receive the permission of local government authorities.[34] Being a secular state has not stopped the country from joining the Organization of the Islamic Conference and the Islamic Development Bank.

The one significant difference from the other republics analyzed in this paper is that Azerbaijan's Muslims are primarily Shi'i. The Shi'i were not allowed to openly practice some elements of their faith during most of the Soviet period. The post-independence era has seen an increase in religious activity in the republic. While any increase in the total number of mosques has been diminished by the destruction of many of these buildings during the conflict with Armenia, there has been growth in attendance and the opening of new religious schools. Azerbaijan also has a legal Islamic party. The Islamic Party of Azerbaijan, a pragmatic organization attacked by some clerics as a party of "non-Islamic cynical bureaucrats" was registered in 1992. A largely Shi'i organization that claims over 100,000 members, it probably has considerably fewer. Far more militant and "fundamentalist" has been the "Tawba" society, which has not been given governmental sanction.

Future interaction with the major Shi'i power in the region, Iran, is more problematic. Relations are clouded by the large Azerbaijani population in Iran and the desire of both countries to assure that the idea of a united Azerbaijan does not gain credence. While there have been problems in the past, at this point Iran does not appear significantly involved in spreading its religious influence into Azerbaijan and has more pragmatic economic interests.

Potential long-term problems

If we look into the future, there are several possible Islamic factors that could negatively impact oil and gas security in Central Asia. Perhaps the most important of these would be an increased Islamic identity aided by external sources. While in itself a Muslim resurgence need not be a major problem, it could become a threat if joined with other social or political forces. Of particular importance could be the use of Islam as a rallying cry by those perceiving themselves as economically and politically oppressed by an "anti-Islamic" regime. Another problem could be the employment of Islamic identity against non-indigenous and other non-Muslim populations in the region reinforcing ethnic-religious tensions. It should be emphasized that these are no major problems for the immediate future, but are issues that may become more salient in the next 10–20 years. Both of these factors could destabilize oil and gas producing governments and could possibly bring to power unfriendly Islamist elements.

The past decade has seen a major growth in interest in Islam after decades of Soviet efforts to weaken its public and private influence. External manifestations of this growth can be seen in the increase in the number of mosques, schools, and Muslim religious organizations. Governments seeking popular support have funded some of these institutions, while others have been built by local private organizations or sustained by foreign financial aid. The opening of new mosques and religious schools had begun during the last years of the Soviet era, but increased exponentially after independence. Studies show that, for example, in Uzbekistan some 3000 mosques had been built or restored by 1992 and 130 main town mosques were operating in Tajikistan that same year.[35] A 1995 analysis, while recognizing problems of statistical reliability found some 1500 mosques (including those under construction in Kyrgyzstan, 500 in Kazakhstan (again, including those under construction), about 300 registered mosques in Tajikistan in 1992, and in 1994 there were 204 registered mosques in Turkmenistan.[36] In 1997 it was reported that there were 4000 registered and 6000 other mosques in Uzbekistan alone.[37]

In addition to these institutional changes, there has also been an increased observance of Islamic rituals. There has been a greater interest in regular prayer and attendance at the mosque on Fridays. Observance of Ramadan has apparently increased. After the years of Soviet control, there has also been growth in the number of individuals making the pilgrimage to Mecca, although the numbers remain quite low. There has also been a major growth in the importation of Muslim religious literature in various languages and the availability to the general populace of these books and pamphlets has greatly increased in recent years. It should be underscored that this pattern is by no means universal and there remains a significant portion of the populace of the Central Asian republics that is either secular or weak in its knowledge of Islamic tenets and lax in its ritualistic practices. In fact, the major efforts of many Muslim "revivalists" have been to expand the knowledge of the basic tenets and practices of Islam among believers.

External groups have aided this increase in Islamic identity. Governmental support for Muslim religious causes has come from Saudi Arabia, the Gulf States, Turkey, Pakistan and other Islamic countries. Aid has included the sending of hundreds of thousands of Korans and financial contributions to the mosques and religious schools. The Saudi government has been particularly active in this regard. In addition, private organizations and individuals, in many cases quite conservative in their religious beliefs, have sought to increase Islamic knowledge and identity in the region. Funds have gone into the construction of mosques and madrasahs and in educating religious teachers and mosque officials. It has been argued that Saudi support has been part of an effort to counter Iranian influence in the region.[38] Central Asian governments have sought to contain this external influence, fearing that it will eventually undermine their authority and increase political Islam.

An increased awareness among Central Asian Muslims of their religious inheritance presents no intrinsic danger to Western energy interests in the region. Islam as a faith need not hinder close economic relations between Western firms and Muslim states, as evidenced by long-term partnerships with strongly Islamic governments in Saudi Arabia, the Gulf, Malaysia, Indonesia and Brunei. What does need to be closely followed is how Islam may provide a religious foundation to popular dissatisfaction in the region. Two particular issues may become especially important in the next two decades, uneven political and economic development and ethno-religious divisions.

Perhaps the most serious future problem may be the "Algerian analogy." Illustrated by Algeria in the 1990s, but evidenced elsewhere, is the use of Islam in conditions where a government is perceived as being corrupt, ineffective, "un-Islamic", and tied to foreign interests. In those circumstances, Islam becomes a rallying cry for those who see themselves as politically and economically deprived by uncaring and insufficiently Islamic authorities. An additional aspect to this pattern is that Muslim religious schools frequently become one of the homes for the discontented. Young men who are unable to enter prestige institutions of higher education gravitate to these schools where they become sources of dissatisfaction against those in authority.

The seeds of this possible scenario are already to be found in most of the Central Asian Republics, although they could take some time to germinate. None of these republics can lay claim to being liberal democratic systems. A recent report by Freedom House stated that only the Kyrgyz Republic could be classified as democratic[39] and even President Askar Akayev told an American audience in 1997 that it could take at least two decades until the republic had a truly democratic society.[40] A review of the United States Department of State country reports on human rights shows a similar pattern throughout the region. Restrictions on the political rights of citizenry vary from state to state with the more egregious records to be found in Turkmenistan, Tajikistan and Uzbekistan. However, all have problems with freedom of the press and other forms of free expression, all limit the ability of the people to change their governments peacefully, and all do not necessarily follow their own constitutions with regard to rights of the accused, and freedom of association and religion.

Beyond issues of political freedom, there is the continuing problem of corruption at both local and national levels. As in other parts of the former Soviet Union, the 1990s saw a major growth in corrupt practices. The involvement of state officials at the local and national levels in such questionable practices is a fact of life in many of the new republics. These activities can only undermine the legitimacy of those in authority, particularly if they continue over time.

Nor can it be argued that at this point in time the economies of the republics are successfully meeting the needs of their people. Like most of the rest of the former Soviet Union, they are going through the painstaking transition from the old planned economies and have not yet reaped the profits from their oil and gas resources. There are some signs of improvement in most of the republics, but according to the World Bank, these states remain at a lower economic base than they had in the Soviet era.

Thus, questions that arise from the Algerian analogy are, at least, unsettling. Conditions today are generally ones of limited democratic freedoms and weak economies. Will these republics be able to exploit their energy reserves in a sufficient and timely fashion to meet popular economic and political pressures? When funds do flow into these countries will they remain in the hands of a small majority, creating greater differentials in wealth leading to demands for greater equity? Will the new profits reinforce tendencies toward corruption and ostentation, which could increase dissatisfaction with the governing elite? Finally, as in Algeria, under these conditions can we expect Islam to be a rallying cry for the politically and economically dispossessed?

A second, and perhaps less dangerous future problem may be the employment of Islam as a symbol of identity in periods of ethnic tension. There were negative reactions to policies of the Soviet period that reorganized territories resulting in splitting ethnic groups, forced collectivization and transplanted non-Asian peoples into the region. As Martha Olcott has noted, however, ethnic violence and hostility were not major problems at the height of the Soviet period, and she states that ethnic toleration predominated.[41] Past patterns of behavior and attitude from the Soviet era have changed, and there remains the possibility of Muslim activists attempting to integrate religious and ethnic identity against "foreign" elements. This has historically been true elsewhere, particularly during periods of economic difficulties and where the non-Muslim groups have been perceived to be economically in more dominant positions. This pattern has been seen in antagonism towards the Chinese in southeast Asia and has been a factor in religious-ethnic alliances among Muslim minorities in Asia.

While communal tensions have increased in many areas of Central Asia, they have usually not been due to a conjunction of religious and ethnic identities. Ethnicity has been a factor in several republics in the post-independence era as the dominant ethnic group has sought to increase its presence in government and the private sector. Thus, there have been complaints of job discrimination by non-Turkmen in Turkmenistan, non-Kazaks in Kazakhstan, non-Kyrgyz in the Kyrgyz Republic, etc. In many cases criticism has come from the Russian minorities in these republics and reinforced their desire to immigrate. There have also been religious tensions generated by the small, but growing presence of Christian evangelists, government efforts to limit the activities of Wahhabis, and traditional Sunni-Shi'i issues.

The one obvious case with religious-ethnic overtones has been the conflict between largely Christian Armenia and Muslim Azerbaijan. Thus, there were demonstrations in the capitol of Azerbaijan against the Armenians with the green flag of Islam waving and religious spokesmen employing Islam as a rallying cry. However, most would not term the conflict as having significant religious causes. As one observer declared, "The religious factor does not play a major role in the conflict. This conflict is rather based on territorial dispute than on religious fanaticism and antagonism."[42] At the same time, the forced deportation by Armenia of some 800 000 primarily Muslim Azerbaijanis has led to strong anti-Armenian and anti-Christian reactions. In the territories taken by the Armenians, mosques have been closed, while in Azerbaijan similar actions have been taken against Christian churches. The situation in Azerbaijan differs from the rest of the region, but there remains the limited possibility of ethno-religious tensions elsewhere, particularly if other economic and social problems are not confronted.

These two long-term issues, the Algerian analogy and religio-ethnic conflict, need to be monitored. They raise problems for energy security today, particularly if economic problems remain unsolved and Islam becomes the battle cry of the dispossessed. In the words of one recent study referring to Uzbekistan, "Both attempts to exploit poor living conditions and the regime's denial of human rights, out of fear of fundamentalism, are internal obstacles to stability in the region."[43] The development of oil and gas resources can aid or exacerbate this situation depending on how governments use the new largesse. Revenues could be employed to alleviate disparities and thus weaken anti-government criticism. On the other hand, revenues could increase disparities and exacerbate corruption. The resultant dissatisfaction could weaken government in oil and gas producing countries and engender opposition to Western companies which are seen as associated with repressive and corrupt regimes. This scenario could endanger future development of the industry.

Notes

1. Six car bombs were placed in various locations in Tashkent with the aim of assassinating President Islam Karimov as his motorcade moved through town to reach a government building where he was to hold a cabinet meeting. The bombings resulted in 13 dead and 128 wounded. According to the government investigations both Islamic and banned democratic opposition had been involved in the plot. The brother of the banned Erk Party leader, Muhammad Solih was among those arrested. The Islamic Movement of Uzbekistan whose members are currently in Afghanistan, led the Islamic incursions in 2000. For more information see: Summary of World Broadcasts, BBC Monitoring Online (hereafter BBC Monitoring Online), CAU120399/21 AJBA/AK (March 12, 1999), Radio Free Europe/Radio Liberty (hereafter REE/RL) Online, vol. 3, no. 37, Part I (February 23, 1999), REF/RL Online, vol. 3, no. 40, Part I (February 26, 1999), REF/RL Online, vol. 3, no. 41, Part I (March 1, 1999), and REF/RL Online, vol. 3, no. 45, Part I (March 5, 1999).
2. Several aspects of the Hanafi School of jurisprudence demonstrate its liberal and tolerant orientation. First, the Hanafis argue that if a Muslim believes in God and the prophethood of Muhammad, but is negligent in performing his religious duties, he is not an infidel. Second, Abu Hanifah believed that the underlying purpose of all Islamic precepts could be understood through rational construction. Therefore, he saw it permissible to carry out Islamic rituals, such as prayer in languages other than Arabic. Third, according to the Hanafi school the principle of socioeconomic necessity overrides the need for religious orthodoxy, thus allowing the postponement or modification of religious duties to accommodate the daily needs of the believer. Fourth, the Hanafi school provides a more tolerant view of matters concerning civil and criminal conduct as compared to the Hanbali, Shafi'I, and Maliki schools. Finally, in addition to the Koran and the Hadith, the Hanafi doctrine places significant emphasis on the role of private opinion and public consensus in reaching decisions that affect the individual and the Muslim community. For more information see: Allamah Shibli Nu'mani, *Imam Abu Hanifah: Life and Work* (Lahore: Institute of Islamic Culture, 1977), pp. 3-4 and 101-2.
3. For more information see: Alexander Bennigsen and Chantal Lemercier-Quelquejay, *Islam in the Soviet Union* (New York: Frederick A. Publishers, 1967).

4. The term Wahhabism has been misused by the Soviet and later Russian authorities to label those Muslim activists that called for the overthrow of the communist and post-communist regimes in Central Asia and the Caucasus.
5. An estimated 40 000 Uzbeks live in Saudi Arabia, many of whom have made substantial financial contributions to Islamic revival in Uzbekistan. In addition the so-called Ahl-I Sunna val Gama'a has made significant monetary contributions. For more information see: *Foreign Report* (June 4, 1993), pp. 4-5 and *Far Eastern Economic Review* (November 19, 1992), pp. 23-4.
6. Some Islamic leaders such as Kazi Akbar Turajonzoda acknowledged the fact that the goal of creating an Islamic state was not achievable for several years since the population has yet to be educated in the tenets of Islam. For more information see: Summary of World Broadcasts, BBC Monitoring, SU/1376, C1/4 (May 12, 1992).
7. *The Current Digest of the Soviet Press,* vol. XLIV, no. 26 (1992), p. 29. See also: Vitaly Naumkin: "Islam in the States of the Former Soviet Union," *Annals,* vol. 524 (November 1992), p. 140.
8. Mufti Muhammad Sadiq Muhammad Yusuf of Uzbekistan was forcibly removed from office in 1993. Earlier Sadiq Kamolov of Kyrgyzstan was removed for acting independently of the government.
9. The Socio-Cultural Association of the Tajiks of Samarkand is a case in point. Created to revive the Tajik heritage and language in Uzbekistan, the association was banned and leaders jailed in 1993–94 and subsequently a government-sponsored organization was set up.
10. The government of Uzbekistan has only recently acknowledged the failure of its religious educational program. BBC Monitoring Online, CAU180399/12 AJBA/MV (March 17, 1999).
11. Public opinion surveys in Kazakhstan and Kyrgyzstan conducted by the United States Information Agency and United States Agency for International Development between 1995–97 provided some early indications in this regard.
12. Turkmenistan and Uzbekistan Country Reports on Human Rights, 1998, US Department of State, Bureau of Democracy, Human Rights, and Labor (February 1999).
13. For more information see: Mehrdad Haghayeghi, *Islam and Politics in Central Asia* (New York: St Martin's Press, 1996), pp. 85-6.
14. The IRP held its founding congress in the city of Astrakhan in the Soviet part of the north Caucasus on June 10, 1990 attended by 150 delegates from Dagestan, Abkhazia, Tajikistan, Azerbaijan, Tatarstan, Uzbekistan, and other republics. The party called for the revival of Islamic tradition, including the Shari'ah in the Muslim–dominated republics. Some also spoke of the formation of Islamic republics.
15. The Economist Intelligence Unit (EIU), (4th quarter 1997), p. 21.
16. The December 1997, May 1988, and February 1999 incidents were widely publicized by the government and the media broadcast footage of the trial of the arrested Muslim activists. For more information see: BBC Monitoring Online, CAU 170598/05 SA/JF (May 15, 1998).
17. BBC Monitoring, SU/1342, B/2 (March 30, 1992).
18. WNC Online, FBIS-SOV-98-029 (January 29, 1998).

19. As a highly secretive organization, very little information has been made available as to the nature and scope of its activities in Central Asia.
20. BBC Monitoring Online, CAU160299/05 (February 16, 1999).
21. BBC Monitoring Online, CAU070598/10 (May 6, 1998).
22. Several members of the so-called Namangan battalion headed by the Jumabay fought alongside the UTO members during the Tajik civil war.
23. See I. P. Kyrgyztan, "Secularism vs Islam", *The World Today*, 48:11 (1992) pp. 208-11.
24. N. Andreev, "Kirgiztan: Grappling with Democracy", *Bulletin of the Atomic Scientist*, 50:1 (January–Febuary, 1994) p. 55.
25. D. Hiro, *Between Marx and Muhammad: The Changing Face of Central Asia* (London: Harper Collins, 1994), pp. 138-9.
26. United States Department of State, Kyrgyz Republic Country Report on Human Rights Practices for 1996 (Washington, DC, 1997), p. 6.
27. Quoted in R. Altoma, "The Influence of Islam in Post-Soviet Kazakhstan" in B. Manz (ed.), *Central Asia in Historical Perspective* (Boulder: Westview, 1994), pp. 175-6.
28. Hiro, *Between Marx and Muhammad,* p. 144.
29. United States Department of State, Turkmenistan Report on Human Rights Practices for 1996 (Washington, DC, 1997), p. 5.
30. Quoted in *Ibid*, p. 182.
31. For more information on the nature of militant Islamic movements in zress, 1944), p. 115.
32. A.Rashid, *The Resurgence of Central Asia: Islam or Nationalism?* (Karachi: Oxford University Press, 1994), p. 100
33. See, for example, Rashid, *The Resurgence of Central Asia*, pp. 159–186 and B. Rubin, "Tajikstan: From Soviet republic to Russian-Uzbek Protectorate", in M. Mandlebaum, *Central Asia and the World* (New York: Council of Foreign Relations, 1994), pp.207-24
34. US Department of State, Azerbaijan Country Report on Human Right Practices for 1996 (Washington, 1997), p.7.
35. Polonskaya L. and A. Malashenko, *Islam in Central Asia* (Reading, Ithaca Press, 1994)
36. D. Trofimov, *Islam in the Political Culture of the Former Soviet Union* (Hamburg: Institut Fur Friedensforschung und Secherheitspolitik, 1995), pp. 21-5
37. M. N. Shahrani, "Reclaiming Islam in Central Asia: Soviet Legacies and Post-Soviet Realities", Working paper Baker Institute, Mimeo (Houston, 1997), p. 9.
38. V. Piacentini, "Islam: Iranian and Saudi Arabian Religious and Geopolitical Competition", in A. Ehteshami (ed.), *From the Gulf to Central Asia (*Exeter: Exeter University Press, 1994), pp. 25-46.
39. Freedom House, "Democracy's Century" (New York, 1999).
40. Economist Intelligence Unit, *Country Report Kyrgyz Republic, Tajikistan, Turkmenistan* (Fourth Quarter 1997), p. 10.
41. M. B. Olcott, "Ethnic Violence in Central Asia: Perceptions and Misperceptions", in R. Sagdeev and S. Eisenhower (eds.), *Central Asia: Conflict, Resolution and Change* (Chevy Chase: CPSS Press, 1995), pp. 115-25.
42. G. R. Sabri-Tabrizi, from the Gulf to Central Asia Azerbaijan and Armenian Conflict and Coexistence' in A. Ehteshami, p. 164.
43. B. Jalali, "Islam as a Political Force in Asia," *IREX* (1999), p. 10.

Part II

Reaching a World Market: Pipelines, Transit Routes and Processing Plants

5

The Economics of Pipeline Routes: The Conundrum of Oil Exports from the Caspian Basin

Ronald Soligo and Amy Myers Jaffe

Introduction: the first musings on Caspian energy corridors

When the Soviet Union began to collapse in 1991, the Caspian region quickly attained salience in the international arena, focused initially around suspicions that the region housed Persian Gulf sized reserves of oil and gas. The oil industry's interest in the area dates from the mid-1980s when Soviet leader Mikhail Gorbachev first seriously raised the prospect of foreign investment to develop the vast unexploited riches of the Caspian area. Then in 1991, the collapse of the Soviet Union rendered the reserves of the newly independent states of Kazakhstan, Azerbaiijan and Turkmenistan of immediate interest.

More than 30 US companies invested billions of dollars in the region in hopes of "striking it big." The prospects of large oil finds in this landlocked and distant region generated a flurry of studies of how the oil would be transported to market, once developed.

Since Caspian hydrocarbon resources are both landlocked and located at a great distance from the world's major energy-consuming regions, the region's producers cannot simply ship oil by tanker from domestic ports to international sea-lanes as is done from the Arab Gulf. Instead, the Central Asian and Caucasus states must rely on expensive pipelines built through neighboring countries as the chief means of transport. A number of routes were deemed possible but almost all of them had serious problems.

Discussion of these problems became a virtual cottage industry for academics and policy makers alike, and early literature on the Caspian energy question focuses in good measure on the political details that might distinguish the most desirable and feasible of the many proposed pipeline routes.[1]

Despite the large amount of ink that was spent describing the many pipeline options for moving oil out of the Caspian region, in reality, few routes maintained a steady audience. At first, discussion focused on multiple pipeline routes,[2] but as the results of early drilling for oil yielded smaller volumes for export than initially expected, talk of many pipelines subsided into a more focused approach.[3] In this phase, beginning around the late 1990s, Turkey began working diligently in the diplomatic domain to narrow the discussion of various routing solutions. Ankara argued that a large rise in Caspian and Russian oil exports that could result from many of the pipeline schemes would potentially bring tanker traffic through the environmentally sensitive Bosporus to dangerous levels, endangering the population of Istanbul, which borders the waterway.[4] Turkey's vociferousness put the matter before several world bodies, including the International Maritime Organization (IMO). Russia has argued that improved management and traffic control equipment would permit safe passage of projected oil exports through the Straits. Free passage through the waterway is guaranteed by the Montreux Convention of 1936.

But Turkey has lobbied hard with the US and the oil companies for the construction of an oil pipeline that would extend from Baku in Azerbaijan to the Turkish Mediterranean port of Ceyhan. Since 1995, the US Government has assertively backed this routing, not only to show support for Turkey, but also because it believes that such a pipeline will enhance economic and political ties in the region and cement its independence from the undue influences of Russia and Iran.[5]

American commentators began to argue that Caspian oil development was a means to weaken Russia's influence on its southern flank by propping up the sovereignty and strength of Central Asian and Caucasus countries.[6] Planting the US "oil" flag in the Caspian Basin and selecting pipeline routes soon became viewed inside the American political elite as a strategic countermeasure to contain the regional power of Russia.

As more attention was given to the Caspian oil transport debate, American concerns shifted to blocking pipeline routing through Iran. US sanctions against Iran were tightened to prevent energy companies from investing in pipelines that would carry Caspian oil or gas to international markets.[7] The US Government has worked behind the scenes with mixed success to thwart foreign companies from joining with Iran's national oil company, NIOC, to construct energy export outlets via Iran.

In 1997, China declared its interest in Kazakh oil, making major investments in two oil fields and proposing a multi-billion pipeline direct route to China. US policy was more ambiguous on Chinese involvement. The US has not opposed oil or gas pipeline routes from Kazakhstan to China and has even given consideration to providing credits to a US firm to participate. However, China is still viewed as a strategic competitor whose activities in the region can be cited as another reason why the US should also have a presence.[8]

For its part, in the early years, segments of the Russian elite argued for the abandonment of political and military responsibilities in Eurasia in favor of either isolationism or stronger economic and cultural links with the West. But these ideas were eventually pushed aside as the West rejected Russia as a European partner and pursued more unfriendly initiatives such as NATO expansion. Russia's foreign ministry became concerned anew with encirclement and Moscow began to take a more proactive stance towards its "near abroad." Top of the list was defending its rights to participation and influence in the development of Caspian resources.

However, despite the rivalry that the US–Russia interest in the Caspian may have generated, it was the close US relationship with NATO ally Turkey that wound up a key driver towards the pipeline transit question.

The US Administration helped choreograph the 1998 Ankara Declaration of support for the Baku–Ceyhan pipeline project by the Turkish president and other regional leaders, including the presidents of Georgia and Azerbaijan.[9] This was followed by a high-profile signing ceremony of the pipeline initiative by the presidents of the USA, Turkey and certain Caspian Basin countries during the summit meeting of the Organization for Security and Co-operation in Europe (OSCE) in Istanbul in November 1999, which US President Bill Clinton was attending.

Since the late 1990s following these events, the focus of the print debate on pipeline routes has remained for the most part political and is now mainly stuck on pros and cons for Baku–Ceyhan route.[10]

Oil as a driving factor: myths and realities

Ironically, a key problem for the success of the Baku–Ceyhan line, and US policy towards the region with it, is the fact that not enough oil has been discovered yet to justify its construction.[11]

A new oil find in Kazakhstan at Kashagan was touted in 2001 as confirming that skeptics might be wrong about the potential of

Caspian resources. Nourlan Kapparov, Vice Minister of Energy and Mineral Resources of the Republic of Kazakhstan, told the press at the 2001 Offshore Technology Conference in Houston that the government of Kazakhstan estimates Kashagan to hold recoverable reserves of between 20 to 27 billion barrels.[12] However, even if Kashagan's reserves are confirmed to be as large as a large field in Saudi Arabia, the story does not end there. The Caspian basin still remains one of the most difficult oil prospecting terrains in the world.

No solution is in sight to the crippling dearth of drilling rigs and other necessary equipment. The problem of drilling rigs is a serious one. Currently only three semi-submersible rigs operate in the Caspian Sea, in contrast to 90 or so in Britain's North Sea. Without more drilling rigs and production platforms, the oilfields of the Caspian cannot hope to reach their optimum production potential in the coming years.

So far, eight years of effort have not eased the critical shortage of drilling equipment. Already, analysts are saying that the Kashagan find, regardless of its size, may not be able to reach optimum production rates until 2015.[13]

The Caspian region is far from major supply centres for exploratory equipment and faces a debilitating shortage of modern drilling platforms and other related supplies. This shortage is worse than almost anywhere else in the world because the region is landlocked and has to rely on extremely limited supply routes, such as the Volga River, for bringing in necessary equipment.

Despite huge demand for equipment, there are only two assembly yards equipped for manufacturing or refurbishing offshore drilling rigs for the region: one at Astrakhan in Russia along the northern Caspian and one in Primorsk, near Baku. Such constraints severely limit the amount of drilling that can take place in the region at any one time. They also mean that oil well completions take considerably longer – in some cases up to two years as compared with 2–3 months in many other oil provinces in other parts of the world. Kashagan's first well, for example, took a year longer to drill than planned.

Obstacles to drilling mean that, while Kazakhstan's resources may be geologically exciting, the region's output could remain constrained for years to come just because several wells cannot be drilled simultaneously. Exploration and production forecasters, Wood Mackenzie Consultants, project that oil production from the Caspian basin could rise to 2.4–3.4 million barrels a day by 2010, up from 900 000 in the late 1990s, with increases primarily from Kazakhstan and to a lesser extent Azerbaijan, but even this assumes that obstacles to drilling and export routing will be eased over time. Wood MacKeuzie's more pessimistic assessment of 2.3 million b/d reflects the possibility that known risks will prevent Kashagan from producing above 1 million b/d over the next decade and possibly beyond. These risks include the difficulty of appraising such a large structure, environmental and bureaucratic challenges, problems of natural gas disposal from the field and the complex hurdles to a major, commercial export route. Wood Mackenzie estimates that production may rise to 4 million b/d by 2020 despite an expected decline in output rates at the Tengiz and Karachaganak fields in Kazakhstan.[14]

Even if the Caspian countries manage to achieve the higher 3.4 million b/d rate of production, it may not justify several large export pipelines to the West. Increased export sales into the Black Sea littoral states such as Romania, Ukraine, Bulgaria and Turkey could be expected to handle at least one-third to half of the expected volume, for example, allowing producers to maximize profits by cutting transport costs to more distant buyers.[15]

Alternative oil pipeline routes: economic factors

The problem of the transport of oil from the Caspian region to consumers beyond the Black Sea remains to be tackled.

So far, Caspian oil producers have dabbled with a variety of export routes, mostly unsatisfactorily. BP is transporting some limited volumes of oil from the Chiraq refurbished pipeline from Baku to the Georgian port of Supsa on the Black Sea. BP would like to enhance the size of this line eventually but is being pressed by the US and Turkish governments to favor the longer, more expensive Baku–Ceyhan route.

Table 5.1 Potential market for Caspian oil by 2010 (in million b/d)

Country	Low estimate	High estimate
Russia (Grozny refinery)	80	80
Ukraine	100	200
Romania	160	380
Bulgaria	200	200
Turkey	226	226
Iran	300	400
Total	1066	1486

Source: Data provided to authors by Planecon, a Washington-based consultancy specializing in energy in the CIS.

BP is leading a consortium of oil companies studying the Baku–Ceyhan route and hopes to have the line in operation by 2006.[16] Chevron announced it would take part in the engineering and construction phases of the project in February, in an endorsement that is expected to help bring the long-awaited pipeline to fruition.[17]

Besides Baku–Ceyhan, several Western oil companies have discussed other bypasses of the Bosporus Strait but with little progress. Several routes have been considered.[18] Although it seems likely that several routes will be completed simultaneously, this approach will bump up against the reality that scale economies for pipeline construction do not favor the implementation of multiple routes for limited volumes. The cost of transporting oil from Baku to Supsa over a pipeline with capacity of 900 000 b/d would be 68 cents a barrel whereas the cost would drop to 50 cents a barrel with a pipeline having a capacity of 1.5 million b/d. Costs for the smaller throughput are 36 percent higher than for the larger one. On the Bosporus bypass route from Kikikoy to Ibrikabana, costs would be 55 cents a barrel for a 500 000 b/d line and only 35 cents a barrel for a 1.5 million b/d line. Costs for the lower throughput are 57 percent higher in this case.

The importance of scale economies for transporting Caspian oil calls into question the wisdom of multiple pipeline routing that has been advocated as the cost effective solution to the threat of disruption of oil exports from the region. These disruptions could result from either acts of terrorism or from government actions of a transit country. However, given the expected level of exports to points outside the Black Sea – perhaps as little as 1.5 million b/d by 2010 – the use of several pipelines will result in substantially higher transport costs. There is clearly a trade-off between lower transport costs and security risk.

Table 5.2 Scale economies in pipeline transport cost of capital

Route	Length miles	Capacity mb/d	Cost/b	% increase in cost
Baku–Supsa	510	900	0.68	36.0
	510	1 500	0.50	
Baku–Ceyhan	1 200	600	2.52	3.3
	1 200	800	2.44	
Samsun–Ceyhan	534	800	1.21	37.5
	534	1 880	0.88	
Kiyikoy–Ibrikbana	114	500	0.55	57.1
	114	1 500	0.35	

Source: Author's calculations.

There are several shorter bypasses that have been considered as alternative routes that could be cheaper than the Baku–Ceyhan route. One would begin at either the Turkish Black Sea port of Samsun or the coal port of Zonguldak and extend across Turkey to the Mediterranean port of Ceyhan, utilizing a mixture of old and new pipelines connecting to the Kirikkale refinery near Ankara. Other possible bypasses include a route in Turkish Thrace from Kiyikoy to Ibrikbana on the Aegean and pipelines from the Bulgarian port of Bourgas to Alexandroupolis in Greece or Vlore in Albania.

Iran has proposed that Azerbaijan and Turkmenistan export their oil to Iran's northern refining centers at Tabriz, Tehran and Arak and "swap" it for exports of Iranian oil from Iran's main Persian Gulf terminal at Kharg Island. The plan has the advantage of the existence of substantial Iranian pipeline capacity that could be reversed. However, US government objections are an important obstacle. Iran is also demanding a swap fee of $2–3 a barrel to make investments to enable its refineries to handle Caspian crude.

The maximum amount of oil that could be swapped would be 400 000 to 500 000 b/d. It is likely that only smaller volumes would be practical. However, industry and local officials report that Malaysia's Petronas or China's CNPC might be willing to invest in an Iranian route that would transport their own future Caspian production while at the same time generating transit fees from other producers once US sanctions are lifted.

China's CNPC proposed and then put on hold construction of a $3.5 billion pipeline from Kazakhstan to China that might connect to future oil facilities in China's Tarim Basin. That project, along with Unocal's cancelled oil and gas pipeline that would have connected to an existing line at Charjou, Turkmenistan through Afghanistan to Pakistan (CAOPP), are considered to be long-range programs that will not be implemented until the next decade. Oil prices must be expected to exceed $16 a barrel for these overland Kazakh shipments to compete with waterborne alternative supplies to China from the Persian Gulf.[19] Exxon, Mitsubishi and CNPC are also studying a natural gas line from Turkmenistan to China.

Despite being the favored option, the Baku–Ceyhan pipeline has its own problems, not least its price tag: at an estimated cost of $3–4 billion . It is by far the most expensive of the Western options.

Assuming that the pipeline would carry 800 000 barrels per day from Baku to Ceyhan for loading onto tankers, Baku–Ceyhan would yield total transport costs of roughly $2.80 per barrel from Baku to Italian ports, according to the authors' calculations.[20] This figure includes capital, construction, operation and onward freight costs but excludes, for purposes of comparison, any tariffs that might be levied by Turkey and Georgia, the two transit countries.

For a point of comparison a bypass pipeline across Thrace from Kiyikoy on the Black Sea to Ibrikbana on the Aegean would be considerably cheaper than the Baku–Ceyhan line. The route is relatively short – only 190 km but is admittedly more complicated than Baku–Ceyhan.[21] Using it would require shipping Azerbaijani oil by pipeline to Novorossyisk or Supsa, shipping it by tanker to Kiyikoy, offloading it there and loading it onto a tanker again at Ibrikbana.

Even so, the total transport cost to Italy of this route – including construction of an 800 000 barrel per day new pipeline across Thrace, expansion of the Baku–Supsa pipeline, and costs associated with off- and on-loading – is roughly $1.90 per barrel, $0.90 less than the comparable figure for Baku–Ceyhan. This figure again excludes any transit fees Turkey or Georgia might charge. The advantage over Baku–Ceyhan, already significant, would be even greater were a larger Thracian pipeline built. This would have the advantage of accommodating Russian as well as Azerbaijani exports. A 1.5 million barrel per day Kiyikoy–Ibrikana pipeline, for instance, would lift the advantage over Baku–Ceyhan to $1.00 per barrel.

There exists another and still cheaper alternative: simply shipping Azerbaijani oil via pipeline to Novorossiysk and/or Supsa and then by tanker through the Bosphorus Strait to the Mediterranean. At $1.40, the cost per barrel of shipping from Supsa to Italian ports by sea alone is $0.50 lower than Kirikoy–Ibrikbana and $1.40 lower than Baku–Ceyhan. This includes the cost of expanding the Baku–Supsa pipeline to 800 000 barrels per day.

Since the sums involved are significant, it is salient to ask who will benefit from the choice of one route versus another. Unless arrangements are made to subsidize the line or minimize tariffs, the producing firms and/or Azerbaijan will bear the full burden of the extra transport costs while Turkey will profit from its construction and from any tariffs that can be levied.

The same exercise for routes from Kazakh oil fields shows similar results. A hook up into the Baku–Ceyhan line for shipment of Kazakh crude will be far more expensive than other Western routes with the long pipeline costing considerably more than $2.75 a barrel compared to only $1.74 for shipments through the CPC pipeline in Russia to the Black Sea and on to Italy.

Table 5.3 Transport cost comparisons for Azeri oil delivered to Europe (assuming a cost of capital of 15%)

Destination-Route *Baku-Rotterdam:*	Cost/b ($)	Cost as a % of bypass route	Cost minus cost of bypass route
Tanker from Supsa	1.91	87	-0.28
Supsa–Turkish bypass	2.19	100	+
Supsa-Samsun–Ceyhan	2.72	124	0.53
Baku–Ceyhan	3.20	146	1.01
Italy			
Tanker From Supsa	1.41	80	-0.36
Supsa-Turkish Bypass	1.77	100	0.00
Supsa-Samsun-Ceyhan	2.30	130	0.53
Baku-Ceyhan	2.78	157	1.01

Source: Author's calculations.

Table 5.4 Transport cost comparisons for Kazak oil from Novorossiysk to Europe (assuming a cost of capital of 15%)

Destination-Route *Baku–Rotterdam:*	Cost/b ($)	Cost as a % of bypass route	Cost minus cost of bypass route
Tanker from Novorossiysk	2.33	89	-0.28
Novorossiysk–Turkish bypass	2.61	100	0.00
Novorossiysk-Samsun–Ceyhan	3.14	120	0.53
Italy			
Tanker from Novorossiysk	1.74	79	-0.46
Novorossiysk–Turkish bypass	2.20	100	0.00
Novorossiysk–Samsun–Ceyhan	2.73	124	0.53

Source: Author's calculations.

For its part, Russia is also aware of Turkey's concerns about congestion in the Bosporus Straits and is talking about opening new export routes for its own oil from its own northernmost ports.[22] Routing from Russia's oilfields to the Adriatic is still an economically viable possibility as well.[23]

The potential of alternative routes through Russia remains a huge "wild card" in the debate over Caspian oil exports. A resurgence of Russian concern with and influence in Central Asia and the Caucasus under the new government of President Vladimir Putin has raised the prospects that increased exports may soon flow as Moscow steps out of the way and removes the kind of obstacles it imposed on transport out of the region in the early 1990s.[24]

However, BP's experience with a Russian oil export route, called the Northern Route, provides an instructive glimpse of potential problems.

The line, which extended from Baku through Grozny and Tikhorestsk to the Russian Black Sea port of Novorossiysk, was supposed to carry 120 000 barrels a day of newly produced oil from Azerbaijan. Ultimately, however, the safety of the line could not be secured. It was not just that security at Grozny could not be attained because of Russia's armed conflict with Chechnya. Routine pilfering from the line by local residents along its extended route meant that BP and its partners were unable to maintain the pumping pressure needed to keep commercial flows going, regardless of the state of war or peace along the route.[25]

In his early days as president, Putin referred to the need for international cooperation in the development of the Caspian resources, leading to optimism in the West. Russia also recently increased Kazakhstan's oil export quota to 14 million tons for 2000, up from a previously specified volume of 10 million tons. Transneft is also reportedly inviting Caspian neighbours to use a new line to Makhachkala on the west shore of the Caspian in Azerbaijan.[26] Given its geographical position, exporting through Russia is the most viable option for Kazakhstan because it obviates the need to cross the Caspian Sea or follow a wide span of its coastline before connecting to existing or proposed pipeline export facilities in third countries.

It is hoped that Russia will be able to deliver on its promise to support a new export system from Kazakhstan that will extend from the large Western-run Tengiz oil field through Russia to Novorossiysk. Initially that pipeline, run by the Caspian Pipeline Consortium (CPC), which involves US, Kazakh and Russian oil company shareholders, will carry 28 million tons of oil per year from Kazakhstan and Russia. The line is already being filled with oil and is expected to be in operation by late 2001.[27]

But the limited ability of the Russian military to protect and operate such lines is highlighted by Moscow's less than successful military operations in Chechyna and its inability to protect public facilities inside Russia.[28] Serious questions remain as to whether Russia itself has the capability to fill the vacuum of power that has prompted the rise in non-state actors and the slide to instability that now plagues parts of the region.

In the spring of 2000, news reports surfaced that the Central Asian republics were discussing the possibility of opening a joint anti-terrorism centre in Moscow.[29] In October 2000, Russia and five of the former Soviet republics met in Bishkek to discuss ways to guard against insurgencies in Central Asia. The meeting was prompted by battlefield successes of Afghanistan's Taliban militia along the Tajikistan border. An accord signed by the leaders of Russia, Kazakhstan, Kyrgyzstan, Tajikistan, Belarus, and Armenia established a more detailed legal framework for the rapid deployment of joint forces against Islamic fundamentalist rebellion in the region.[30] The framework builds on an existing, but vague institution called the Collective Security Council of the Commonwealth of Independent States. Uzbek leader Karimov was notably absent from the accord.

Diplomats say that the USA has also begun trying to establish a regional body – to include Georgia and Turkey – to maintain security for oil pipeline routes, presumably bypassing Russia and Iran.[31] Among US strategic specialists, however, the extension of the PFP program into Central Asia has raised new concerns. It has been argued in US policy circles that local conflicts could easily draw Russia and any Western-sponsored or Turkish-led body into an unwanted confrontation if these larger patrons were to support different sides.[32] Russia's military support and presence in Abkhazia in Georgia is one case in point.[33] Turkey's previous support of the Azeri war effort in Karabakh and Russia's of Armenia is another.

Thus, it seems advisable for all concerned to re-evaluate strategic priorities and see where common ground exists. There is no point in routing oil expensively all the way to Ceyhan in order to prevent a conflict between Turkey and Russia over the Bosporus but by doing so creating the underpinnings for such conflict in protecting that same pipeline.

Options to Asia

Asian oil demand is expected to rise considerably between 2000 and 2010. At the same time, oil production in Asia will make few, if any, gains. Thus, Asia will have to import an increasing amount of oil from other world regions. This oil "deficit" in Asia, that is the difference between the amount that will be consumed and the amount produced, is expected to grow by approximately 8 million b/d by 2005 over the deficit that prevailed in 1995 and by 11–13 million mb/d over 1995 levels, by 2010. This large gap means that Asian buyers will have to pay prices that will attract oil from other regions in the world.

In recent years, Asian markets have carried a price premium over European markets. Table 5.5 shows that prices for Far East markets over the ten-year period, starting in 1988, were, on average, 72 cents per barrel higher than for European buyers. In Table 5.5, we have plotted

Table 5.5 FOB price of Arab Light – 34

Year	Europe	US	Far East- Far East	Europe	Percentage difference
1988	13.22	13.06	14.16	0.94	107.1
1989	16.63	16.91	16.23	-0.4	97.6
1990	21.47	20.31	21.13	-0.34	98.4
1991	16.78	16.49	17.35	0.57	103.4
1992	17.19	17.30	17.78	0.59	103.4
1993	14.21	14.53	15.63	1.42	110.0
1994	14.64	14.68	15.39	0.75	105.1
1995	15.67	15.66	16.71	1.04	106.6
1996	19.44	19.73	19.39	-0.05	99.7
1997	16.06	15.99	18.74	2.68	116.7
Average	16.53			0.72	

Source: Price Scorecard data base of *Petroleum Intelligence Weekly*, a newsletter published by Energy Intelligence Group, New York, New York.

monthly Saudi freight on board(F.O.B) prices as computed by PIW for European and Asian delivery. To allow for the lag inherent in the Saudi pricing formula, we have plotted the Far East price for a given month against the European price for one month later.[34] The price gap is especially visible for the post-Gulf War period.

The price anomaly between the two markets would suggest that some Persian Gulf suppliers are price discriminating, charging European buyers a lower FOB price than Far East buyers. Since most Persian Gulf suppliers are producing close to capacity and presumably would sell as much as possible in the higher priced market, it is Saudi Arabia, which does have spare capacity and is viewed as the swing (or marginal) supplier, that has an incentive to price discriminate if it is possible to do so.[35]

As long as this premium is maintained, it will add to the appeal of shipping Caspian supplies to Asia. Since Europe has many alternative suppliers of oil from various parts of Africa as well as the Western Hemisphere, it may pay Caspian exporters to diversify to other markets. The Far East, on the other hand, seems destined to become ever more dependent on Mid-East oil and could provide an attractive alternative.

Determining whether Caspian oil would earn the greatest net returns by building a pipeline to the Gulf and then having the oil shipped on to the Far East or by transporting it to the Mediterranean depends very much on how the oil would be delivered to the Mediterranean and on the reaction of other producers.

Transport costs for Azeri oil to Italy, by way of a 1.5 million b/d bypass pipeline through Turkish Thrace, are in the neighborhood of $1.77 per barrel. Building the Baku–Ceyhan pipeline would increase the cost to $2.78 a barrel. For Khazak oil the comparable costs would be even higher.[36] Caspian oil will compete in the Mediterranean (and elsewhere in Europe) with supplies from the Mid-East as well as Africa.

Oil from the Mid-East is shipped to the Mediterranean by way of the Sumed pipeline which has a capacity of 1.5 million b/d. Oil deliveries above this level must be shipped around South Africa at a cost of roughly $2.22 per barrel. Since transport costs from the Western Hemisphere and Africa are lower, Mid-East oil shipped around South Africa will be the marginal supplier to Europe.

Given these transport costs, Caspian oil would be competitive with marginal supplies from the Mid-East at FOB prices roughly equal to those in the Gulf, if it is shipped through the Bosphorus or via the bypass pipeline through Turkish Thrace but not if it is shipped via a Baku–Ceyhan pipeline. If oil is shipped through a Baku–Ceyhan pipeline, Caspian oil producers would be forced to accept discounted returns in order to offer buyers prices competitive with alternative supplies that have lower transport costs.[37]

In the long run, however, if European demand consistently results in shipments of Mid-Eastern oil round South Africa, one must assume that the Sumed pipeline would be enlarged. In other words, producers of Caspian oil cannot count on competing at the margin with such Mid-Eastern shipments indefinitely. The most likely competition will come from West Africa and Western Hemisphere producers. The transport costs for these sources will be in the neighborhood of $0.75–1.00 per barrel. Thus, in the long term, Caspian oil will have to sell at a discount to these other sources by an amount equal to the difference in transport costs to the European market.

If oil prices in European and Asian markets were the same except for differences in transport costs of the marginal supplier, our calculations suggest that, generally, Caspian oil would net more if shipped to the Mediterranean as opposed to the Gulf for onward shipment to Asia except in the case of the more expensive Baku–Ceyhan route. The transport costs of Kazakh oil to Asia are calculated at around $3.00 per barrel from Iran's Kharg Island.

However, European and Asian prices have not been equal over the past decade. From 1990 to 1997, Gulf FOB prices for Asian delivery have been set higher, on average by 83 cents a barrel, than for European delivery.[38] If this price differential were to continue, Asian exports via the Gulf would be competitive with the Mediterranean market for Caspian oil, except if the oil were delivered to the Mediterranean by shipping it through the Bosphorus.

A further complication concerns the effect of Caspian oil on the European price if it is delivered to the Mediterranean. If the marginal supplies come from the Mid-East via South Africa, profit considerations would require that oil to be shipped to Asia. However, there is evidence that Persian Gulf suppliers, most notably Saudi Arabia, might not be willing to have their share of the European market reduced. Instead, for several years, Saudi Arabia has taken steps to ensure that its oil remains competitive in distant markets by subsidizing buyers' transportation costs. In this case, Mediterranean prices would fall, reducing net returns further for Caspian oil (and other suppliers as well).

If West African producers become the marginal supplier in Europe, their alternative is to ship oil to Asia at a cost of around $1.50 a barrel. They will shift their sales when the net returns in Asia exceed those in Europe, namely when Asian prices less transport costs are greater than European prices less transport costs. West African suppliers would be willing to discount European sales by up to the differential in transport costs between Europe and Asia, roughly 40–75 cents a barrel. Caspian producers need to factor in this possibility in deciding the most profitable route.

The special case of China

China is the second largest energy consumer in the world, after the US, and is the world's most populous country. In 1986, China's State Planning Commission, acknowledging that its domestic oil industry could not maintain oil self-sufficiency in light of the country's growing energy demand, officially gave the go-ahead to allow foreign crude imports.[39] However, it wasn't until 1993 that China became a net oil importer for the first time. Import rates have risen slowly over time and today, China's oil imports currently average around 1.5–1.7 million b/d. They are expected to grow to between 2 million b/d and 4 million b/d over the next ten years.[40]

In 1996, facing this trend of rising demand for oil and flagging domestic oil production, China unveiled a plan to attain around a third of its energy needs through international exploration and acquisition activities.[41] China's first steps included strengthening ties with oil suppliers Iraq and Iran, and initiating investment in international oil fields in such locations as Sudan, Venezuela and Peru.

China also began looking for closer and more stable sources of energy imports and developed a strategy of forming borderless economic regions. Gaye Christofferson offers an explanation of this policy, asserting it is part of a non-hegemonic regional agenda, motivated by economic development priorities.

> "China's strategy for Central Asia and the Asia Pacific has not been formulated unilaterally but rather in consultation with countries in each of these regions. This strategy involves the formation of natural economic territories that transcend borders, extending from China's domestic economy into surrounding countries. Called the Northwest Economic Circle and the Northeast Economic Circle, they open up inner border areas to international trade, with the hope that the interior will gain the same benefits as the coastal region. Oil and gas pipelines are the sinews that integrate and link these natural economic territories."[42]

Others offer differing explanations of China's interests in the Caspian region. Some, like Geoff Kemp, suggest a more geopolitical interpretation, noting that China's extensive border with Kazakhstan means it must concern itself with foreign competition in the region.[43] Others believe China must also concern itself with separatist movements by Muslims in its own sensitive Xinjiang region that could be supported by any future Western-backed Kazakh regime.[44] The growing interdependence of the Xinjiang region and Central Asia is demonstrated by the rise in trade, which reached $950 million in 1998.[45] China is also said to view its activities in Central Asia as a potential land bridge to the Persian Gulf whose waterborne oil supplies are now patrolled and protected by the US Navy.[46]

China made its first investment in Central Asia in June 1997. The China National Petroleum Corporation (CNPC) agreed to purchase 60 percent of Kazakhstan's Aktyubinsk Oil Company for US$4.3 billion and announced plans to build a US$3.5 billion, 3000 km pipeline linking western Kazakhstan with its own Xinjiang region.[47] In announcing its investment, China said it hoped to secure significant, long-term supplies of crude oil which would not only make a proposed Kazakh–Xinjiang pipeline more economically feasible, but also render economically attractive planned eastbound pipelines which would link the Xinjiang province with China's energy – demanding, industrial heartlands.[48] However, actually building the pipeline would prove to be more problematic than expected.

China is faced with the same endemic problems that have prevented the building of significant pipelines proposed by other countries and consortiums in Central Asia. Not only are the economics of the pipelines tenuous, mainly due to the lack of proved reserves in the region, there are also matters of ethnic and social unrest in almost all of the newly formed states. This regional instability has made it difficult to find investors willing to commit to building the infrastructure essential for transporting the energy resources to market.[49] In the case of an export route to China, this threat included not only instability in Central Asian countries but also possible troubles in the Xinjiang region itself from Uihgur separatists who have already claimed attacks on oil installations and convoys in the autonomous region.[50] Nearly 8 million people spread across the northwest Zungaria plateau, the southern Tarim Basin, the southwest Pamir region, and the eastern Kumul-Turpanern Hami corridor, regard themselves as Uighur, against a total population of 16 million.[51] China must consider the trends among this Muslim population in considering its positions toward the predominantly Muslim Central Asian states.[52]

Still, despite the obstacles, China will still have to weigh the security benefits of over land routes against the economy of sea-borne shipments. As mentioned above, international oil prices must exceed $14–16 a barrel for overland pipeline shipments from China's Tarim Basin and Kazakstan to compete with waterborne imports from the Persian Gulf.[53] Under conservative assumptions, the cost of transporting Tarim Basin oil to the Guangdong province will be around $2.84 a barrel, excluding right of way costs, assuming enough oil to support a 1 million b/d pipeline (costs would rise to $4.48 if a 30 in, 500 000 b/d pipeline were constructed instead). Given that production costs at the field are roughly $10 a barrel, the total cost of Tarim Basin crude in Southern China will be at least $13 a barrel and probably more given right of way costs (costs to Shanghai are similar). Given tanker costs of approximately $1.00 a barrel from the Middle East, Tarim Basin oil would be competitive with Middle East imports at around $12–13 a barrel, the equivalent of international market prices for North Sea Brent crude of around $14.00 a barrel.

For Kazakh crude, the equation is more complicated. The 7200 km pipeline that has been proposed to cross Kazakhstan and China would imply a transport cost of $4.90 per barrel while costs for shipments via Iran are calculated at around $3.00 a barrel, both excluding export tariffs and right of way costs. In the case of a Bosporus route to Europe, these transport costs are generally higher than transportation costs for

Kazakh oil to Europe, implying that Kazakstan producers would need a considerable subsidy before they would shift oil from the more profitable Mediterranean market to the Chinese market. This will be true despite the fact that Asian oil markets generally carry a price premium to Mediterranean prices.

Only in the case of the Baku–Ceyhan route versus an Iranian route, would the existence of an Asian price premium mean that Kazakh producers could earn more profits selling their oil to China via Iran.[54] In the case of an expensive overland route from Kazakstan to China, the cost disadvantage would have to be overcome through support from the Chinese government since this option would be the least profitable of any export route that might be available to Kazakh oil producers. The issue for policy makers in China will be whether the security benefits of this diversification is worth the cost in terms of higher total oil import costs.

Natural gas: equal export troubles for US policy

The issue of natural gas exports from the Caspian basin is facing no less complex and difficult issues than the oil pipeline routes. By 2020, the Caspian region could be producing upwards of 29 billion cubic feet a day of gas, up from 11 bcf/d currently.[55] But this potential growth is highly dependent on the development of secure, accessible markets for this gas. Financing and political risks must also be overcome.

Market availability rather than productive capacity is likely to be the constraining factor for the foreseeable future, and a lack of access to export markets currently plagues gas producers in Azerbaijan, Kazakhstan, Turkmenistan and Uzbekistan. So far, despite promising initiatives in the late-1990s, US diplomacy has failed to loosen the stranglehold Russia maintains on natural gas exports from the region.

In 1999, the US Government backed efforts to establish the Trans-Caspian Pipeline (TCP). The $2 billion gas line would carry up to 30 billion cubic meters of natural gas per year from Turkmenistan to Azerbaijan under the Caspian Sea to Georgia and Turkey. Several private energy companies have looked at the feasibility of the project, including the Transcaspian Gas Pipeline Project, a grouping of Bechtel, General Electric and the Royal Dutch Shell Group. While technically feasible, the project still faces stiff competition from other better organized, cost-effective competitors, including a $3.2 billion Russian–Italian–Turkish project called Blue Stream which would bring

Russian gas to Turkey via a 1,200 kilometre long pipeline beneath the Black Sea.

In early June 2000, the Transcaspian Gas Pipeline Project announced it would close its Istanbul and Baku offices and reduce spending dramatically following President Niyazov of Turkmenistan's refusal to commit to the project.[56] US diplomacy on behalf of the TCP continued but by November, Turkmen President Saparmurat Niyazov had reached agreement with Russia's gas monopoly Gazprom to sell it as much as 30 billion cubic meters of natural gas a year.[57] The agreement, taken together with the groundbreaking of the Russian–Italian–Turkish Blue Stream pipeline, is seen as major blow against any additional US-backed initiatives. Turkmenistan also has existing agreements to export gas to Ukraine and to Turkey via Iran.

Lack of agreement between Azerbaijan and Turkmenistan over what share of capacity each should have in the joint Trans-Caspian natural gas export line to Turkey remains a major stumbling block. Moreover, political tensions between Azerbaijan and Turkmenistan make negotiation of the final plans for the TCP extremely difficult.[58] Iran and Russia also have pre-existing "take or pay" gas agreements with Turkey that take precedence over proposed projects and involve pipeline infrastructure that already exists.[59]

Blue Stream, which partners Russia's state gas monopoly Gazprom with Italy's ENI conglomerate, has announced that it has arranged $1.7 billion credits from Banca Commerciale Italiana, Mediocredito Centrale and West LB with an additional $660 million expected from the Japan Bank for International Cooperation and Japan's Ministry of International Trade and Industry (MITI).[60] Construction of the pipeline has already begun, giving Russia a further advantage in enlarging its already sizable share of the Turkish gas market. The success of this project is considered a major blow for US-organized projects in Central Asia by taking up a large proportion of the potential market in Turkey. Inside Turkey, however, despite the progress bringing Blue Stream on line, some last minute questions remain about increasing dependence on Russian gas, highlighted by a major corruption scandal allegedly involving the Blue Stream project.[61]

One trump card that could reduce future Turkish gas purchases from Russia is the possibility of cheaper Azeri supplies. BP is also trying to move ahead plans to export gas to Turkey from its large Shah Deniz field in Azerbaijan. Turkey signed a natural gas purchase arrangement with Azerbaijan on March 12, 2001 stipulating that Ankara would buy 233 billion cubic feet of gas a year under a 15 year contract.[62] BP's partners in the Shah Deniz field include regional parties, including a joint venture between Russia's Lukoil and ENI's Agip, as well as Turkey's TPAO, Azerbaijan's Socar, Iran's OIEC, Statoil and TotalFinaElf. The BP project's potential received a boost in May 2001 when it was endorsed by the Cheney energy task force report.[63]

Complicating gas export matters further is the fact that several major fields in Kazakhstan, including Tengiz, Karachaganak and Kashagan, need to find outlets for associated and non-associated natural gas production. Kazakhstan is important to Russia's Gazprom as a transit route for Turkmen gas to reach the Russian natural gas pipeline network. But, there is some talk that Kazakh gas might make economical supply for Gazprom to feed to certain Russian markets, potentially reducing Russia's need for Turkmen supplies. American companies might be forced to consider gas sales to the Russian monopoly if alternative export options cannot be identified.[64] In April, the US Trade and Development Agency awarded a $600 000 grant to Kazakhstan's Minister of Energy to fund a study of the strategic uses of its natural gas, including possible export projects.[65] Any US pressure on Kazakhstan to deny Turkmenistan access to Russia's pipeline system would presumably muddy the waters for Russia's current dominance in the Central Asian gas game.

Conclusion

In this chapter, we have focused mainly on the economic and technical aspects of Caspian export pipelines. We have calculated the costs of exporting oil through a number of proposed lines, including those that are designed to bypass the Turkish Straits. Our conclusions are as follows.

Limitations on drilling infrastructure and recent disappointing finds suggest that the region will not be able to generate sufficient export volume to support large-scale export lines in the near and perhaps even intermediate term. As a result, reliance will be on make-shift solutions, such as using existing lines which can be refurbished and expanded or the use of oil swaps, as has been proposed with Iran.

Given reasonable expectations for economic growth, neighboring countries such as the Ukraine, Romania, Bulgaria and Turkey can absorb much of the projected export surplus of Caspian oil over the next decade. Projected increases in oil demand from these countries, combined with exports to supply refineries in Grozny, Russia and northern Iran could absorb 1–1.5 million barrels of oil a day by 2010. While total regional production could reach 3.5 million b/d by 2010, this projection depends on optimistic assessments of the quantity of reserves that lie in the shallow waters of the Kazak offshore sector. If these expectations are borne out, exports could total 2.5–2.8 million b/d by 2010. However, given the difficulties of developing Caspian oil, it is unlikely that production will support exports of more than 2.8 million b/d by 2010. This could leave as little as 1–1.5 million barrels of Caspian oil that would have to be exported beyond the littoral states of the Black Sea or Iran.

There are significant scale economies to pipeline throughput which are sacrificed when several smaller lines are built instead of one larger one. The benefits of multiple routes as a means of reducing the financial risk of temporary closures of pipelines must be weighed against this cost. For reasonable assumptions about the frequency and severity of disruptions, the certain costs of higher transport costs exceed the expected value of such losses. On the other hand, if risks involve not the acts of terrorists but acts of governments, the existence of multiple routes will reduce the bargaining power of governments of transit countries to squeeze post-contract concessions from pipeline operators.

Given economies of scale and the likely magnitude of increases in the volume of Caspian oil (including Russia) that will be exported via the Mediterranean, it is likely that only one large capacity export pipeline from each of the major producing countries, Azerbaijan and Khazakstan will be needed, at least until 2010.

Of the routes to the Mediterranean that are designed to bypass the Turkish Straits, the pipeline from Baku to Ceyhan has the highest cost/barrel of the routes investigated, at least one dollar per barrel more than a bypass route through Turkish Thrace. Extending the Baku–Ceyhan line to carry Russian or Kazak crude would permit a larger capacity pipeline to be built and would lower transport costs. Nonetheless, given the relationship between tanker and pipeline costs, the Baku–Ceyhan route will still always be more expensive than alternatives involving shorter pipelines and more reliance on tanker transport.

Depending on where Caspian oil is finally shipped, a large capacity bypass pipeline could be a relatively inexpensive substitute to transit through the Turkish Straits and should be considered as a means of transporting projected increases in oil exports from the Caspian region. The economic viability of a bypass would be increased if shippers had to bear the true social cost of transiting the Turkish Straits, that is, the expected value of damages borne by the residents of Istanbul to their person and property as well as the cost of delays due to congestion. It is the Montreux Treaty, which allows all ships to transit the Straits without bearing these costs, that makes transiting the Turkish Straits so attractive to shippers. Revision of the Montreux Convention will be difficult, since it will require that countries using the Turkish Straits agree on how to share both the benefits of reduced congestion and the costs of environmental externalities.

Notes

1. Rosmarie Forsythe, "The Politics of Oil in the Caucasus and Central Asia", *Adelphi Papers*, No. 300, 1996; Rajan Menon, "In the Shadow of the Bear: Security in Post-Soviet Central Asia", *International Security*, Vol. 20, No. 1 (Summer 1995); Graham Fuller, "Central Asia: The New Geopolitics" (Santa Monica: Rand, 1992); John Roberts, "Caspian Pipelines" (London: Royal Institute of International Affairs, 1996); Ian Brimmer, "Oil, Politics: America and the Riches of the Caspian Basin", *World Policy Journal*, Vol. 15, No. 1 (Spring 1998).
2. For a detailed discussion of the history of this period, see Jennifer Delay, "The Caspian Oil Pipeline Tangle: A Steel Web of Confusion", *Oil and Geopolitics in the Caspian Sea Region*, edited by Michael P. Croissant and Bulent Aras 43–81. Also, discussion of multiple routes in Laurent Rusekas.Laurent Ruseckas, "State of the Field Report: energy and politics in Central" Access Asia Review, Vol. 1, No. 2, NBR Publication, (National Bureau of Asian Reasearch, Seattle, Washington, 1998).
3. Ronald Soligo and Joe Barnes, "Baku-Ceyhan Pipeline: Bad economics, Bad Politics, Bad Idea *Oil and Gas Journal*, Vol. 96, No. 43. (1998) pp. 29–34.
4. Author's interviews with US State Department officials show this latter concern to be cited as more important than the others, although public pronouncements do not emphasize it. For a more detailed discussion of the problem of the Bosporus, see R. Soligo and A. M. Jaffe, 'The Economics of Pipeline routes', Baker Institute working paper, Spring 1998, available at www.bakerinstitute.org
5. Speeches by Ambassador John Wolfe and his staff at various meetings attended by author. See also texts avaible online at URl<http://www.state.gov>
6. D.Morgan and D.Ottoway, *Washington Post*, 6 July 1997. See z. Brzezinski, *The Grand Chessboard* (New york : Basic Books 1997). A good critique of this school is provided by O. Harries, 'The Dangers of Expansive Realism', *The National Interest*, No. 50 (Winter 1997/1998), pp. 3–7.
7. The US Congress passed legislation, the Iran–Libya Sanctions Act (ILSA) of 1996, that would allow it to impose sanctions on third parties which invested in Iran's oil and gas industry. Other US laws restrict such investments by US companies to $40 million. This policy is nicely described by Washington analyst Robert Ebel as "ABI: anywhere but Iran". See R. E. Ebel, *Energy Choices in the Near Abroad: the Haves and Have-Nots Face the Future* (Washington, DC Center for Strategic and International Studies, 1997): and G. Kemp, "The Persian Gulf Remains the Strategic Prize",*Survival*, Vol. 40, No. 4) (winter 1998), pp. 132–49.

8. Most US authors discussing geopolitical competition in the Caspian mention China on the list, among them S. F. Starr, "Power Failure: American Policy in the Caspian", The National Interest, Spring 1997. For a good survey of China's moves, see Xiaojie Xu, "The oil and Gas Links between Central Asia and China: A Geopolitical Perspective", OPEC Review, March 1999; or G. Christoffersen, 'China's Intentions for Russian and Central Asian Oil and Gas", NBR Analysis Series (National Bureau of Asian Research), Vol. 9, No. 2, March 1998.
9. Signed on October 29, 1998. Complete text available on the US Department of Energy Website at www.energy.gov/HQPress/releases98/octpr/pr98161a.htm.
10. J. Delay, "The Caspian Oil Pipeline Tangle". B. Aliriza, "US Caspian Pipeline Policy: Substance or Spin?", CSIS, Aug. 2000, available online at www.csis.org/turkey/CEU000117.html.
11. B. Aliriza, 'US Caspian Pipeline Policy, (n.10).
12. Press Conference at the OTC in Houston organized by the US Department of Commerce.
13. Author's inteviews with shareholders of the Kashagan field, September 19 and October 3, 2000.
14. Wood Mackenzie Forecasting Service, November 2000, provided to authors by email by this Edinburough UK based consulting service.
15. For economic comparisons and options, see R. Soligo, and A. M., "The Economics of Pipeline Routes: The Conundrum of Oil Exports from the Caspian Basin", Baker Institute working paper, (April 1998,) avaible online at URL <http://www.bakeriinstitute.org>.
16. Authors interviews with consortium members, January 2001, in Washington DC.
17. Douglas Frantz, "Chevron Talks to Azerbaijan about Pipeline", The New York Times, February 9, 2001.
18. Extensive literature exists on the proposals for various routes including excellent surveys by the Center for International Strategic Studies and the International Energy Agency. Other authors are John Roberts, Ian Brimmer and Laurent Rusekas.
19. For more details on the economics of Chinese routes, see Ronald Soligo and Amy Myers Jaffe, "China's Growing Energy Dependence: The Costs and Policy Implications of Supply Alternatives", Baker Institute Working Paper, April 1999, available at www.bakerinstitute.org.
20. For more detailed discussion of transport costs, see Ronald Soligo and Amy Myers Jaffe, "The Economics of Pipeline Routes", Baker Institute working paper, Spring 1998 available at www.bakerinstitute.org.
21. For more discussion, see Joe Barnes and Ronald Soligo, "Baku–Ceyhan Pipeline (n.3).
22. See Vijai Maheswari, "Baltic Oil Access Wakens New Russian Pipeline Dream", *Financial Times*, 30 March 2000, p. 38.
23. Industry sources in Moscow say studies of the route are being undertaken by Russian firms.
24. Fitchett, J., "A resurgent russian Influence grips former Soviet Central Asia", *International Herald Tribune*, July 9, 2000, p. 5..
25. Author's interviews with oil company executives involved in the BP consortium, September 19, October 3 and November 12, 2001.

26. Op cit Fitchett, note 24.
27. "In the Caspian, it's all pipelines and No Oil' (n. 26); "PIW Kazakh Discovery Eclipses Azeri Pipeline Progress', *Petroleum Intelligence Weekly,*. Author's interviews with shareholders for the various pipelines, various dates between August and October, 2000, also November 12, 2000.
28. For discussion of the decline of the Russian military, see R. Pipes, "Is Russia Still an Enemy?", Vol. 76, No. 5 (Sep./Oct. 1997).
29. Op cit Fitchett.
30. "Neighbors Concerned about Afghanistan", *Washington Post,* October 12, 2000, p. A 19.
31. Author's interviews with officials from US Department of State, August 3, 2000.
32. For a detailed discussion of US military involvment, see R. Sokolsky, and T., Charlick-Paley, "NATO and Caspion Security: A Mission Too Far" RAND Coporation, Santa Monica, CA, 1999 and R. Bhatty, and R. Bronson, "NATO's Mixed Signals in the Caucasus and Central Asia." *Survival,* Vol. 42, No.3 (Autumn 2000), pp.129–45.
33. Pipes, "Is Russia Still An Enemy?", (n. 28).
34. Soligo R. and A. M. Jaffe, "A Note on Saudi price Discrimination" Energy Journal Article Volume 21, January 2000, p. 121–34.
35. For more detailed discussion, see Soligo, Jaffe op cit.
36. All cost estimates are based on a useful life of the pipeline of 30 years and a discount rate of 15 percent.
37. These conclusions assume that the qualities of the two are equiva-lent. To the extent that Caspian oil is of a higher quality than Gulf oil, it would sell at a premium which might be large enough to offset the higher transport costs on a Baku-Ceyhan pipeline.
38. See A. M. Jaffe and R. Soligo, "Saudi Arabian Price Discrimination", Energy Journal, October, 1998.
39. Gaye Christoffersen, "China's Intentions for Russian and Central Asian Oil and Gas," *Analysis, The National Bureau of Asian Research.* Vol. 9, No. 2, (1998) p. 6.
40. Ronald Soligo and Amy Myers Jaffe, "China's Growing Energy Dependence" (n.19)
41. "China's CNPC Leaps on to Global Oil Production Stage," Petroleum Intelligence Weekly, June 9, 1997, p. 3.
42. Ibid., p. 5.
43. Geoffrey Kemp, *Energy Superbowl: Strategic Politics and the Persian Gulf and Caspian Basin,* (Washington: The Nixon Center for Peace and Freedom, 1997).
44. Dru Gladney, "China's Interest in Central Asia", in *Energy and Conflict in Central Asia and the Caucasus,* edited by Robert Ebel and Rajan Menon, The National Bureau of Asian Research (Oxford, UK: Roman & Littlefield Publishers, 2000).
45. Gladney, ibid.
46. Xiaojie Xu, "The Oil and Gas Links Between Central Asia and China: A Geopolitical Perspective," *OPEC Review,* March 1999.
47. Tony Walker, and Robert Corzine, . "China Buys $4.3bn Kazak Oil Stake," *Financial Times* June 5, 1997, p. 9.
48. Amy Myers Jaffe and Martha Brill Olcott, "The Geopolitics of Caspian Energy", in *The Euro-Asian World: A period of Transition,* edited by Yelena

Kalyuzhnova and Dov Lynch (London: Macmillan Press – now Palgrave, 2001).

49. Rajan Menon, "Treacherous Terrain: The Political and Security Dimensions of Energy Development in the Caspian Sea Zone," *Analysis, the National Bureau of Asian Research.* Vol. 9, No. 1, (1998) p. 10.
50. "Central Asia: China's Strike," *The Economist (US Edition),* August 16, 1997, p. 32.
51. See Justin Jon Rudelson, *Oasis Identities: Uighur Nationalism Along China's Silk Road* (New York: Colombia University Press, 1998) .
52. Dru Gladney, "China's Interest in Central Asia" (n.44).
53. For more details on the economics of Chinese routes, see Ronald Soligo and Amy Myers Jaffe, "China's Growing Energy Dependence.[19]
54. Soligo, Jaffe op cit.
55. Forecast provided to author by email by Edinburgh, UK-based consultants Wood Maokensie Consultants' Caspian Service, November 2000.
56. David Stern, "Gloom Over Pipeline Plan: Turkmen Opposition May Scupper US Backed Proposal," *Financial Times*, June 8, 2000, p. 12.
57. James Dorsey, "Turkmenistan Deal May Kill Pipeline Backed by the US," Wall Street Journal, November 19, 2000, p. A22.
58. Authors, interviews with US diplomats active in the Caspian region indicate that this political obstacle is viewed as the major barrier to the TCP.
59. I. Joseph, 'Caspian Gas Exports: Stranded Reserves in a Unique Position, Baker Institute Working Paper 1998, available at www.bakerinstitute.org.
60. Aliriza, "US Caspion Pipeline Policy" (n. 10).
61. Michael Lelyveld, "Ankara Examining Russian Energy Project" RFE/RL News Service, May 30, 2001. A corruption scandal is brewing in Turkey, focused on alleged favors in contracting for the $3.2 billion Blue Stream pipeline. The investigation over accusations has led to a delay in final construction of the line and the resignation of Turkey's energy minister. Turkish prosecutors have raided the offices of state-owned pipeline companies.
62. Hugh Pope, "Turks to Buy Azerbaijani Gas in Boost to US-backed Plan", *Wall Street Journal,* March 13, 2001, p. A 21.
63. For the full text of report, see www.whitehouse.gov, "National Energy Policy" Report of the National Energy policy group, May 2001, The report recommends the following: "The NEPD Group recommends that the President direct the Secretaries of State, Commerce and Energy to support the efforts of private investors and regional governments to develop the Shah Deniz gas pipeline as a way to help Turkey and Georgia diversify their natural gas supplies and help Azerbaijan export its gas via pipeline that will continue diversification of secure energy supply routes."
64. Author's discussions with Kazakh producers, October 13, 2000.
65. "Russia Closing In On Central Asian Natural Gas Business", *Petroleum Economist,* June 13, 2000, p. 74.

6

Domestic Use of Energy: Oil Refineries and Gas Processing

Andrei Kalyuzhnov, Julian Lee and Julia Nanay

Introduction

Local refineries and gas processing facilities play an important role for the Caspian Sea region economies (CSRE), determining what products are available for the domestic market and thereby influencing consumption patterns. The governments of the region are interested in supporting and promoting these industries for a variety of economic and political reasons. Governments must worry about maintaining a cap on domestic energy prices as well as sustaining jobs in the local energy industry.

Refineries in the Caspian area are struggling to overcome their legacy of outdated technology from the Soviet era. While there is enormous potential for the Caspian area to become a refining centre, expensive and inadequate crude supplies, poor product qualities, and poor payment records contribute to their troubles today.

Prior to the break-up of the former Soviet Union (FSU) in 1991, the ten functioning oil refineries in Azerbaijan, Georgia, Kazakhstan, Turkmenistan, and Uzbekistan were part of a broader integrated, regional network, designed to function as part of a monolithic, centrally controlled Soviet oil industry. Breaking up this unified industry has proven much more difficult than breaking up the underlying political union.

The countries of the Caspian region aspire to become increasingly independent from Russia's sphere of influence. But this is not easy to accomplish because of the difficulties in creating independent energy systems and markets (see Chapter 3). Without independent and efficient petroleum industries, their political gains are somewhat illusory.

Today there are 12 refineries in the five countries of the Caspian Region (see Figure 6.1). Since 1991, Georgia and Uzbekistan are the only

Figure 6.1 Oil refineries in the Caspian region

two countries to have built new refineries. Turkmenistan is the only country to be able to finance a costly upgrade of one of its two refineries. As a result, it will have the largest up-to-date facility in the region.

The natural gas processing, transportation and distribution infrastructure inherited by the Caspian region countries also reflects the commercial legacy of the planned economy of the former Soviet Union. Thus, the existing infrastructure does not meet the needs of the individual countries as sovereign territories. Caspian countries are struggling to realign their domestic gas infrastructure to better meet internal demand and to allow their surplus gas, where it exists, to reach foreign markets.

Under the Soviet Union, the republics of the Caspian region – and in particular Turkmenistan and Uzbekistan – served the role of major suppliers of natural gas to fuel the industries and power plants of the Russian Federation and other parts of the Soviet Union. As a result, a network of major gas trunk lines was built to carry gas from the fields developed in these two republics northwards to Russia, passing through western Kazakhstan on the way.

The gas markets of the Central Asian republics themselves were relatively poorly developed. Little domestic infrastructure exists outside of the pipelines extending north to Russia and surprisingly, relatively little has been done in the Caspian region to change this situation. Domestic utilization of gas resources remains low, while gas exports have, until very recently, been curtailed by deteriorating political and commercial relations between the Caspian republics and Russia.

This chapter addresses the basic challenges facing five Caspian basin countries – Azerbaijan, Georgia, Kazakhstan, Turkmenistan and Uzbekistan – as they gear up to create independent domestic energy markets. Discussion focuses on existing and planned facilities and an assessment of whether those facilities will be able to meet local requirements for energy. We begin with a discussion of the outlook for the Caspian basin refining industry and then address the challenges facing each of the five individual countries surveyed. A detailed presentation of the natural gas industries in the region follows, including some analysis covering future investment plans. Finally, some comments on the future challenges to the countries in meeting domestic energy needs are presented.

Refineries: outlook and challenges

Refineries in the Caspian region are geographically remote from the world markets for crude oil and products. Although the outlook for exporting crude oil appears good, as has been demonstrated by the TengizChevroil joint venture in Kazakhstan (Chevron, ExxonMobil, LukArco/BP) and the CPC pipeline investment, moving refined product is much more difficult. This difficulty offers the Caspian region refining industry a high level of natural-price protection, because competing supplies from outside the region must travel over long distances to reach this market. Futhermore, producing the right quality of petroleum products for export markets will prove difficult for all but two of the refineries – one each in Turkmenistan and in Uzbekistan – with the rest of the region being burdened with outdated old facilities. The Caspian refining industry cannot compete for the sophisticated requirements of European markets.

As in the past, Kazakhstan, Turkmenistan and Uzbekistan are primarily producers today. Azerbaijan is a producer and a transit country. Georgia's main role is as a transit country, although it produces small volumes of oil and gas. Armenia, Kyrgyzstan, and Tajikistan lack sufficient resources and are unlikely to take part in the regional competition of oil and gas development.

Given their remote, land-locked position and the inevitability of growing domestic demand for oil products, the countries of Central Asia and the Caucasus must continue to rely on their own refineries. The ten plants built before 1991 remain in various states of disrepair. Prior to 1991, there was little access to the latest Western technologies. Instead, the refineries were constructed with Soviet design and manufacturing processes (the only exception to this is Atyrau Refinery in northwestern Kazakhstan, built in 1945, using equipment imported from the United States under the Lend-Lease program). In 1991 the secondary oil processing capacities (in percentage of primary crude distillation) were as follows: Azerbaijan 16.3 percent, Georgia 13.1 percent, Kazakhstan 30.6 percent, Turkmenistan 15.6 percent, and Uzbekistan 48.5 percent. Thus, the refineries were essentially hydroskimmers with minimal capacity to convert heavy fuels into light products. The output mix of the refineries was largely composed of heavy products such as residual fuel oil.

In 1991, many of the region's refineries were largely dependent on Russian crude oil. The percentage of Russian crude oil in refinery throughput in the republics of the Caspian region was as follows: Azerbaijan 25 percent, Georgia 86 percent, Turkmenistan 4 percent, and Uzbekistan 85 percent. Even Kazakhstan, the second biggest regional oil producer after Russia, relied on Russian crude for 74 percent of its crude input (*Khartukor and Surovtsev*). At the present time, this dependence remains. In addition, the reduced availability of Russian oil (Goskomstat of Russia, 1999, p. 395) means that the refineries are running well under their nameplate capacity.

Today, the refining sector in the Caspian region is facing numerous problems. The share of heavy fuel oil in refinery output is, on average, 35–40 percent (Nigmatullin, 1998, p. 72; Guluzade, p. 76) versus 20–25 percent in Western Europe and 10 percent in the US. Refineries have limited capacities for converting bottom-of-the-barrel fractions of oil into light products (Table 6.1). They rely largely on catalytic reforming and hydrotreating processes rather than catalytic cracking, hydrocracking and thermal operations.

According to the authors' calculations, catalytic cracking, hydrocracking, and thermal operations represent only 12 percent of crude charge capacity, compared to 32 percent in the UK and 30 percent in Germany (calculations based on Oil and Gas Journal, December 20, 1999, p. 58).

Meanwhile, gasoline quality in the Caspian region is well below European standards. Caspian area refineries mainly make low-octane, leaded gasoline. At the present time, this is not a big problem, because most vehicles in the FSU are designed for this type of fuel, and refined products are mainly consumed in domestic markets. However, poor quality gasoline will be a problem, when more cars are imported from abroad and emission standards become more stringent (*Oil and Gas of Kazakhstan* , 2000, p. 75).

The refineries' petroleum products are high in sulfur and thereby cannot be profitably sold in export markets (*Oil and Gas of Kazakhstan*, 2000, p. 75). Diesel and heavy fuel oil, because of their high sulfur content, cannot be used for power stations in Europe (unless fitted with flue-gas desulfurization) and can be sold only as a cheap feedstock for further processing.

The narrow slate of refined products in combination with a fixed crude slate means that refiners cannot react to seasonal changes in consumption patterns. That is, they cannot adjust to the need for more light products during the summer and greater quantities of winter type diesel fuel during the cold seasons.

Compared to similar types of plants in Europe, energy consumption and losses in the Caspian area are high, in some cases up to 7–8 percent of the feedstock (EU Consortium- TACIS, 1995).

Investment in refining in the region has lagged, mainly because governments are unable to finance major revamps, and foreign investors are reluctant to invest in downstream businesses. It is more attractive

Table 6.1 Refineries – capacities as of January 1, 2000

Country	Crude	Vacuum distillation	Coking	Charge capacity, barrels per calendar day Thermal operation	Catalytic cracking	Catalytic reforming	Cat hydro cracking	Cat hydro refining	Cat hydro treating
Azerbaijan	441 808	137 200	38 529	...	71 342	24 466	...	...	67 492
Kazakhstan	427 093	12 1037	24 997	30 071	38 356	59 452	...	....	207 353
Turkmenistan	236 970	71 231	28 568	...	15 151	32 540	...	...	33 300
Georgia	108 836	24 809	...	...	...	10 276	...	...	10 800
Uzbekistan	222 271	45 672	17 667	9 585	...	23 487	...	...	30 804

Source: *Oil and Gas Journal*, Decembers 20, 1999.

to export crude than to sell products into the domestic market, where customers are often unable to pay (Kalyuzhnova, 1998, 2001; EIU, 2001). But some ambitious investment projects are under consideration, such as a Japanese plan for a major restructuring of Azerbaijan's industry.

At present, the Caspian region has a surplus of refining capacity compared to domestic demand, calling into question the economic viability of many of the region's refineries (EIU Country Report – Kazakhstan, January 2001, p. 28). This has stifled any interest in downstream investment. In addition, there is a surplus of fuel oil producing capacity, and a lack of capacity to produce the products which are required: middle distillates and gasoline. Because local governments prefer to achieve self-sufficiency in domestic oil products supplies, which means precisely in the products which are lacking, they will try to prevent any shutdowns of these "dinosaur" facilities and will seek investors for their modernization. The refining sector is seen by governments as creating employment and helping in the diversification of exports (*Oil and Capital*, 2000, p. 24), while cancelling the need for high cost imports. Furthermore, the often difficult political relations between neighboring countries and the remoteness of these countries from the major world markets for oil and oil products, argue for these governments' pursuit of self-sufficiency.

Azerbaijan

Azerbaijan has two refineries with a total capacity of 442 000 b/d: Azerneftyanajag (203 000 b/d) and Azerneftyag Baku (239 000 b/d). Both are located in the vicinity of Baku and are very old plants, built 40–70 years ago. In the past, Azerbaijan processed oil in excess of its own needs and supplied products to the rest of the USSR. Despite recent interest in upgrading Azerneftyag, Azerbaijan's two refineries remain so run down that they are only able to function at below 40 percent of capacity, processing 164 000 b/d (8.205 million tonnes) in 2000. In 2000, the two refineries produced 536 800 tonnes of gasoline, 1.958 million tonnes of diesel, 754 700 tonnes of kerosene, and 87 000 tonnes of lubricants (Baku press report, January 29, 2001).

Azerneftyanajag was built in 1953 and upgraded in 1965. Azerneftyag was built mostly in the 1930s, but some of its units are even older. Between 1994 and 2000, $16.9 million of Azerneftyag's revenues were reinvested in the refinery to undertake upgrades in its technology, storage tanks, and loading facilities and to install a bitumen plant. The latter project was undertaken by US company Petrofac and Austria's Pernier and will permit the production of 250 000 tonnes per year of asphalt for road construction, of which 175 000 tonnes per year are intended for export. (Baku Sun News Agency, November 12, 2000, US Embassy/Commerce Dep. January 22, 2001). The asphalt is earmarked for road construction under the European Union's (EU's) TRACECA (Transport Corridor Europe Caucasus Asia) program. In addition, based on a $500 000 grant provided by the US Trade and Development Agency (TDA), US firm Merichem and Refinery Services has begun a feasibility study on modernizing the kerosene and diesel fuel units at the Azerneftyag plant, so as to improve product yields to meet European specifications. Still awaiting takers at Azerneftyag is the installation of additional lubricants manufacturing capacity, a project with a price tag of about $300 million. This would provide much needed aviation fuel, meeting the standards required for the major airlines that refuel in Baku.

Azerbaijan estimates that upgrades at the two refineries, which will permit it to process 260 000 b/d, will cost $600–$700 million (US Energy Information Administration, May 2000).

As the above developments indicate, some attention has been devoted to the refining sector in Azerbaijan. Supplementing these efforts is yet another proposed project, this one being promoted by Japanese companies. In 1998, Nichimen Corp., Tokyo, and Chiyoda Corp., Yokohama, began work on the master plan for modernizing the two refineries. In May 2000, they presented their recommendations to the Azeri government (Reuters, June 2, 2000).

Combining the two refineries is one option being proposed. Future production would be focused on transportation fuels and specialty lubricants, including jet fuel, rather than fuel oil, since the latter will largely be replaced in the power sector by natural gas. Azerbaijan's master plan has set an optimistic date of 2003 for the country's gasoline specifications and usage to be brought in line with European standards, but this is an ambitious schedule, which is not likely to be met. Although the modernization of the refineries would be financed by Japan's Bank for International Cooperation (JBIC) – with Nichimen being the financial arranger and Chiyoda arranging engineering and construction – final decisions on procedure are pending. The magnitude of the broader Japanese plan, which aims to integrate Azerbaijan's oil refining, petrochemicals and gas refining sectors and undertake their modernization in a phased approach over the next decade, has led to slower progress in taking decisions by the government.

The master plan also envisions the construction of an 855 km oil-products export pipeline from Baku to the Georgian Black Sea coast, by which 60 000 b/d of products will be sent to the European market by 2010.

With high oil prices in 1999, Azerbaijan was exporting its oil instead of stockpiling it for winter refining needs. But these exports left the country exposed and it was caught short during the winter of 1999–2000, when the country experienced serious shortages of fuel oil in its power sector. The government issued a decree on June 19, 2000, forcing the diversion of Socar's oil from lucrative export markets to domestic refineries to build up fuel oil stocks for the country's winter power needs.

One plan under consideration is to adjust Azerbaijan's domestic capacity to refine poorer quality crudes from the region – primarily Kazakhstan – freeing up Azeri State company Socar's crude for export markets. This could give a boost to the availability of superior quality crude from Socar's share of the AIOC development for the planned Baku–Tblisi–Ceyhan (BTC) pipeline.

Oil production in Azerbaijan reached 280 000 b/d in 1999, below the nameplate capacity of its two refineries. Domestic consumption was 125 000 b/d, down from a peak of 170 000 b/d in 1990 (BPAmoco, 2000).

Georgia

Georgia has two refineries with a total capacity of 109 000 b/d, of which only one is functioning. The country's main refinery is located in Batumi, the capital of the autonomous republic of Adzharia (106 000 b/d). It was built in the 1930s and has been shut down for several years. A second, much smaller plant, built in the 1990s, is located in Sartichala (4 000 b/d), 30 km east of Tblisi. It began operations in 1998, and has been largely idle since June 2000. It should resume operating in the second half of 2001.

Georgia has attracted some interest from foreign investors in its refining sector because of the country's strategic location as a transit hub for crudes from the Caspian region.

CanArgo Energy Corp., Calgary, has a 51 percent interest in the Sartichala plant, called the Georgian American Oil Refinery (GAOR). GAOR is near CanArgo's Ninotsminda oil field, which accounts for much of Georgia's 2 200 b/d of oil production, and which supplies GAOR's crude needs.

This small refinery produces fuel oil, diesel, and low octane gasoline for the local market. CanArgo is financing a refinery upgrade that includes a new catalytic reformer, which will permit the production of high octane gasoline.

The refinery at Batumi, which mainly operated on Russian and Azeri crudes, may remain shut down because modernizing the refinery is too costly. Mitsui & Co. Ltd., Tokyo, tried to drum up interest in modernizing the Batumi refinery, which would have cost $250 million. Mitsui was forced to drop the project, however, when it was unable to organize investor interest and could not obtain Georgian government guarantees. Marubeni Corp. and JGC Corp., both based in Tokyo, also dropped out of an earlier modernization proposal because of the same lack of interest and a failure to obtain guarantees.

Another local group has suggested constructing a new $400 million refinery in Supsa, but this project remains dormant. The refinery, as envisioned, would receive its feedstock from oil shipments through the existing Baku–Supsa pipeline. This pipeline will transport about 130 000 b/d of oil from Azerbaijan's AIOC development. The planned refinery would have an initial capacity of 60 000 b/d, ramping up in phases to 240 000 b/d. Azerbaijan's state oil company, Socar, expressed interest in becoming a stakeholder if such a refinery were to be built. Itochu Corp. of Tokyo, which at one point considered participating in a plant at Supsa with its equity-crude production from Azerbaijan, is no longer pursuing this option. In fact, no new refineries need to be built in Georgia because they would struggle to compete with highly efficient refineries in Europe, where there is overcapacity. The Supsa refinery, like the plant at Batumi, is likely to remain on the drawing boards for the foreseeable future. Companies will prefer to export crude, and not refined products, from the ports at Supsa and Batumi. Georgia's railroads will continue to be the economic, preferred transport option for delivering crude to Batumi, as the pipeline delivery option would require a significant increase in volumes before it would become economic to build.

Production of 2200 b/d in 2000 is expected to rise to 4000 b/d in 2001. Georgian oil consumption is about 23 000 b/d (figures provided by the Georgian Government).

Kazakhstan

Kazakhstan has three refineries with a total capacity of 427 000 b/d. The Pavlodar (in northeast Kazakhstan) and Shymkentnefteorgsyntez (ShNOS; in south central Kazakhstan) refineries have capacities of 163 000 b/d and 160 000 b/d, respectively. They were built to process crudes from Western Siberia, delivered via the Omsk–Pavlodar–Shymkent–Chardzou pipeline.

The oldest refinery is located in Atyrau (104 000 b/d) in western Kazakhstan, close to the Caspian Sea. This is the only refinery in Kazakhstan designed to use local crudes, although ShNOS now also relies on domestic production.

In 1999, Russia, for various political reasons, supplied only 721 200 tonnes (14 400 b/d) of oil to Kazakhstan. As a result, the Pavlodar refinery, the newest Kazakh plant, which came onstream in 1978, was forced to run at 9 percent of design capacity. In 2000, Russian political concerns were appeased and crude supplies were increased to nearly 40 000 b/d. Pavlodar, which is the refinery closest to Russia, has also suffered from competition from Russia's Omsk refinery (part of Russian integrated company Sibneft), located 350 km to the north. Deliveries of Russian crude to Pavlodar dropped after the Omsk refinery expanded its capacity in recent years.

In 2000, Pavlodar's US-based owner, CCL, with an 87 percent interest in the plant, became embroiled in an ownership struggle with the Kazakh government, reminiscent of the struggle which Canadian Hurricane Hydrocarbons is facing in 2001 with the ShNOS refinery. In November 2000, the plant's ownership was transferred to Kazakh producer, Mangistaumunaigaz (MMG, 51 percent) and the state (49 percent). Mangistaumunaigaz has excellent ties within Kazakh government circles. This has put the refinery's operations on much more solid ground, giving it access to MMG's crude production. MMG is one of Kazakhstan's largest producers, holding fields like Zhetybay and Kalamkas. MMG's Indonesian partners have now relinquished their stake in these producing fields to domestic Kazakh interests.

Pavlodar has the best processing facilities among the three Kazakh plants (catalytic cracking, thermal operations and coking). Pavlodar's output consists of over 20 different types of products: various gasoline grades, including unleaded Ai-91 and Ai-95; various grades of summer and winter diesel fuel; jet fuel; bitumen; LPG, and others. Major purchasers of Pavlodar's refined products in central, northern and southern Kazakhstan include: Ispat-Karmet, Aluminum Kazakhstan, Eurasian Energy Company, Bogatyr Access coal mine, Alautransgaz, Almaty Airport, and airports in Astana, Karaganda, Kokshetai, Ust-Kamenogorsk, and Petropavlovsk (Interfax, October 29–November 5, 1999).

The Shymkentnefteorgsyntez (ShNOS) plant was designed to process mainly Western Siberian oil, which used to account for 80 percent of its feedstock. It has access to railed crude deliveries from Uzbekistan and from the Chinese National Petroleum Company's (CNPC's)/Access Industries Aktyubinsk fields in the west. But the refinery now relies largely on oil from Canadian Hurricane Hydrocarbons and Lukoil's Kumkol fields.

ShNOS processed 3.4 million tonnes (68 000 b/d) of oil (42 percent of design capacity) in 1999. This dropped to 2.9 million tonnes (58 000 b/d) in 2000 (Research Kazkommerts Securities, January 2001). ShNOS supplies about 65 percent of the refined products used in the southern regions of Kazakhstan. It also sells products in Kyrgyzstan, where ShNOS has a representative office. The refinery produces diesel, gasoline (Ai-80, Ai-85, Ai-92, and Ai-95), kerosene, and fuel oil. Close to 50 percent of output is consumed in Almaty. A catalytic-cracking complex to increase light oil products from 65 percent to 85 percent of its output slate is planned for the refinery.

ShNOS plans to invest $14 million, generated in part from its own profits, in refinery improvements this year, up from $6 million in 2000. ShNOS will also ask the European Bank for Reconstruction and Development (EBRD) for an $80 million loan to undertake major upgrades like the installation of a catalytic cracking plant. Work on this plant has already begun (Interfax, May 18–24, 2001). Before serious progress can be made, ShNOS's major shareholder, Canadian Hurricane Hydrocarbons, which owns 88.37 percent of the plant, may have to overcome its ongoing disputes with various Kazakh entities.

The 104 000 b/d Atyrau refinery is in a paradoxical situation. Oil extraction in the western part of Kazakhstan is rising, but refinery output is declining. In 1998, Atyrau processed 2.7 million tonnes (54 000 b/d) of crude, or 52 percent of capacity. In 1999, this figure dropped to 1.9 million tonnes (38 000 b/d), or 37 percent of design capacity. In 2000, there was an increase to 2.19 million tonnes (43 800 b/d), or 42 percent of capacity.

Built in 1945, Atyrau is the simplest of the country's three refineries and uses equipment from the United States, imported under the post-War Lend-Lease program. This is the only Kazakh refinery in which the state, through Kazakhoil, holds a majority stake (86.49 percent) – nearly equal to Hurricane's share in ShNOS. It takes crude from the Mangyshlak, Tengiz, Martyshin, Karazhanbas, Kalamkas, Buzachi, and other fields. Some of these fields have a high metal and sulfur content, and if their role increases in supplying the refinery, this could pose a problem. Atyrau is not equipped for sulfur removal.

Eventually, Atyrau's location could bring the refinery significant advantages: it is less than 100 km from the new offshore East Kasahagan development. Modernization projects at the refinery in the 1960s and 1970s added a 420 000 tonne catalytic reforming unit, a 720 000 tonne delayed coking unit, and a 140 000 tonne coke calcinations unit. (Interfax Business Report, January 12–18, 2001). Atyrau currently produces gasoline (A-76, A-80, Ai-91, and A-93), diesel, heating oil, aviation kerosine (TS-1), and fuel oil. About 40 percent of its output, however, is fuel oil, reflecting its sizable crude slate of heavier oil.

The refinery requires significant investments to install a catalytic cracker, which will allow it to process 86 000 b/d and boost the production of light products to 80 percent of capacity. A $308 million two-year upgrade is planned, to be financed as follows: Kazakhoil ($68 million) and Japanese Marubeni ($240 million), with the Kazakh government providing $200 million in guarantees. The production of gasoline is slated to increase from 316 000 tonnes to 660 000 tonnes; aviation kerosene, from 43 000 tonnes to 86 000 tonnes; winter diesel, from 291 600 tonnes to 500 000 tonnes. At the same time, fuel oil production will be cut to 397 800 tonnes from about 900 000 tonnes now. In May 2001, Kazakhoil and Marubeni signed an agreement that the feasibility study for the refinery's reconstruction will be completed by the end of 2001, to be followed by a two-year reconstruction phase. Japan's JGC will undertake the engineering work (Interfax, May 18–24, 2001).

Plans have been announced for two new refineries in Kazakhstan: a $1.5 billion plant in Mangistau (150 000 b/d) and a $480 million export refinery (50 000 b/d) at the Zhanazhol field near Atyubinsk. Based on current utilization of existing plants and expected growth, however, it is hard to envision support in the near term for investment in these refineries.

In 2000–2001 high world oil prices negatively influenced the supply of crude oil for Kazakhstan's refineries as producers began to favour export markets. In the initial stage of the domestic crude shortage, the Kazakhstani government tried to introduce a quota for oil exports, but this idea was dropped along with a plan to protect the domestic market through export duties, which would have varied according to world oil prices. The Kazakh government officially states that it would like oil producers to supply 30 percent of their production to domestic refineries, but in actuality, the government appears to accept around 20 percent. In fact, the average rate for foreign companies is more like 10 percent.

The oil companies who are owners of Kazakhstani refineries are increasingly finding incentives to supply crude to their facilities (Kazakhoil supplies about 50 percent of its production to Kazakhstani refineries, and Pavlodar's owner, MMG, supplies 45–50 percent). Moreover, Hurricane Hydrocarbons and Kazakhoil have announced plans to develop their own gasoline station networks. MMG already has its gasoline station network, under the brand name Helios.

Kazakhstan's oil production was 630 000 b/d in 1999 and reached 707 000 b/d in 2000, well in excess of its nameplate refining capacity. Domestic consumption in Kazakhstan has dropped sharply from 430 000 b/d in 1990 to about 130 000 b/d in 1999 and 2000 (BPAmoco, 2000).

Turkmenistan

Turkmenistan has two refineries with a total capacity of 237 000 b/d. They are located at Chardzou in northeastern Turkmenistan (120 000 b/d) and at Turkmenbashi on the Caspian Sea (116 000 b/d). In 1999, they refined 4.5 million tonnes (90 000 b/d) of crude oil, 13 percent less than in 1998. In 2000, the Turkmen government planned to refine 6.6 million tonnes (132 000 b/d).

The Chardzou refinery is a simple hydroskimming facility, designed to process heavy and high sulfur crudes from Western Siberia for re-export to neighboring countries. Its location was determined by the availability of low cost gas for feedstock and its yield is dominated by heavy fuel oil. The plant is not commercially viable (World Bank, 1993).

The Turkmenbashi refinery was built in 1943, from the resiting of a refinery from Georgia (World Bank, 1993). Some of its equipment dated back to 1929 (Institutional Investor Focus, 1997). The delayed coking unit was of German design and French construction (World Bank, 1993). It is undergoing a $1.5 billion modernization, which includes the installation of a $300 million, 1.8 million tonnes/year (t/yr) catalytic cracker by France's Technip and Iran's National Iranian Oil Co. (NIOC) and a $139 million, 750 000 t/yr catalytic reforming unit by Japan's Nichimen and Chiyoda, Turkey's Gama, and financed by Japan's Eximbank. The upgrade will also include a $186 million, 80 000 t/yr lubricants unit, which is to be built by a German branch of Technip and financed by German banks, and a $200 million, 90 000 t/yr polypropylene unit to be built by Japan's Itochu, Nissho-Iwai and JGC.

The 750 000 t/yr catalytic reforming unit came onstream in May 2000. The 1.8 million t/yr catalytic cracker was completed in April 2001. As a result, the refinery can now produce 920 000 t/yr of high octane gasoline, 255 000 t/y of diesel, 280 000 t/yr of heating oil, and up to 345 000 t/yr of LPG. A complex of auxiliary units to service the plant have been installed, including a seawater desalination plant and a steam furnace to satisfy the plant's water and steam requirements. By end-2001, the 80 000 t/yr lubricants unit and the 90 000 t/yr polypropylene unit should be in operation. Ireland's Emerol Ltd is currently reconstructing the vacuum unit and building storage facilities. One final addition will be a $150 million hydrocleansing unit (Interfax Business report, April 9–15, 2001).

The revamping of the Turkmenbashi refinery, while costly, will mean that Turkmenistan will have the most modern refinery in the Caspian region. This upgrade was organized by Israeli company, Merhav, which was also instrumental in lining up the finance. Merhav has been active in Turkmenistan's agricultural sector and used the refinery project as a stepping stone to additional activities in the country's energy sector. The most important of these was the TransCaspian Gas Pipeline Project (TCGP), which failed to materialize but in which Merhav was the project coordinator.

The modernized refinery at Turkmenbashi will be able to produce gasoline, lubricants and polymers that meet world standards. By 2005, the plant will be able to refine 6 million t/yr or 120 000 b/d. By 2010, an increase to 9 million t/yr or 180 000 b/d is planned. The refinery's output will hit 2 million t/y or 40 000 b/d of gasoline, 80 000 t/yr of lubricants, and 90 000 t/yr of polypropylene.

Oil production in 1999 reached 150 000 b/d, which is less than Turkmenistan's nameplate refining capacity. Domestic consumption of 90 000 b/d, is about the same as it was in 1990 (BP Amoco 2000).

Uzbekistan

Uzbekistan has three refineries with a total capacity of 222 000 b/d. Before the country's independence, its two refineries in Fergana (106 000 b/d) and Alty-Arik (66 000 b/d) relied on crude from a pipeline that originated in Omsk, Western Siberia and delivered oil to Uzbekistan by way of Chardzou, Turkmenistan. By 1995, these crude imports were largely eliminated, although product imports from Russia continued until 1998.

Uzbekistan achieved self-sufficiency in supplying its domestic products' demand with the August 1997 completion of a new 50 000 b/d refinery in Karaoul Bazar, 55 km east of Bukhara. It was the first grass-roots refinery built in the post-1991 FSU. Along with Georgia's 2 400 b/d refinery at Sartichala (1998), it is one of two plants in this region constructed entirely with Western technology.

The Bukhara refinery was built by Technip, Marubeni, and JGC with Japanese participation in its financing. The $400 million refinery has run on gas condensates produced from the Kokdumalak field, 94 km away. Kokdumalok accounts for 70 percent of Uzbekistan's liquids production.

The refinery is equipped with units for atmospheric distillation, naphtha hydrodesulfurization, gas-oil hydrodesulfurization, kerosine sweetening, regenerative reforming, sour-water treatment, and sulfur recovery. It also has a gas plant, one control station, and two electricity substations. It now produces gasoline for export as well as gasoline, diesel, and kerosine for the domestic market. The Uzbekistan government has plans to double the refinery's capacity.

In 1997, Mitsui and Toyo Engineering undertook a $200 million desulfurization capacity expansion project at another refinery in Fergana, to permit the production of low-sulfur diesel. Texaco is involved in a joint venture to produce and market Texaco-branded lubricants from the Fergana refinery.

The third refinery at Alty Arik needs to be mothballed or completely rebuilt.

Uzbekistan is now able to export limited volumes of product by rail to neighboring countries.

Oil production in 1999 reached 190 000 b/d, which is less than the country's nameplate refining capacity. Domestic consumption of 145 000 b/d in 1999 is significantly below the 1990 consumption of 255 000 b/d (BPAmoco 2000).

Natural gas in the Caspian region

A logical link between the refineries and gas processing is the question of the internal energy consumption by the CSRE. Increased natural gas production (Chapter 3) required the availability of processing and gas distributing capacities. However, the existing facilities are insufficient for processing the gas production and transmission to the customers.

The natural gas industry has a similar background, as a refinery sector – built in the Soviet era, the gas processing sector in every Caspian region republic was orientated towards the Soviet economic system needs. For example, Kazakhstan has three gas processing plants (total annual capacity 6.7 billion cubic meters of gas), namely the Tengiz gas processing facility (total annual capacity 3.0 bcm), the Kazakh gas processing facility (total annual capacity 1.5 bcm), and the

Zhanazhol gas processing facility (total annual capacity 0.7 bcm). In Kazakhstan, the growth in gas production potential could be envisaged from the contribution of the Karachaganak, Tengiz and OKIOC projects.

Gas trunk pipeline infrastructure

The Soviet era gas trunkline infrastructure was designed to carry natural gas northwards from the fields discovered in southern Turkmenistan and along the Amu Darya river basin along the border between Turkmenistan and Uzbekistan. These lines, known collectively as the Central Asia–Centre gas pipeline, cross into Kazakhstan to the west of the Aral Sea, traverse western Kazakhstan, before crossing into Russia at Aleksandrov Gay. They are joined at Bayneu in Kazakhstan by a fifth line, which carries gas from fields along Turkmenistan's Caspian Sea coast and some additional volumes from fields in southwest Kazakhstan.

A second corridor of gas export pipelines began in southern Uzbekistan and followed the Central Asia–Centre pipeline as far as the Aral Sea where it turned northwards along the western shore of the Aral Sea and across Kazakhstan, entering Russia near Orsk (see Figure 6.2). In 1997, the flow of this pipeline was reversed in order to carry gas from Russia's Orenburg gas processing plant to markets in Kazakhstan.

The diameter of the major south–north gas export pipelines varies from 40 in (1.02 m) to 56 in (1.42 m) (Table 6.2).

The Central Asia–Centre gas pipeline system has been allowed to deteriorate since the break-up of the Soviet Union. Turkmenistan found itself effectively excluded from gas export markets in Western Europe once it became an independent country. The gas pipeline infrastructure was divided among new national companies on a territorial basis. Thus, Russia's Gazprom became the new owner of all the natural gas trunk pipelines on Russian soil. At a stroke, Turkmenistan was cut off from its gas export markets in the rest of the former Soviet Union and, more importantly, in Western Europe.

Following the suspension of Turkmenistan's gas exports through Russia in 1997, the unused Central Asia–Centre trunk gas pipeline was allowed to deteriorate. The effective capacity of the pipeline is thought to be around 40 bcm/yr, compared with a design capacity of 67.5 bcm/yr, (Reuters 2001).

In addition to the Central Asia–Centre gas trunkline, a network of lines carry gas eastwards from fields in southern Uzbekistan to consumers in the industrial heartland of the Fergana valley, Tajikistan,

Figure 6.2 Gas in the Caspian region (pre-transition): locator map (key producing area).
Source: Centre for Global Energy Studies (2001).

Table 6.2 Trunk gas pipelines in Central Asia (2001)

From	To	Length (km)	Diameter (inches)	Diameter (mm)	Capacity (bcm/yr)	Capacity (mcm/day)	
Turkmenistan	Russia	1 200~	40/56	1 020/1 420	67.5	185.0	'Central Asia–Centre'
Okarem (Turkmen.)	Beineu (Kaz.)	1 000	48	1 220	5.4	15.0	
Uzen (Kaz.)	Aktau (Kaz.)	140	40	1 020	3.6	10.0	
Makat (Kaz.)	N. Caucasus	380*	56	1 420	25.5	70.0	
Orenburg (Russia)	Europe	415*	48	1 220	58.4	160.0	Crosses Kazakhstan
Kartali (Russia)	Kustanay (Kaz.)	265*	48	1 220	5.4	15.0	
Bukhara (Uzbek.)	Ural (Russia)	1 450~	40	1 020	14	38.5	Reversed in 1997
Bukhara (Uzbek.)	Almaty (Kaz.)	1 200	40	1 020	13	35.5	
Gazli (Uzbek.)	Chimkent (Kaz.)	600	48	1 220	13	35.5	
Korpedzhe (Turkmen.)	Kord Kui (Iran)	190	40	1 020	4	14.3	

* Kazakh portion only ~ Distance to Russian border

Source: *Russian Petroleum Investor* (various issues) and CGES estimates.

Kyrgyzstan and Kazakhstan. These pipelines bear little relation to present-day international borders, frequently crossing and re-crossing between newly independent countries. This feature has caused numerous problems with one side accusing the other of illegally taking gas from the line.

A new pipeline was opened in 1997 linking gas fields along Turkmenistan's Caspian Sea shore to Iran. This is the first gas export pipeline from Central Asia that avoids Russian territory. This small 190 km pipeline had an initial capacity of just 4 bcm/yr, but this is to be increased to 8 bcm/yr by 2002. A second gas pipeline from Turkmenistan to Iran was reportedly opened at the end of 2000, linking Artik (which lies on the domestic gas pipeline linking Mary to Ashgabad) with Loftabad across the border in northern Iran (IRNA News Agency, 2000).

To the west of the Caspian Sea, the existing gas trunk pipeline network was designed to carry gas from Russia to consumers in the republics of the Caucasus. One pipeline, with a diameter of 1 020 mm (40in), brings gas from Central Asia around the northern shore of the Caspian, while a second line, with a diameter of 1 420 mm (56 in) carries gas southwards from Russia's Astrakhan field. Three further pipelines, each with a diameter of 720 mm (28 in) carry gas southeast from Rostov-on-Don. All these pipelines converged in the vicinity of Mozdok in Ingushetia and Grozny in Chechnya.

From Mozdok (see Table 6.3), two lines ran southwards across the Caucasus mountains to Tblisi in Georgia, whence distribution lines carried gas into Azerbaijan, Armenia and the Azerbaijani enclave of Nakichevan. A second line ran eastwards from Grozny to the western shore of the Caspian Sea at Makhachkala. It then followed the coast southwards to Baku.

Azerbaijan is also served by a gas pipeline from Iran. This 1020 mm (40in) pipeline runs from Rasht (on Iran's IGAT-1 and IGAT-2 trunk pipelines) via Astara on the Azerbaijan–Iran border to Ali Bayramly, where it joins Azerbaijan's internal gas network. This line was used in the latter years of the Soviet era to import gas from Iran, but remained idle throughout the 1990s. There were suggestions that the direction of flow through the line could be reversed and that it might be used to carry Azerbaijani oil south to refineries in northern Iran, but nothing came of these suggestions. Azerbaijan also considered using the line to import gas from Iran during the winter of 2000/2001, but it was found to have deteriorated to such an extent that it needs replacing. Parts of

Table 6.3 Trunk gas pipelines in Azerbaijan (1998)

From	To	Length in Azerbaijan (km)	Diameter (inches)	Diameter (mm)	Capacity (bcm/yr)	Capacity (mcm/day)	
Mozdok (Russia)	Kazi Mahomed	240	48	1 220	13	35.6	
Qom (Iran)	Kazi Mahomed	297	48	1 220	10	27.4	Mothballed since 1993
Kazi Mahomed	Kazakh	378	40	1,016	10	27.4	
Kazi Mahomed	Kazakh	378	48	1 220	13	35.6	
Kazakh	Georgia	120	20/32/40	508/813/1 016	10	27.4	
Kazakh	Armenia	38	20/40	508/1,016	7	19.2	Unused since 1992
Yevlakh	Nakhichevan	290	28	710	4.5	12.3	

Source: *Oil and Gas of Azerbaijan* (1998).

the line had been dismantled, while along other sections houses had been built over the line.

Gas processing and distribution

The Caspian region is characterized by a general lack of gas processing infrastructure, with relatively few processing facilities in the region. Gas distribution within the individual republics is highly variable. In Azerbaijan, for example, although the gas pipeline network is extensive (covering some 85 percent of the population) gas is hardly available outside the Baku region (IMF, 2000). In Kazakhstan, despite sizable gas reserves, much of the country is not served with gas pipelines, while the south relies on gas imported from neighboring countries. In Turkmenistan, the domestic gas distribution network has been significantly expanded since independence, raising the proportion of households supplied from 40 percent in 1990 to 92 percent by the end of 1999 (IMF, 1999).

Azerbaijan

Azerbaijan's gas is processed by the state oil company, Socar, while Azerigas, the state gas concern, is responsible for the transportation, storage and distribution of gas to customers.

Azerbaijan has two underground gas storage facilities at Karadag and Kalmas, both located to the southwest of Baku. The two facilities have a combined capacity of 3 bcm. In 1999, Azerigas and Sofregas estimated the cost of rehabilitation of the Kalmas and Karadag facilites and their expansion to a combined capacity of 7.5 bcm at $81 million and $191 million respectively (*Oil and Gas of Azerbaijan,* 1998)

Azerbaijan's gas from fields in the Caspian Sea is brought ashore through two pipelines, one from the AIOC (Azerbaijan International Operating Company – a consortium of foreign companies developing the Azeri, Chirag and deep-water section of the Guneshli fields) operated Chirag field via the Neft Dashlary oil and gas complex and the other from the Narimanov and Bulla-Deniz fields. Both lines carry gas to the Karadag processing plant close to Baku. Under the terms of the contract negotiated with the AIOC, all associated gas is delivered free-of-charge to Socar.

Although the Karadag gas processing plant has a nominal treatment capacity of 6.5 bcm/yr of gas and 675,000 t/yr of condensate, actual capacity is thought to be around 4.5 bcm (CGES, 2001).

Neither of Azerbaijan's two gas storage facilities have gas treatment plants and, as a result, gas fed into the distribution network is often contaminated with water and liquid hydrocarbons, as is the gas fed directly into the system from the gas fields without prior treatment. In a study of Azerbaijan's gas market completed by Norway's Statoil and Socar in 1998, it was noted that, "Only a third of the gas produced by Azerbaijan today is cleaned and treated, with the rest sent unprocessed. This causes corrosion in the pipelines, and treatment capacity must be upgraded to protect the transport infrastructure" (News article on the Statoil website.)

Azerbaijan's gas distribution system is in dire need of refurbishment. Azerigas has estimated that the total refurbishment of the system would require an investment of $150 million.

Azerbaijan's gas pipes suffer from a high degree of corrosion, and losses from the system are high. The World Bank estimates that around 5 percent of the gas put into the system is lost through leaking pipes, although the International Energy Agency (IEA) quotes Azerigas as saying the figure was 8 percent in 1997. However, Azerigas judged that two-thirds of this was due to theft or tampering with meters. Rehabilitation of the gas system is a high priority for the government of Azerbaijan.

In 1996, the World Bank approved a $20.2 million Gas System Rehabilitation Project (World Bank, 1996) to be funded through the International Development Association. While most of the money is to be used to install or refurbish gas meters, approximately 50 percent of the total ($5.1 million) is to be used to rehabilitate cathodic protection and replace seriously corroded pipe on the Apsheron peninsula.

Kazakhstan

Kazakhstan has three gas processing plants with a total annual capacity of 9.8 bcm of gas. The Tengiz gas processing facility, located at the Tengiz oil field in northwest Kazakhstan, processes crude oil from the field, removing and purifying gas from it. The facility has the capacity to produce 11 tonnes per day (approximately 6.0 bcm/yr) following the installation of additional facilities during 2000 (*Oil and Gas Journal,* June 12, 2000, pp 64–72). The Kazakh gas processing facility, located at Novy-Uzen in southwest Kazakhstan, has a total annual capacity of 6.0 bcm), while the Zhanazhol gas processing facility, located on the Zhanazhol field has a total annual capacity of 0.8 bcm. Both the Tengiz and Zhanazhol facilities handle crude oil as well as gas.

Kazakhstan's gas has a relatively high sulfur content, which is both corrosive and noxious. Much of the processing of Kazakhstan's crude involves the removal of the sulfur as well as removal of liquid fractions.

There are three underground gas storage facilities in Kazakhstan. One is located in the northwest of the country at Birzai, while the other two are in the south at Chimkent and Atyrtyubin.

Kazakhstan's trunk gas pipeline network consists of three separate systems. The first of these is a 400 km section of the Central Asia–Centre gas pipeline system that carries gas northwards from Turkmenistan, across western Kazakhstan to the Russian export network at Aleksandrov Gay. Joining this line, and branching from it, are the pipelines from Turkmenistan's western oilfields, which runs from Okarem to Bayneu and the pipeline that runs around the northern shore of the Caspian Sea from Makat via Atyrau to Russia's Astrakhan region.

The second part of the system consists of the Bukhara–Ural pipeline that runs from Uzbekistan to Orsk in Russia. A branch from this line serves the Aktyubinsk region of western Kazakhstan.

The direction of flow in the Bukhara–Ural pipeline was reversed in 1997 in order to bring Russian gas into western Kazakhstan to replace supplies that had previously been received from Turkmenistan in payment for gas transiting Kazakhstan en route to Russia. This trade was suspended in March 1997 with a consequent loss of transit fees to Kazakhstan that had totalled some 3.1 bcm in 1995 and 3.6 bcm in 1996.

The western network of pipelines is also used to gather and distribute gas from Kazakhstan's own fields in the west of the country. Indeed, much of the gas produced in Kazakhstan is exported to Russia, previously on Turkmenistan's behalf in exchange for gas from Turkmenistan supplied to southern Kazakhstan, but more recently in exchange for supplies from Russia itself.

There is also a dedicated pipeline that carries output from Kazakhstan's Karachaganak gas/condensate field in northwestern Kazakhstan to Orenburg in Russia.

The third section of Kazakhstan's gas pipeline network connects the south of the country to gas fields in Uzbekistan and Turkmenistan. Two pipelines, one from Gazli and the other from Bukhara, converge on Chimkent in Kazakhstan. From there, a 1 020 cm (40in) pipeline carries gas to Kazakhstan's former capital at Almaty. The pipeline also supplies gas to Bishkek, the capital of Kyrgyzstan, dipping in to that country en route to Almaty.

Kazakhstan's trunk gas pipeline network is in urgent need of rehabilitation, with an average wear rate of 70 percent and losses from the pipelines in the west of the country estimated at 11 percent. Kazakh officials calculated in 1996 that refurbishment of the country's gas pipelines would require an investment of around $350 million, while the World Bank has estimated that refurbishment of the Central Asia–Centre pipeline alone would cost $110 million (*IEA*, 1998, p. 226).

Turkmenistan

Turkmenistan has no underground gas storage facilities, relying on production from its plentiful fields to meet demand. There are gas processing facilities at the Turkmenbashi refinery in the west of the country and additional plants associated with the individual gas fields, where primary processing is carried out.

Gas from the Dauletabad field in the south of the country, which is high in sulfur, carbon dioxide and wax, is processed at the field to remove these impurities before entering the country's transmission and distribution network.

Turkmenistan's gas pipeline infrastructure is divided into two distinct systems, one in the west and the other in the east.

The western system runs northwards from Okarem, carrying associated gas from the fields of western Turkmenistan northwards to a processing facility at Turkmenbashi and onwards into Kazakhstan where it joins the main Central Asia–Centre trunk gas pipeline at Bayneu. A new 4 bcm/yr pipeline linking the Korpedzhe gasfield in western Turkmenistan to the Iranian gas network at Kord Kuy was commissioned in December 1997. If sufficient gas can be allocated to this pipeline from western Turkmenistan and if Turkmenistan and Iran can agree on payment terms, it is expected that the capacity of this line will be increased to 12 bcm/yr.

In the east of the country, the main gas pipeline runs northwards from the giant Dauletabad field on the border with Iran. The pipeline carries gas from Dauletabad, Shatlyk and other fields in Turkmenistan to Kiva, just across the border in Uzbekistan. Two lines between Shatlyk and Khiva date from the mid-1970s, while a third line was built a decade later. From Khiva the lines run northwest, following the course of the Amu Darya river, carrying gas to Kazakhstan and Russia.

A separate pipeline carries gas from the Shatlyk field to the capital, Ashgabad and also serves towns in between. A second line from Shatlyk carries gas eastwards to the power plant at Mary.

Uzbekistan

Uzbekistan's gas is high in sulfur and requires extensive treatment before it can be used. Most of the country's gas is processed at the Mubarek and Shurtan plants, which have capacities of 35 bcm/yr and 30 bcm/yr respectively. Two smaller processing plants are located at the Alan field (capacity 5 bcm/yr) and the Uchkyr field (capacity 0.9 bcm/yr), both located in the southwest of the country (CGES, 2001).

There are four underground gas storage facilities owned and operated by the state gas company, Uztransgaz, although not all are in Uzbekistan. The largest of these storage facilities is in the Gazli field, located on the trunk gas pipeline that runs along the Uzbekistan/Turkmenistan border. This facility has a storage capacity of some 3.9–4.0 bcm and is used to meet demand in the country's industrial heartland. The North Sokhskoye facility, located in the Fergana region of eastern Uzbekistan has a capacity of 1.2 bcm in two sites, one on either side of the Uzbekistan/Kyrgyzstan border. A third facility at Poltoratskoye on the border with Kazakhstan has a capacity of 0.35 bcm, while a fourth facility used by Uztransgaz is located at the Mali Su-IV gas field in Kyrgyzstan, close to Andijan at the head of the Fergana valley.

Uzbekistan's gas pipeline network originates in the south of the country, in the area between Bukhara, Mubarek and Karshi, where most of the country's gas fields are located. From this region, two 1 020 mm (40 in) pipelines carry gas northwestwards along the course of the Amu Darya river into Kazakhstan and Russia. A third line carries gas from Gazli and follows a similar route to northern Uzbekistan, whence it runs in a more westerly direction across Kazakhstan, carrying gas to the Russian export network at Alexsandrov Gay.

From Bukhara, a 1 220 mm (48 in) pipeline carries gas northeastwards into southern Kazakhstan, supplying the Kyrgyz capital, Bishkek, en route to Almaty. This line is joined at Chimkent in Kazakhstan by two further lines from Bukhara (one of 1 020 mm and the other of 1 220 mm), which serve the Uzbek capital, Tashkent, before crossing into Kazakhstan. Tashkent is also served by a third pipeline that originates at Mubarek. Two further pipelines from Mubarek carry gas to Uzbekistan's Fergana Valley, crossing Tajikistan en route.

Uzbekistan's domestic gas distribution network is extensive. The system covers most of the country and includes 250 gas distribution stations (IEA, 1998). Since independence, the gas distribution network has been extended to the country's rural areas, opening up new markets. However, only around one-third of the country's households were connected to the gas grid in 1997.

Investment plans

The gas markets around the Caspian Sea are relatively small, while large markets that could be supplied with Caspian gas are a long way away. Nevertheless, most of the gas-related investment plans in the Caspian region countries have centered on large-scale export pipelines rather than on projects to supply the local market. Such projects are far more attractive economically than increasing supplies to highly subsidized local consumers who often do not pay for the gas they consume. However, none of these large-scale gas export projects has yet moved beyond the feasibility study stage.

Instead, several Caspian countries have for the time being chosen to sell their natural gas to Russia at cheap rates because this remains the only option to monetize production at this time. In particular, Turkmenistan and Kazakhstan currently sell natural gas to Russia. In November 2000, Turkmen President Saparmurat Niyazov had reached agreement with Russia's gas monopoly, Gazprom, to sell it as much as 30 bcm of natural gas a year (Dorsey, 2000.) Kazakhstan is also exporting gas from its Karachaganak field to processing facilities in Orenburg, Russia and more exports are under discussion. Russia's Gazprom benefits directly from receiving the gas from the Caspian in an effort to free up more domestic Russian gas for export to profitable markets in Europe.

Despite efforts to diversify exports away from Russia, the Caspian countries have had little success to date. Turkmenistan's plans to export gas across Afghanistan to Pakistan and India, through Iran to Turkey and Europe or beneath the Caspian Sea have so far come to nothing. Likewise, proposals for huge gas pipelines from the Caspian to China and beyond remain little more than dreams. As Graham Batcheler of Texaco pointed out, no single country in the Caspian region, with the possible exception of Turkmenistan, is in a position to undertake the construction of a major gas export pipeline from the region on its own (Batcheler, 1998, pp. 207–19).

The Caspian republics are, after ten years, at last beginning to turn their attention to utilizing some of their gas resources domestically, although these plans are still far from realization.

Azerbaijan

Surprisingly perhaps, for a country that has recently discovered huge gas reserves of its own after having restricted domestic gas use in the face of rising import costs, Azerbaijan's gas investment plans focus more on export options than on supplying additional volumes to the domestic market. The government of Azerbaijan feels it necessary to establish a foothold in the Turkish gas market as a matter of urgency to support higher volumes of gas exports in the future.

That said, rising oil production from the Chirag field (and from the Azeri field when it is developed) will yield increasing volumes of associated gas. Under the terms of the AIOC's license, associated gas is supplied free of charge to Socar. Additional gas processing capacity is currently being installed at the Neft Dashlary oil development to allow it to process the full 3 mcm/day of associated gas produced at Chirag. The first phase of the development of the Azeri field envisages the conversion of the existing 20 in oil pipeline to shore to carry gas, enabling the utilization of the associated gas from the new field. However, it is unclear just how much of this gas might be used for re-injection into the oilfield.

The World Bank is engaged in a $20.2 million project to help rehabilitate Azerbaijan's gas system (World Bank, 1996). The project aims to rehabilitate part of the country's gas distribution network in the Baku region, and to improve the efficiency of gas delivery, accounting and use.

A number of Western oil companies, including Statoil, Exxon, Conoco, BP and Shell have undertaken studies on the development of Azerbaijan's upstream and downstream gas industries. A "gas master plan" submitted by Statoil, Socar and Azerigas in April 1998 noted that Azerbaijan will continue to suffer a gas deficit for several years until new fields are brought on stream and said that Azerbaijan urgently needs to increase its gas processing capacity to reduce the proportion of corrosive, untreated gas fed into the system.

Following the fuel crisis experienced in Azerbaijan in the winter of 1999–2000, during which blackouts became a frequent occurrence in Baku, the government of Azerbaijan has sought urgent solutions to the country's ongoing domestic energy problem.

Many of the immediate solutions to the problem focused on securing imports of oil and gas from other Caspian region producers, principally Russia, over the winter of 2000–2001 and on increasing the volume of fuel oil storage. Nonetheless, the more efficient utilization of the country's own gas resources forms part of the government's longer-term plans. The capacity of the gas compression facilities at the offshore Neft Dashlary oil complex was to be increased to nearly 3 mcm/day by November 2000 in order to allow full utilization of all associated gas from AIOC's operations at the Chirag field. The project was completed by Socar in February 2001 when three new compressors were installed (Turan, 2001).

Furthermore, Azerigas was instructed to rehabilitate the country's gas pipelines before the onset of winter. In July 2000, Azerigas invited bids for the construction of a new, 10 mcm/day gas compressor station at the Karadag underground storage facility and a 90 km, high-pressure gas pipeline to carry the produced gas to a gas-fired power station at Severnaya to the north of Baku.

Kazakhstan

Kazakhstan has ambitious plans for the development of its gas transmission and distribution network. These plans centre on making the country self-sufficient in gas by linking the gas fields in the west of the country to the centres of gas consumption in the south and east.

The construction of more than 5 500 km of new gas transmission lines has been proposed by Kazakhgaz (*Russian Petroleum Investor*, 1996, pp. 38–42). One line would link Karachaganak and other fields in northwestern Kazakhstan, via the new capital at Astana to Pavlodar, Semipalatinsk and Ust-Kamenogorsk in the east. A second line would link the existing western and southern pipeline networks with a new line running from Chelkar, north of the Aral Sea, to Chimkent. A third proposed line would link Amangeldy and the other undeveloped gas fields around Aktyrtobe, via Almaty to Ust-Kamenogorsk. It is estimated that these projects will cost well in excess of $2 billion, and no real progress has been made since they were first put forward by Kazakhgas in 1996.

The World Bank has put forward a more modest set of priorities for investment in Kazakhstan's gas sector (World Bank 1997, quoted in IEA, 1998, pp. 225–6). These projects include:

- the capture and utilization for power generation of flared gas at the Zhanazhol and South Turgay fields;
- the development of the Amangeldy and other fields to supply gas to Kazakhstan's southern gas distribution system;
- the rehabilitation of the Kazakh section of the main Central Asia–Centre gas transmission line from Turkmenistan to Russia;
- the installation of metering equipment on Kazakhstan's borders; and
- the rehabilitation of the gas distribution network in the south of the country.

An early priority of the Kazakh government is to build a short section of new gas pipeline in the south of the country to bypass Kyrgyzstan. Kazakhstan has frequently accused its southern neighbour of taking gas from the line without fully compensating Kazakhstan. Kyrgyzstan pays for the transit through Kazakhstan of its gas imports from Uzbekistan with exports of electricity and water to cities in southern Kazakhstan. However, Kazakhstan claims that Kyrgyzstan has failed to supply agreed volumes of power and water.

Construction of the Kyrgyz bypass was to have begun by the end of 1999 but disagreements between Kazakhstan and Tractabel (the Belgian company that won the contract to take over Kazakhstan's gas distribution network in 1997) prevented work from starting. Tractabel won the concession to operate both of Kazakhstan's gas pipeline networks for a 15-year period and agreed to invest $600 million to modernize and extend the pipeline system (Eastern Bloc Energy, 1997, p. 17). However, the deal was always unpopular with some of Kazakhstan's parliamentary deputies and quickly became unworkable. Tractabel left Kazakhstan in April 2000, a year after the Kazakh government froze utility prices (EIU, 2000 pp.19–20) and before any work had been carried out on the upgrading of Kazakhstan's gas pipeline network.

A key part of Kazakhstan's gas policy is for oil producers in the country to utilise associated gas rather than flare it, as is common at present. If the flared gas were marketed, it would boost Kazakhstan's effective domestic production by more than 3.2 bcm. The chief problem faced by producers of associated gas is how to find a commercially attractive solution to the gas utilisation problem. Although Kazakhstan's domestic gas consumption exceeds local supply, the producers and consumers are often far apart and not linked by existing pipelines. Furthermore, the payment record of gas consumers in Kazakhstan is generally poor and there is no guarantee that producers will be paid for whatever gas they do supply.

Turkmenistan

Turkmenistan's agreements to increase gas supplies to Russia and Ukraine, which envisage exports of 40 bcm during 2001, have not yet put a strain on the country's export pipeline capacity. Turkmenistan used to export up to 85 bcm to Russia and the Ukraine under the Soviet system. However, if Gazprom is successful in negotiating a sales and purchase agreement lifting the export volume to 50 bcm/yr, Turkmenistan is likely to need to carry out refurbishment of the gas export pipelines to Russia which have suffered from a lack of investment and use in recent years.

Turkmenistan has 38 000 tonnes of gas liquefaction capacity at the Naipsky gas processing complex and the Turkmenbashi oil refinery and has plans to increase this substantially. The first phase involves the expansion of liquefaction capacity at Turkmenbashi to 365 000 tonnes by mid-2001 and the construction of new plants at the KoturTepe and Korpedzhe gasfields in western Turkmenistan, capable between them of producing a further 330 000 t/yr of liquefied petroleum gas (LPG) by 2001. Alongside these new processing plants contracts have been awarded for the construction of storage and transportation infrastructure. Iran's Pars Energy was awarded the contract to build and operate liquefied gas terminals and storage facilities as Turkmenbashi, Serakhs (on the border with Iran) and Serkhetabat (on the border with Afghanistan). By 2003, Turkmenistan aims to increase gas liquefaction capacity by a further 350 000 t/yr with the completion of a gas processing plant at the Kirpichli field, south of Khiva in the west of the country.

Separately, Turkmenistan has reportedly awarded a $10 million contract to Ukrgazstroy of Ukraine to build a 50 km loop in the gas export trunkline carrying gas northwards to Russia. *Russian Petroleum Investor* (2000, p. 43) reported that this pipeline would allow Turkmenistan's gas exports to bypass Uzbekistan, but this is clearly not the case as the length of new pipe needed to achieve this would be in the region of 400 km. A 50 km loop would more likely bypass a short stretch where the Turkmenistan's gas export pipeline passes across a small region of Uzbek territory around the town of Khiva.

Uzbekistan

Although the top priority in the oil and gas sector for Uzbekistan is to boost reserves through further exploration with foreign partners, a number of gas infrastructure projects have been included in Uzbekneftegaz's investment plans for the period 2000–2005.

Of the nine projects listed, two include an element of boosting gas production, two more are aimed at increasing the production of liquefied gas in the country, and the fifth is designed to boost the extraction capacity from the Gazli underground storage facility.

By 2003, Uzbekistan aims to have boosted production of LPG by almost 800 000 t/yr from its gas processing plants at Shurtan and Mubarek. With only around one-third of households in Uzbekistan connected to the domestic gas distribution pipelines, LPG plays an important role in the country's gas consumption. The attractiveness of LPG for producers is enhanced by the fact that consumers pay cash on receipt for LPG, circumventing the non-payment problem for energy supplies that plagues the post-Soviet republics.

An initial gas liquefaction plant, with a capacity of 500 000 t/yr is already under construction at the Shurtan gas processing plant. The liquefaction plant, along with other facilities, is being built by a consortium comprising ABB Lummus Global of Sweden, Mitsui and Nissho Iwai of Japan. This initial plant will just about meet the country's current LPG consumption of 500 000 t/yr, almost all of which is imported from Russia.

Conclusion

After disintegration of the Soviet Union, all former soviet republics faced a problem: most of their industries were highly integrated in the single economy and their enterprises (including oil and gas) were part of the technologically interdependent system. In the case of oil, the entire chain, from the oil well to the petrol station, was vertically integrated and coordinated. Although different levels were under different ministries, such as Ministry of Oil and Gas, Ministry of Oil Processing and Petrochemical Industry, and Soyuznefteexport (foreign oil trade), all of them were coordinated by Gosplan. The justification for the initial construction of these refineries was based on the needs of the Soviet era and the requirements of the Soviet economy, rather than on the particular domestic or industrial needs of each country.

Today all refineries in this region are confronted by the challenges of moving into a new and independent era. They are saddled with old technologies and equipment and shortages of crude. They remain embroiled in a non-payment crisis in which their customers fail to pay for oil products received.

The high oil prices in 1999–2001 on the world market affected these refineries negatively. Oil exports offer higher and quicker profitability than domestic refining and consumption (Anglo-Caspian Services, 2000, 2001).

The countries of Central Asia and the Caucasus will have to rely in some measure on their own financial resources to complete the necessary refinery improvements. The countries of the Caspian Sea region will have to develop opportunities within their regional markets. Theoretically, the total regional market in the above mentioned countries is more than 70 million consumers but, practically, this is a segmented underdeveloped market. The refining sector of the Caspian region desperately needs real economic integration and co-operation among these countries. Individual country political ambitions, however as well as aspirations for regional power and control, might not allow this idea to be developed into a plausible scenario in the near future.

Taking into account the size of Caspian oil reserves, with economic integration and cooperation, the region has the potential to become a center for refining. In addition to serving their domestic markets, these refineries could provide Russia, Turkey, Iran, and Europe with a range of petroleum products.

The gas processing and distribution infrastructure of the Caspian region countries was also designed to serve the needs of the Soviet Union, rather than those of a collection of independent countries. The main pipeline corridor in the region is the Central Asia-Centre gas pipeline, used during the Soviet era to carry gas from Uzbekistan and Turkmenistan northwards to Russia. Although the line lay virtually idle between the middle of 1997 and late 1999, it is now in use again as Turkmenistan has resumed gas exports to Russia and Ukraine.

The gas distribution networks in the countries of the region vary greatly. Azerbaijan's network is extensive, covering 85 percent of the country, yet gas supplies are limited to the Baku area due to supply shortages. At the other extreme, the potentially large gas-consuming regions in Kazakhstan are not connected to the country's gas fields and have to rely on expensive imported gas. A key feature of the country's future gas plans is the utilization of domestically produced gas in the local market and plans exist, on paper at least, to dramatically expand the country's gas distribution network.

The newly independent countries of the Caspian region are only slowly moving towards refurbishing, rationalizing and updating their domestic gas transportation and processing infrastructure. For those countries with significant gas reserves, large-scale export-oriented projects seem to have taken most of the attention of the host governments, although none of these projects has yet seen any material progress on the ground. Projects such as the trans-Caspian gas pipeline from Turkmenistan to Turkey and the Turkmenistan–Afghanistan–Pakistan gas pipeline show little sign of progressing at the present time.

Countries such as Kazakhstan and Azerbaijan have identified the need to utilize their own gas resources locally and are beginning to take steps to make this desire a reality. The refurbishment and extension of local networks has been hampered by a lack of funds locally and the difficulty of attracting foreign investment into a sector plagued with non-payment problems. All the countries of the region need to take steps to improve the collection of payments for gas supplies, since this is one of the keys to generating domestic investment funds and attracting outside financing for gas infrastructure projects. In addition to extending the gas distribution networks to cover a larger proportion of their populations, the countries of the Caspian region also need to install more gas processing capacity to clean the produced gas before it is put into the pipelines, since failure to do so in the past has led to extensive corrosion of the pipes and a reduction in the capacity of the gas transportation and distribution networks.

Acknowledgements

Part of this chapter was published as an article in "Oil and Gas Journal", August 21, 2000 and reproduced here with the kind permission of the Chief Technology Editor-Pipelines/Gas Processing of "Oil and Gas Journal".

References

Anglo-Caspian Services (2000) "Power. Engineering: Capacity Needs Resources", in *Caspian, Azerbaijan: 2000* (Anglo-Caspian Services Ltd, London).

Anglo-Caspian Services (2001) "Oil Refining in Kazakhstan", in *Caspian, Kazakhstan: 2000–2001* (Anglo-Caspian Services Ltd, London).

Baku press report (2001), January 29.

Baku Sun November 12, 2000,

Batcheler, Graham (1998) "Caspian Gas: are alliance the Way Foward?" in Caspian Oil and Gas Summit, (CGES Publication, Merchant Taylors, London).

BPAmocoalive (2000) *Statistical Review of World Energy,* June.

CGES (Centre for Global Energy Studies), (1998) *Breaking the Stranglehold.* (CGES Publication, London).

CGES (Centre for Global Energy Studies) (2001), *Caspian Gas* (CGES Publication, London).

Connell, Dave, Ormiston Bob, Amott Nick, Cullum Irene (2001) "Gas-Plant update Moves Tengiz Field", *Oil and Gas Journal,* June 12, pp. 64–72.

Dorsey, James (2000) "Turkmeniustan Deal May Kill Pipeline Backed by the US", *Wall Street Journal,* November 19, p. A22.

Eastern Bloc Energy (1997) *A Monthly Review of Oil and Energy in the CIS, and Eastern Europe* Vol. X, No. 5.

EIU (Economic Intelligence Unit) (2001) *Country Report: Kazakhstan,* January.

EIU (Economic Intelligence Unit) (2001) *Country Report: Azerbaijan,* January.

EU Consotrium–TACIS, *Oil Refining, Gas Processing and Petrochemicals in Kazakhstan*, Almaty: EU Consortium- TACIS, 1995.

FSU Energy (various issues) *Petroleum Argus.*

Goskomstat of Russia (1999) *Russia in Figures,* Moscow.

US Energy Information Administration www.eia.doe.gov

Stat oil web site: www.statoil.com/ *bgNews & Topics *bgTopics *bgAzerbaijan – centre of the oil world *bga developing gas market

IEA (International Energy Agency) (1998) *Caspian Oil and Gas* (IEA Publication, London).

IMF (1999) *Staff Country Report,* No. 99/140, December.

IMF (2000) *Staff Country Report,* No. 00/121, September.

Institutional Investor Focus, 1997.

Interfax Business Report, April 9–15, 2001.

Interfax Business Report, January 12–18, 2001.

Interfax News Agency July 12, 1999.

Interfax, October 29–November 5, 1999

Interfax, May 18–24, 2001.

IRNA News Agency, Tehran, December 6 2000

Guluzade, K. (1998) "Sufferings of Baku Refineries," *Neft I Gas Caspia* (Caspian Oil and Gas), October(in Russian).

Kalyuzhnov, Andrei and Nanay, Julia (2000) "Caspian Are Refineries Struggle to Overcome Soviet Legacy", *Oil and Gas Journal,* August 21, pp. 62–6.

Kalyuzhnova, Yelena (1998) *The Kazakhstani Economy: Independence and Transition* – New Pelgrave,

Kalyuzhnova, Yelena (2001) "Kazakhstan. 1999–2000. Tributaire. Du Pétrole", *Le Courrier Des Pays De l'Est,* N 1010, Novembre-Décembre 2000, pp. 55–67 (in French).

Khartukov, Eugene and Surovtsev, Dmitry (1992) "Ex-Soviet Oil on the Global Market: Beware of the Dog!", *OPEC Bulletin,* Vol. XXIII, No. 6, June, pp. 13–24.

Nigmatullin,M. "Kazakhstani Refineries: New Achievements, New Problems". *Neft I Gas Caspia* (*Caspian Oil and Gas*), October (in Russian).

Oil and Capital (2000) "Turkmen Target: 18 per cent annual Growth Rate", *Oil and Capital. Russia and CIS Energy Magazine,* No. 2, pp. 23–6.

Oil and Gas of Azerbaijan (1998) Socar. pp. 159–184.

Oil and Gas of Kazakhstan (2000) "Reconstruction of Atyrau Refinery is Postponed Until 2003", in *Oil and Gas of Kazakhstan,* No. 3–4 (15–16), Almaty, pp. 72–5.

Radler, Marilyn (1999) "1999 Worldwide Refining Survey", *Oil and Gas Journal,* December 20, pp. 58–61.

Research Kazkommerts Securities, January 2001.

Reuters (2001) English News Network, March 6.

Reuters (2000) Daily Brief , Baku, June 2.

Russian Petroleum Investor (1996–97) "Alamty Offers Foreign Investors Opportunity to Run Kazakhstan's Gas Pipelines", December/January, pp. 38–42.

Russian Petroleum Investor (2000) "The Caspian Region", Vol. IX, Issue 7,August, p. 43.

Turan News agency (2001), *Expansion of Gas-compressing Station on Oil Rocks Completed,* Baku, February 9.

US Embassy/Commerce Department (2001), *Press Release,* January 22.

US Energy Information Administration (2000) *Azerbaijan,* May.
US Energy Information Administration (2000) *Press Release,* May.
World Bank (1993) *Turkmenistan Energy Sector Review,* November.
World Bank (1996) *Press Release No 97/1131 ECA,* September.

7
Convergent Economies: Implications for World Energy Use

Patrik T. Hultberg and Robin C. Sickles

Introduction

The neoclassical model predicts that countries converge to their own steady states. Assuming identical technologies across countries, this implies that exogenous differences in savings (investment), employment, and education cause the observed differences in levels of income and rates of growth. However, countries differ not only in accumulation rates, but also use different technologies. In fact, hardly any group of countries fits the assumption of identical technologies. The existence of a technology gap may therefore present an additional opportunity for growth through technology flows. If so, then a nation's ability to adopt and absorb new knowledge must also be considered. Indeed, if "follower" countries are characterized by large technology gaps and low and variable absorption capacities, then predictions about rate of growth will be ambiguous. Abramovitz (1986) proposes that the ability of countries to take advantage of the catching-up potential depends on their respective "social capabilities"; that systematic variations in social institutions make some countries better or worse at catching up. The institutional economics literature also highlights the importance of the security of property rights and the efficiency of government policies as determinants of countries' growth rates (North, 1990; Olson, 1982). The empirical importance of institutions in the growth-accounting framework has been shown in cross-country studies (Barro, 1991; Knack and Keefer, 1995; Scully, 1988).

We use a standard model augmented to include technology gaps and differing adoption capabilities.[1] The possibility of adopting technology from more advanced countries is added through a catch-up term. This adoption potential may be compromised due to varying political and social rigidities. We present empirical tests of these ideas using panel data. These tests use methods that are consistent with the dynamic frontier literature. In particular, we use an extension of the least squares dummy variable (LSDV) methodology in which one slope coefficient is allowed to vary across countries and regions. The included fixed effects are meant to capture all inevitable country heterogeneity due to varying social and political institutions. This estimation was performed on countries for which data is available through the Penn World Tables.

Our results allow us to determine the length of time required for particular countries in the sample to converge to the US per capita income level, which is world standard. These catch-up times are then used for the main purpose of this chapter, namely to predict increases in energy use that would be necessary if, given exogenous rates of populations growth, rates of development were such that per capita energy consumption converged to the US level. Based on forecasts from the Energy Information Administration, we allocate the energy use among the various categories "oil," "coal," and "other" to forecast oil consumption by country. World energy demands are then developed and compared to baseline estimates from the Department of Energy. We find remarkable similarity between our forecasts and those from the US Department of Energy through the year 2015, when our forecast ends.

The next two sections of the chapter briefly discuss the growth model and its estimation. The fourth section highlights the data and the econometric model. Results and energy forecasts are reported in the fifth section, which is followed by a conclusion.

Theoretical model

The model used in our estimation is a modification of the Solow growth model that allows for the transmission of technological knowledge across national borders.[2] The standard model predicts that countries converge to steady states determined by levels of accumulation and the depreciation rate. In addition to having different accumulation rates, however economies also differ in levels of technology. This introduces the possibility that technology flows may provide additional growth. That is, adoption of technology from abroad is a possible mechanism through which the capital stock of a nation increases, as better technology improves the productivity of the existing stock of capital. The difference from the standard Solow model is that technology adoption from abroad reduces the effective rate of depreciation, which leads to higher growth. These results are similar to those derived for capital and labor mobility; mobility raises an economy's convergence toward steady state and technology flows might augment the level of that steady state.[3]

A model with technology adoption

The estimation builds on the standard neoclassical model with a Cobb–Douglas production function

$$Q_{it} = A_{it} K_{it}^{\beta_1} L_{it}^{\beta_2} H_{it}^{\beta_3}$$

where output Q depends on technology A, physical capital stock K, employment L, and human capital H (Mankiw *et al.*, 1992). All countries are represented by i, $i = 1,\ldots, N$, in each time period t, $t = 1,\ldots,T$. We use the common specification of the evolution of exogenous world technology and number of workers so that

$$A_{it} = A_{i0} e^{\gamma t}$$
$$L_{it} = L_{i0} e^{\eta t}$$

We include human capital as a factor of production, but other authors have shown how it might affect the growth process through different channels.[4] We consider human capital growth in our derivation, but we also include its level in the estimation. The only difference from the standard model appears in the equation for capital evolution. The evolution of capital depends on an exogenous saving rate, the depreciation rate, and a technology catch-up term, $\xi(T,T^{W})$, so that

$$K_{it} = sQ_{it} - \delta K_{it} + \xi(T,T^{W})_{it} K_{it}$$

We assume here that new investment may embody differences in technical design so that a new "machine" may be more efficient than an old "machine" even if there is no difference in physical capacity. That is, in our setup, technology from abroad makes existing and new capital stock more productive and therefore increases the capital stock (capital measured in efficiency units). We specify the catch-up term as a logarithmic function of the inverse ratio of labor productivity, $Y_i = (Q_{it}/L_{it})$, to the "desired" level of labor productivity, Y_i^*, which differs between countries $\xi_{it}(T, T^{W})_{it} = \rho_i \ln(Y_{i,t-1}^*/Y_{i,t-1})$. Using a desired level of labor productivity reflects the belief that all countries are not able to obtain the same level of productivity.[5] For example, the Latin American nations may not be able to adopt the entire technology gap between themselves and the US because of institutional inefficiencies.

Log linearizing and differencing the production function and substituting for the growth rate of capital yields that the growth rate of per worker output depends on the growth of factor inputs as well as the productivity gap,

$$y_{it} = \phi + \beta_1 k_{it} + \beta_2 l_{it} + \beta_3 h_{it} + \rho[1nY^*_{i,t-1} - 1nY_{i,t-1}] \tag{7.1}$$

where $\rho_i = \beta_1 \theta_i$ is the country-specific technology adoption rate and $\phi = (\gamma - \beta_1 \delta)$ is net exogenous technology growth.

To capture some of Abramovitz's (1986) ideas of "social capabilities," countries may also differ in ability to recognize or use the available technology. This is included into the model as a term that acts to reduce the available technology gap to economies. The term used is similar to what frontier production literature refers to as "efficiency"; and we refer to it in the same way. It is understood that this term captures much more than mere production slack, as it encompasses the institutional framework, adjustment costs, international openness, and so forth. So, to account for varied institutional rigidities, we postulate that the desired or maximum level of labor productivity, controlling for institutional features, is some fraction of the leader's productivity, and that the fraction is determined by the nation's level of inefficiency

$$Y^*_{it} = \frac{Y^L_t}{E_{it}} \Rightarrow 1nY^*_{it} = 1nY^L_t - 1nE_{it}$$

where Y^L_t is the leader's labor productivity and E_{it} is the inefficiency parameter.[6] Substituting into Equation (7.1) and rearranging yields the equation that is estimated

$$y_{it} = \phi - \rho_i 1nE_{i,t-1} + \beta_1 k_{it} + \beta_2 l_{it} + \beta_3 h_{it} + \rho_i[1nY^L_{i,t-1} - 1nY_{i,t-1}] \tag{7.2}$$

That is, the growth rate of GDP per worker for country *i* depends on the rate of growth of factor inputs, the common rate of exogenous technological change minus capital depreciation, country-specific inefficiency, and the technology gap between the leader and the follower countries lagged one period. Interpretation of the parameters are straightforward: β_1, β_2, and β_3 show the elasticity of per worker GDP to a change in the growth of factor inputs; ρ_i, is the adoption of available technology from abroad and the (estimated) inefficiency measure,

$\rho_i \ln E_{i,t-1}$, shows the reduction in growth of labor productivity due to political and social factors that reduces the available technology gap.[7]

The key to this model is that it allows for countries to either leap ahead or fall behind since countries may differ in both technology adoption rates and inefficiency levels. Figures 7.1–7.3 in the Appendix show various simulations of this model to provide a more intuitive explanation of it compared to the standard neoclassical model (Figure 7.1), where the marginal product of capital leads to convergence of output levels. Figures 7.2 and 7.3 show the effect of different adoption rates and inefficiency levels. Our technology catch-up term leads to initially higher rates of growth depending on the catch-up parameters, but in the end it is the familiar diminishing marginal product of capital that closes the gap.

Data and econometric model

For the empirical estimation we predominantly use variables from the Summers and Heston data set (Penn World Tables Mark 5.6). Number of workers is the labor variable. The number of workers was found by multiplying each nation's population by its labor force participation rate.[8] For physical capital growth we use the share of investment in output as a proxy. The rate of growth of depreciated capital stock is missing for several nations and time periods, so its use was not possible. Implicit in the use of this proxy is that the capital–output ratios are constant across time and countries so that the growth rate of physical capital will be proportional to the investment ratio.[9] This assumption could overstate country heterogeneity because countries are not allowed to move along their isoquants. However, our estimation focuses on the technological change aspect of growth as in Abramovitz (1986), which should not be seriously affected by the constant capital–output assumption since the argument concerns country isoquants' differentiated rate of contraction toward the origin. Also, the factor shares are held fixed across time and countries, assuming countries cannot vary their technology, which may introduce a specification bias. For the human capital variable, we use the percentage share of total population that attained secondary education from Barro and Lee (1993). Secondary schooling is favored over primary education since many countries in the sample are likely to have reached their upper limits for primary education.

In terms of econometric issues, most of the empirical convergence literature has used cross-country data but we choose to use a pooled data set (lately the literature has moved towards the use of panel data). Panel data have some very desirable attributes. For example, panel data formulation supports all the steady state arguments made in the cross-country literature and is in fact more appropriate since it assumes that the accumulation rates are constant over a shorter time period. Also, the fact that we can control for unobservable individual country effects when using panel data should create a cleaner relationship between the included economic variables. Pooled data provide more information, more variability, less multicollinearity among the variables, more degrees of freedom, and more efficiency (see Baltagi, 1995). In addition, the panel can identify and measure effects that are not observable in pure cross-sections or pure time-series data.

Having chosen a pooled data, an issue is whether individual effects should be considered fixed or random. In a random effect framework the effects are assumed to be uncorrelated with the exogenous variables included in the model, which is not an appropriate assumption for cross-country studies. Consequently, we use a fixed effect framework. Actually, the fact that such correlation exists is a further argument for the use of panel data. A problem with ordinary least squares (OLS) estimation (such as LSDV) is that a lagged dependent variable exists on the right-hand side of the estimable equation, a problem common to many economic relationships that are dynamic in nature. The problem is that since y_{it} is a function of the disturbance, $y_{i,t-1}$ must also be a function of the disturbance; that is, a right-hand side regressor is correlated with the error term. This implies in general that OLS is biased and inconsistent. So for the typical panel where N is large and T is fixed, the within (LSDV) estimator will be biased and inconsistent. It would be consistent if T goes to infinity, but this is unlikely in a panel data setting.[10] Several solutions for this problem have been suggested in the econometric literature (see Baltagi, 1995, for an overview). The obvious way to remove the problem is to use an instrumental variable technique. For example, Arellano and Bond (1991) argue that to get a consistent estimate of a lagged dependent variable for large N and finite T, one needs to (a) first difference to eliminate the individual effects and (b) use lagged differences or levels as instruments. This is straightforward: the problem, in our estimation, is that we want to leave the individual effects. Further, Ahn and Schmidt (1995) point out that there are additional moment conditions that are ignored by the IV (Instrumental Variable) estimators suggested by Arellano and Bond. Ahn and Schmidt therefore suggest a Generalized Method of Moment 'GMM' estimator. Their (GMM) estimation is asymptotically equivalent to Chamberlain's (1982, 1984) optimal minimum distance (MD) estimator. A fact that we utilize since Islam (1995) compares the MD estimator with LSDV in a Monte Carlo study using the same data set as us. Islam's result is that LSDV, although consistent in the direction of T only, performs very well. We use Islam's simulation results and conclusions as the motivation for our LSDV estimation.

Results

The model described above (Equation 7.2) is estimated using a fixed effect panel data estimator in order to capture the inevitable country heterogeneity due to political and social institutions. The results of these estimations are given in Table 7.1 and contrasted to the estimation using initial income as an explanatory variable (which is the common variable in the convergence literature). Including fixed effects led to highly significant results for almost all countries (with the exception of the Netherlands and Mexico). When considering the three regions separately, a different regional heterogeneity ranking is obtained. However, the change in estimated fixed effects is accompanied by technology adoption rates of different magnitudes across the three regions. This indicates that fixed effects may pick up the countries' different abilities to incorporate new technology as well.

To explore whether the fixed effects in fact contain the ability of nations to adopt new technology, we estimate the model using an extension of the LSDV methodology. In particular, we allow one slope coefficient (the technology adoption parameter) to vary across countries and regions (Cornwell, *et al.*, 1990).[11] We thus estimate both adoption speeds and "inherent" inefficiency levels as country-specific parameters.[12] The added fixed effect (whether five year or annual pooling is used) yields highly significant negative coefficients for all countries, confirming our hypothesis that the US is the productivity leader in our sample(s).

We test whether adoption rates differ across countries by including an interactive dummy variable for each country's technology gap. This produces two general results for the five-year pooled data: approximately half of the fixed effects become insignificant at 5 percent, and only two of the 38 different slope coefficients are statistically significant. For the annual data the results are even less significant. Furthermore, several adoption rate parameters are nonsensical, being either negative or greater than one. We attribute the weakness of these results to the reduced degree of freedom stemming from insufficient

Table 7.1 Least squares dummy variables, 5-year pooled data

	Using initial income				Using technology gap			
	All	EU	EA	LA	All	EU	EA	LA
Constant	2.821	2.693	2.727	3.903	–0.264	0.009	–0.325	–0.139
	(0.268)	(0.289)	(0.509)	(0.619)	(0.094)	(0.075)	(0.147)	(0.184)
Inv/GDP	0.015	0.007	0.019	0.017	0.015	0.005	0.018	0.018
	(0.002)	(0.002)	(0.004)	(0.004)	(0.002)	(0.002)	(0.003)	(0.004)
Labor	-0.506	–0.582	–0.291	–0.621	–0.311	–0.366	–0.268	0.102
	(0.250)	(0.265)	(0.492)	(0.488)	(0.259)	(0.280)	(0.468)	(0.530)
Education	0.002	0.001	0.003	0.001	0.001	–0.001	0.001	–0.007
	(0.002)	(0.001)	(0.004)	(0.003)	(0.002)	(0.001)	(0.004)	(0.005)
Initial Inc.	-0.301	–0.269	–0.304	–0.408				
	(0.029)	(0.030)	(0.058)	(0.064)				
Tech. Gap					0.409	0.380	0.371	0.583
					(0.038)	(0.043)	(0.064)	(0.087)
EU	-0.154	–0.126			–0.232	–0.211		
EA	-0.297		–0.309		–0.512		–0.463	
LA	-0.235			–0.381	–0.412			–0.828
R^2	0.65	0.81	0.68	0.53	0.66	0.80	0.71	0.57
F	6.93	13.57	5.31	3.79	7.15	13.28	6.15	4.27
P	0.001	0.000	0.000	0.000	0.000	0.000	0.000	0.000

Notes: EU–Europe; EA–East Asia; LA–Latin America.

data points. We can, however, reject the hypothesis that all technology adoption rates are the same at the 5 percent significance level.[13] Despite this we choose to consider only a separate technology adoption rate for the three regions.

Technology adoption rates

The results for five-year adoption rates are Europe, 0.367; East Asia, 0.322; and Latin America, 0.597.[14] That is, before considering institutional inefficiencies, Europe closes 36.7 percent of the initial technology gap every five years. The numbers indicate that Latin America has been more successful at adopting foreign technology than Europe and East Asia – a surprising result. However, recall that we have separated out the technology adoption that presumably is included in the growth of physical and human capital. Also, we can speculate that Latin America has adopted technology faster than Europe because it might be further behind, and that "older" technologies might be easier to adopt than new production techniques. This does not explain why Latin America has a greater adoption rate than East Asia. Perhaps, again we are speculating, East Asia's technology adoption is to a larger degree embodied in new capital, and the large amount of foreign direct investment to Latin America might have contributed significantly to the region's technology adoption. The amount of foreign direct investment is less for the East Asian countries.[15]

Forecasting world energy demand

We use the estimates above to forecast energy consumption by assuming that the rest of the world's per capita energy consumption levels is catching up with the United States. Forecasts are prepared according to the following method. Using the US per capita energy consumption data as the frontier, growth rate of per capita consumption of each of the countries is computed with previously determined catch-up time.[16] Population growth rates are based on World Bank estimates and enable us to construct a projection of future populations. The forecast of total energy is carried out for every five-year period using 1994 as the base year. We assume that US energy consumption is growing at its population growth rate in order to maintain constancy in its per capita energy consumption. World energy consumption is the sum of the consumption of all of the countries and that of the US. Comparisons of per capita consumption and total consumption of the US versus the world indicate that per capita consumption of the world is upward sloping and is converging to the frontier country, the US. The temporal pattern of total energy consumption is consistent with the implications of convergence in that the world's total energy consumption is growing at a faster rate than that in the United States. We can decompose the major components of energy demand in our convergence-based forecasts. Consumption of petroleum products in the various countries used in our forecasts is based on *Energy Balances of OECD Countries, 1994–1995* and *Energy Statistics and Balances of non-OECD Countries, 1994–1995* (OECD, 1997a, 1997b). Catch-up time is used to forecast the consumption of petroleum products as with the forecasts of total energy consumption in coal equivalents. We summarize our forecasts at the regional and world level (Table 7.2) and the estimates from the US Department of Energy's Energy Information Administration in Table 7.3. These show remarkable overlap. Clearly our modeling effort has succeeded in closely replicating the forecasts from the Department of Energy, an agency of the federal government with substantially more resources than those devoted to our modeling exercise. This in itself is an interesting result.

Forecasts for the year 2005 and 2010 reveal that if production from non-OPEC provinces continues to grow at a rate commensurate with expansion seen over the past decade, the amount of oil from the Middle East needed to meet rising world oil demand requirements could be significantly reduced. Non-OPEC production has expanded by 1 – 1.5 percent annually on average since 1988 through a combination of technological advances in drilling systems and unearthing new basins in South America in deep water and elsewhere. Should this trend continue, non-OPEC production would likely reach 54 million barrels per day (b/d) by 2005 and 58 million b/d by 2010 including rising Caspian basin production.

Under this moderate non-OPEC expansion scenario, the expectation is that oil will be oversupplied by the years 2005–10. This is under both the high- and low-demand growth cases. The period is likely to witness a substantial increase in the amount of production capacity that will have to be shut in by OPEC or other producers to defend even moderate price levels. Under this scenario, Caspian basin oil production will not be critical for maintaining moderate oil prices for at least another decade, assuming, as seems reasonable, that historically persistent competition continues within OPEC.

Table 7.2 World total oil consumption by region (forecasts based on convergence in world per capita energy use to US 1997 levels – million barrels per day)

Region	History		Projections			Average annual percentage change, 1994–2015
	1994	2000	2005	2010	2015	
Western Europe	13.3	14.9	16.3	18.1	20.1	2.4
Asia	16.9	18.7	20.8	23.1	25.8	2.5
EE/FSU	6.1	6.5	7.0	7.6	8.2	1.6
Africa/Rest of world	6.0	6.4	7.4	8.3	9.3	2.6
Western Hemisphere	23.4	25.8	28.6	31.9	35.8	2.5
Total World	65.6	72.4	80.1	89.0	99.3	2.4

Notes: EE/FSU–Eastern Europe/Former Soviet Union.

Table 7.3 World total oil consumption by region (forecasts based on energy information administration – million barrels per day)

Region/Country	History			Projections				Average annual percentage change, 1995–2015
	1990	1994	1995	2000	2005	2010	2015	
Industrialized countries								
North America	20.4	21.3	21.3	23.4	25.1	26.4	27.4	1.3
United States[a]	17.0	17.7	17.7	19.4	20.7	21.6	22.1	1.1
Canada	1.7	1.7	1.7	1.9	2.0	2.1	2.3	1.4
Mexico	1.7	1.8	1.8	2.1	2.4	2.7	3.0	2.6
Western Europe	12.9	13.6	13.9	14.3	14.8	15.1	15.4	0.5
Industrialized Asia	6.2	6.8	7.0	7.7	8.3	8.9	9.4	1.5
Japan	5.1	5.7	5.7	6.4	6.9	7.3	7.8	1.5
Australasia	1.0	1.2	1.3	1.3	1.4	1.6	1.7	1.4
Total industrialized	39.5	41.7	42.2	45.4	48.2	50.4	52.3	1.1
EE/FSU								
Former Soviet Union	8.4	4.8	4.4	4.9	5.8	6.7	7.7	2.7
Eastern Europe	1.6	1.2	1.3	1.5	1.5	1.7	2.0	2.0
Total EE/FSU	10.0	6.1	5.8	6.4	7.3	8.5	9.6	2.6
Developing countries								
Developing Asia	7.6	10.5	11.1	13.9	17.6	20.9	24.9	4.1
China	2.3	3.1	3.3	4.4	5.5	6.9	8.6	4.9
India	1.2	1.4	1.6	1.9	2.4	2.8	3.3	3.8
Other Asia	4.2	5.9	6.2	7.6	9.7	11.2	13.0	3.7
Middle East	3.4	3.9	4.1	4.4	4.9	5.4	6.0	1.9
Africa	2.1	2.3	2.3	3.1	3.6	4.0	4.4	3.2
Central and South America	3.4	3.8	3.9	4.7	5.6	6.5	7.5	3.3
Total developing	16.5	20.5	21.4	26.0	31.7	36.8	42.7	3.5

Table 7.3 World total oil consumption by region (forecasts based on energy information administration – million barrels per day) *cont*

Region/Country	History			Projections				Average annual percentage change, 1995–2015
	1990	1994	1995	2000	2005	2010	2015	
Total world	66.0	68.3	69.4	77.8	87.2	95.6	104.6	2.1

Sources: History: Energy Information Administration (EIA), International Energy Annual 1995, DOE/EIA-0219(95) (Washington, DC, December 1996). Projections: EIA, Annual Energy Outlook 1997, DOE/EIA-0383(97) (Washington, DC, December 1996), Table A21; and World Energy Projection System (1997).

[a] Includes the 50 States and the District of Columbia. US territories are included in Australasia.

Notes: EE/FSU = Eastern Europe/former Soviet Union. Totals may not equal sum of components due to independent rounding. The electricity portion of the national fuel consumption values consists of generation for domestic use plus an adjustment for electricity trade based on a fuel's share of total generation in the exporting country.

The above conclusion is illustrated in Table 7.5 (Table 7.4 shows the low-growth forecasts), which projects anticipated production levels for various players in the international oil market under a moderate production growth scenario that matches historical trends for price and rate of capacity expansion. The non-OPEC figures assume that non-OPEC growth will continue at an annual rate of 1.4 percent, the rate of the past decade, and provide a forecast of non-OPEC production of 54 million b/d in 2005 and 58 million b/d in 2010. By adding government-projected outputs for OPEC countries, it is possible to illustrate the overall surplus between OPEC's production goal and the volume of OPEC oil necessary to balance supply with demand. The discrepancy between the two, as expressed in the line for the residual share left for Saudi Arabia, serves as a measure of market oversupply. It can be assumed that Saudi Arabia will want to produce at levels similar to the 1997 base case or some amount above that level. In many cases shown, Saudi Arabia's residual share is indicated as either a negative number or a number substantially below the 8.7 million b/d of current production. This implies that under many scenarios, Saudi Arabia and other Persian Gulf producers will have to shut in significant volumes of production capacity to balance supply with demand and defend oil price levels.

However, in a high-demand scenario where oil use rises by 3 percent per annum between 2000 and 2010, subtracting Caspian oil would lead to a significant tightening of oil markets from current levels. In other words, rising exports from the Caspian Basin could play a significant role as a marginal supplier in arresting a jump in the price of oil under conditions of strong oil demand and high growth.

The implications of this forecast for oil producers seeking to raise output between 2005 and 2010 are relatively pessimistic. Under a scenario where oil demand growth reaches 80 million b/d in 2005 and 89 million b/d in 2010, oil markets could wind up oversupplied by a wide margin. For example, the residual share for Saudi Arabia is negative in all scenarios, including those where increases in production from the Caspian basin are assumed to be zero. Such an outcome will obviously not occur. However, the analysis suggests that Saudi Arabia and other members of OPEC will have to shut in significant volumes of productive capacity – ranging from 12 million b/d to 15 million b/d – to balance supply with demand in 2005 and 2010 under a moderate non-OPEC growth scenario. By comparison, OPEC only has around 1–2 million b/d daily of production capacity shut in at present.

Under a low non-OPEC growth scenario forecast by the US Department of Energy, OPEC would have to shut in between 5 and

Table 7.4 Global oil demand and supply balance for 2005 and 2010: low non-OPEC growth

	1997 Base	2005 With Caspian				2005 Without Caspian				2010 With Caspian				2010 Without Caspian			
		Low	H-S	Mod.	High	Low	H-S	Mod.	High	Low	H-S	Mod.	High	Low	H-S	Mod.	High
Rate of demand increase		1%		2%	3%	1%		2%	3%	1%		2%	3%	1%		2%	3%
Global demand	73.50	79.50	80.00	85.00	89.50	79.50	80.00	85.00	89.50	83.50	89.00	94.00	103.00	83.50	89.00	94.00	103.00
Global supply	73.00	79.50	80.00	85.00	89.50	79.50	80.00	85.00	89.50	83.50	89.00	94.00	103.00	83.50	89.00	94.00	103.00
Other non-OPEC	42.00	44.50	44.50	44.50	44.50	44.50	44.50	44.50	44.50	44.50	44.50	44.50	44.50	44.50	44.50	44.50	44.50
Caspian	0.80	2.50	2.50	2.50	2.50	1.00	1.00	1.00	1.00	3.50	3.50	3.50	3.50	1.00	1.00	1.00	1.00
OPEC total	30.30	32.50	33.00	38.00	42.50	34.00	34.50	39.50	44.00	35.50	41.00	46.00	55.00	38.00	49.50	48.50	57.50
OPEC liquids	2.50	3.00	3.00	3.00	3.00	3.00	3.00	3.00	3.50	3.50	3.50	3.50	3.50	3.50	3.50	3.50	3.50
Iran	3.65	4.00	4.00	4.00	4.00	4.00	4.00	4.00	4.00	4.50	5.00	5.00	5.00	4.50	5.00	5.00	5.00
Iraq	1.20	4.50	5.00	5.00	5.00	4.50	5.00	5.00	5.00	5.00	6.00	6.00	6.00	5.00	6.00	6.00	6.00
Kuwait	2.00	3.00	3.50	3.50	3.50	3.00	3.50	3.50	3.50	3.50	4.00	4.00	4.00	3.50	4.00	4.00	4.00
UAE	2.30	2.50	3.00	3.00	3.00	2.50	3.00	3.00	3.00	3.00	3.50	3.50	3.50	3.00	3.50	3.50	3.50
Venezuela	3.40	6.00	6.00	6.00	6.00	6.00	6.00	6.00	6.00	6.50	7.00	7.00	7.00	6.50	7.00	7.00	7.00
Other OPEC	6.00	7.50	8.00	8.00	8.00	7.50	8.00	8.00	8.00	7.50	8.00	8.00	8.00	7.50	8.00	8.00	6.00
Residual Saudi	8.70	2.00	0.50	5.50	10.00	3.50	2.00	7.00	11.50	2.00	4.00	9.00	18.00	4.50	6.50	11.50	20.50

Table 7.5 Global oil demand and supply balance for 2005 and 2010: moderate non-OPEC growth

	1997 Base	2005 With Caspian				2005 Without Caspian				2010 With Caspian				2010 Without Caspian			
		Low	H-S	Mod.	High	Low	H-S	Mod.	High	Low	H-S	Mod.	High	Low	H-S	Mod.	High
Rate of demand increase		1%		2%	3%	1%		2%	3%	1%		2%	3%	1%		2%	3%
Global demand	73.50	79.50	80.00	85.00	89.50	79.50	80.00	85.00	89.50	83.50	89.00	94.00	103.00	83.50	89.00	94.00	103.00
Global supply	73.00	79.50	80.00	85.00	89.50	79.50	80.00	85.00	89.50	83.50	89.00	94.00	103.00	83.50	89.00	94.00	103.00
Other non-OPEC	42.00	51.50	51.50	51.50	51.50	51.50	51.50	51.50	51.50	54.50	54.50	54.50	54.50	54.50	54.50	54.50	54.50
Caspian	0.80	2.50	2.50	2.50	2.50	1.00	1.00	1.00	1.00	3.50	3.50	3.50	3.50	1.00	1.00	1.00	1.00
OPEC total	30.30	25.50	26.00	31.00	35.50	27.00	27.50	32.50	37.00	25.50	31.00	36.00	45.00	28.00	33.50	38.50	47.50
OPEC liquids	2.50	3.00	3.00	3.00	3.00	3.00	3.00	3.00	3.00	3.00	3.50	3.50	3.50	3.50	3.50	3.50	3.50
Iran	3.65	4.00	4.00	4.00	4.00	4.00	4.00	4.00	4.00	4.50	5.00	5.00	5.00	4.50	5.00	5.00	5.00
Iraq	1.20	4.00	4.50	4.50	4.50	4.50	4.50	4.50	4.50	5.00	6.00	6.00	6.00	5.00	6.00	6.00	6.00
Kuwait	2.00	2.50	3.00	3.00	3.00	2.50	3.00	3.00	3.00	3.50	4.00	4.00	4.00	3.50	4.00	4.00	4.00
UAE	2.30	2.50	3.00	3.00	3.00	2.50	3.00	3.00	3.00	3.00	3.50	3.50	3.50	3.00	3.50	3.50	3.50
Venezuela	3.40	6.00	6.00	6.00	6.00	6.00	6.00	6.00	6.00	6.00	7.00	7.00	7.00	6.00	7.00	7.00	7.00
Other OPEC	6.60	7.50	8.00	8.00	8.00	7.50	8.00	8.00	8.00	7.50	8.00	8.00	8.00	7.50	8.00	8.00	6.00
Residual Saudi	8.70	-4.00	-5.50	-0.50	4.00	-2.50	-4.00	1.00	5.50	-7.00	-6.00	-1.00	8.00	-5.00	-3.50	1.50	10.50

7 million b/d of capacity, except under the high-growth scenario for 2010, where emerging production from the Caspian basin is set to zero. Under this high-growth scenario, OPEC need only shut in an incremental 2 million b/d. This forecast indicates that maintenance of moderate prices is feasible for the period between 2005 and 2010 even if a major non-OPEC province is removed. In other words, under the convergence forecast scenario and other scenarios, Caspian basin production will not be critical for maintaining moderate oil prices for at least another decade, assuming, as seems reasonable, that historically persistent competition continues within OPEC.

Conclusion

We argued that performing growth accounting with only the common factors of production is not sufficient to explain the growth process since the long-run scenario of fully diffused technology has not arrived. Since countries differ in both technology and institutions we chose to use a model that contains three growth effects in addition to varying accumulation rates. Each nation is faced with a technology gap approximated by the difference to the leader in per worker output, which can increase the productivity of capital. We also include heterogeneous absorption capacities and adoption rates in the growth model. Thus a nation might not take advantage of the catch-up potential if it either fails to adopt foreign technology or technology absorption is seriously compromised due to the nation's level of inefficiency.

Estimations of our model yield results that are comparable to previous research as well as significant country heterogeneity and regional adoption rates. For example, Europe, Latin America, and East Asia faced on average a technology gap of 0.58, 1.34 and 1.65, respectively, over the 1960–85 period. Including adoption rate and inefficiencies, the net annual growth effect is roughly 0.5 percent for Europe, 0.6 percent for Latin America, and 2.0 percent for East Asia. Another way to discuss our findings is in terms of catch-up times. We found the required times for the nations to catch up with both their inefficiency frontiers and to the leader's frontier, the latter requiring declining inefficiency levels. We then used these heterogeneous catch-up times to benchmark the rates of growth of different countries within the world economy to the standard of energy intensity used in the Unites States. Based on the hypothesis that countries within the world economy are converging to the energy intensive production technology utilized in the US we constructed forecasts of energy use and decomposed these into specific demand forecasts for oil demand. Interestingly enough, these are found to be in close agreement with those generated from the Department of Energy's Energy Information Agency.

Our forecasts show that world oil demand will grow to 80 million b/d by 2005 and 89 million b/d by 2010, up from 65.6 million b/d in our base year of 1994. The implications of this forecast for oil producers seeking to raise output between 2005 and 2010 are relatively pessimistic. Given projections for the rise in oil production from OPEC countries, oil markets could wind up oversupplied by a large margin. OPEC or some other coalition of countries will likely have to shut in a significant portion of their productive capacity to balance available supply to the world's requirement for oil consumption. Energy security is enhanced in markets where there is considerable competition within and without OPEC, and where large amounts of shut-in productive capacity exist.

Acknowledgement

The authors would like to thank Lily Fu and Chris Belfi for their valuable research assistance and James Griffin for helpful comments. Particular thanks are extended to Amy Jaffe for editorial oversight, institutional perspective, and substantive suggestions. The usual caveat applies.

Appendix

The fact that the convergence time will be identical to the Solow–Swan model, but that the convergence path is very different, can be seen if our model is simulated (see Figures 7.1–7.3). The simulations show the effect on the convergence path when an economy does or does not adopt technology when assuming identical steady states for all economies (that is, identical saving rates). Figure 7.1 shows a simulation of the traditional Solow model using three economies which differ in initial capital stock, while Figure 7.2 shows the effect of different adoption rates and Figure 7.3 shows the effect of differing inefficiency levels.

Notes

1. An important catalyst was to consider a model that incorporates overtaking among nations as discussed in Hultberg and Postert (2000), Quah (1993), and Chari *et al.* (1996). The inclusion of technology adoption, with and

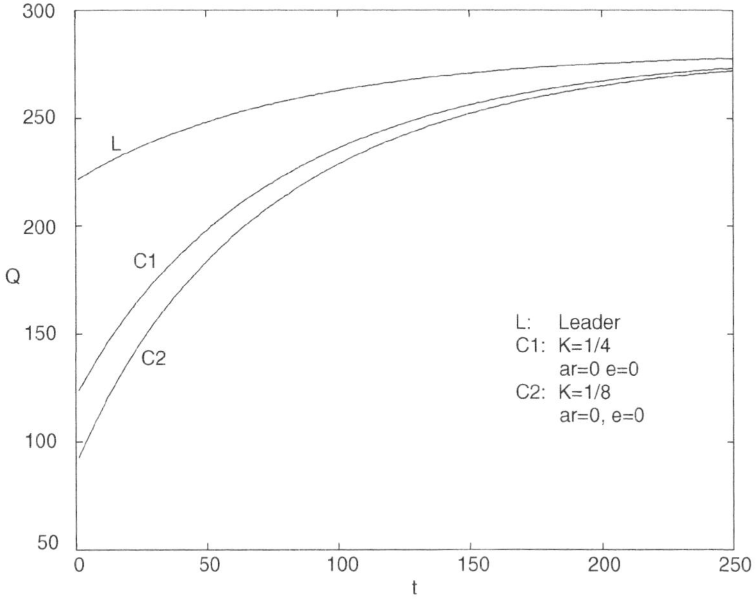

Figure 7.1 Simulations of growth paths: neoclassical model

without institutional inefficiency, slightly modifies the standard results for nations' steady states and rates of convergence (Hultberg, 1999).

2. For more detailed information about this model, see Hultberg (1999).
3. The results are similar to those obtained by Barro and Sala-i-Martin (1995) in their model of labor mobility. They make the unrealistic assumption that people are more mobile than physical capital, while we make the no less unrealistic assumption that both are perfectly immobile.
4. Several possibilities have been suggested (Benhabib & Spiegel, 1994; Kyriacou, 1991). Levine and Renelt (1992) find that average level of secondary education enrollment is a robust determinant of per capita GDP. The only other two robust explanatory variables in their study are investment share of GDP and initial real GDP per capita. We include employment growth as well.
5. It would be better if the rate of catch-up was determined by relative levels of total factor productivity (Solow residual), but since this is both harder to obtain and is likely to be highly correlated with labor productivity we use the above definition.
6. The difference comes from the technology function, which is redefined as $\xi(\ln(Y),\ln(Y^w),E)_t = -\rho\ln(EY_t/Y^w_t)$, where $E \geq 1$, and thus acts to reduce the available technology gap. Accordingly the economy may run out of available technology before its capital intensity is equal to the leader nation. An

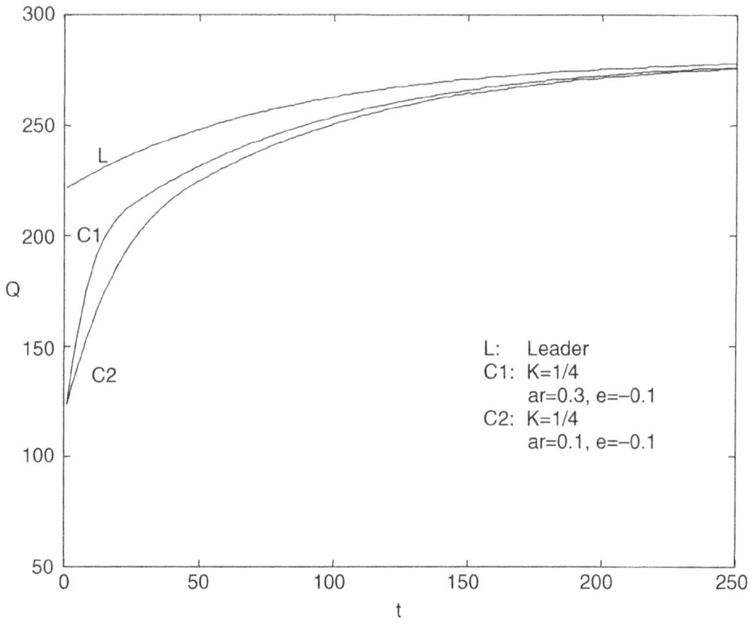

Figure 7.2 Simulations of growth paths: different adoption rates

alternative to this approach would be to make the adoption rate, ρ, a function of absorption capacity.

7. In the estimation we use both 5-year and annually pooled data. The parameters must of course be interpreted accordingly.
8. A measure of labor input such as hours of work is preferred, but this variable was not available. From Summers and Heston (1991), number of workers = (*RGDPCH / RGDPW*) * *POPULATION.*
9. The growth rate of capital is given by, $k_{it}= (I_{i,t-1}/ Y_{i,t-1})$ z, where z is a constant representing the unchanging capital–output ratio. This is an assumption that finds validation in Dowrick and Nguyen (1989) for the OECD sample and Oroczo *et al.*, (1996) for the Latin American countries.
10. The existence of a lagged dependent variable on the right-hand side makes the LSDV an inconsistent estimator when asymtotics is considered in the direction of *N* going to infinity. However, if we consider the asymtotics in the direction of *T*, then LSDV is consistent and equivalent to MLE.
11. The general panel data model with heterogeneity in slopes and intercept takes the following form: $y_{it} =X_{it}'\beta+W_{it}'+\delta_i +\varepsilon_{it}$,1,...,*N* and *t*=1,...,*T*. The difference from the standard model is then that *W* has coefficients, σ_i, which varies with the individual (country).
12. The methodology is similar to studies of firm heterogeneity that usually estimate frontier functions and firm-specific inefficiency levels (Schmidt and

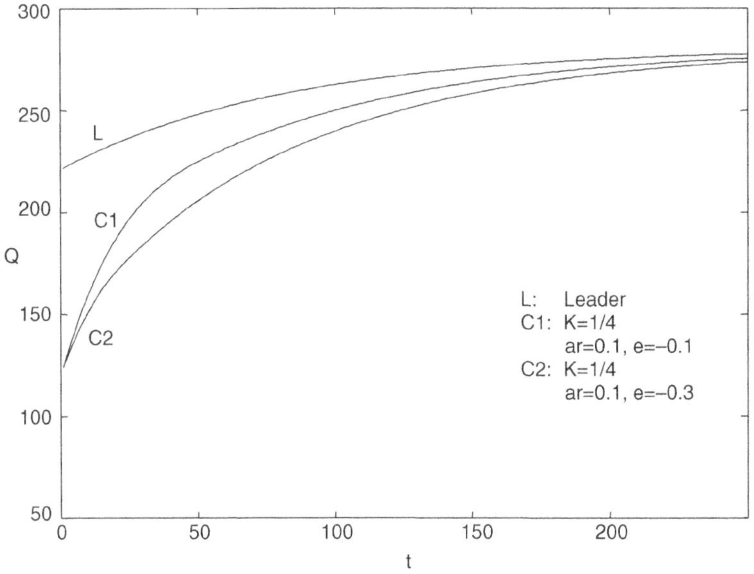

Figure 7.3 Simulations of growth paths: different inefficiency levels

Sickles, 1984; Cornwell *et al.*, 1990). We tried to provide a dynamic interpretation of the inefficiency levels by using a time dummy, but when splitting the sample in two (1972–73), the results are insignificant. Using an index of institutional environment as the basis for trend break yields some significant results, but in most cases not enough information is available.

13. Table 7.1 suggests that the Latin American adoption rate might be greater than the other two major regions. Indeed, if we include an interactive regional dummy we can reject the equality of Latin America's adoption rate with that of Europe and East Asia at the 99 percent significance level. We are unable to similarly reject the equality of adoption rates across Europe and East Asia.
14. Performing the same estimation for each region we obtain the following adoption rates: Europe, 0.380; East Asia, 0.371; and Latin America, 0.583. The estimated adoption rates for the annual data are 0.100 (0.099 in regional estimation) for Europe, 0.037 (0.058) for East Asia, and 0.119 (0.108) for Latin America.
15. To test the robustness of these measures we estimate the model using annual data as well. The annual results are also significant, except for East Asia. It is also for East Asia that the annual results differ from the 5-year panel results.
16. The per capita energy consumption and total energy consumption data in 1994 are from United Nations (1996). The growth rates of countries not in

Table 7.2, including India, China, Russia, Eastern Europe and other countries in the former Soviet Union, and those in Africa are calculated as weighted averages of the rest of the countries since those three countries were not included in the former catch-up time forecast.

References

Abramovitz, M., "Catching Up, Forging Ahead, and Falling Behind", *Journal of Economic History*, 46 (1986) 385–406.

Ahn, S.C., and Schmidt, P., "Efficient Estimation of Models for Dynamic Panel Data", *Journal of Econometrics*, 68 (1995) 5–27.

Arellano, M., and Bond, S., "Some Test of Specification for Panel Data: Monte Carlo Evidence and an Application to Employment Equations", *Review of Economic Studies*, 58 (1991) 277–97.

Baltagi, B.H., *Econometric Analysis of Panel Data*, (England: John Wiley & Sons, 1995).

Barro, R.J. and J-W. Lee, "International Comparison of Educational Attainment," *Journal of Monetary Economics*, 32, (1993) 363–94.

Barro, R.J. *and X. Sala-i-Martin, Economics Growth*, (New York,: McGraw-Hill) (1995).

Barro R.J. and Sala-i-Martin, X, "Converqence", *Journal of Political Economy*, 100 (1992) 223-51

Benhabib, J., and Spiegel, M.M., "The Role of Human Capital in Economic Development: Evidence from Aggregate Cross-Country Data", *Journal of Monetary Economics*, 34 (1994) 143–73.

Chamberlain, G., "Multivariate Regression Model for Panel Data", *Journal of Econometrics*, 18 (1982) 5–46.

Chamberlain, G., "Panel Data," in Z. Griliches and M. Intriligator (eds), *Handbook of Econometrics*, (Amsterdam: North-Holland, 1984) 1247–1318.

Chari, V.V., Kehoe, P.J., and McGrattan E.R., "The Poverty of Nations: A Quantitative Exploration", *Federal Reserve Bank of Minneapolis*, Research Department Staff Rep. No. 204, (1996)

Cornwell, C., Schmidt, P., and Sickles, R.C., "Production Frontiers with Cross-Sectional and Time Series Variation in Efficiency Levels", *Journal of Econometrics*, 46 (1990) 185–200.

Dowrick, S., and Nguyen, D., "OECD Comparative Economic Growth, 1950–85: Catch-up and Convergence", *American Economic Review*, 79 (1989) 1010–30.

Hultberg, P.T., "An Alternative Model of Growth: Efficiency and Catch up", mimeo, University of Wyoming (1999).

Hultberg, P.T., Nadiri M.I., and Sickles, R.C., "An International Comparison of Technology Adoption and Efficiency: A Dynamic Panel Model", *Annales d'Economie et de Statistique*, 55–56 (1999) 449–74.

Hultberg, P.T., and Postert, A.K., "Forging Ahead and Falling Behind": Can the Neoclassical Model of Growth Explain the Empirical Evidence?" mimeo, University of Wyoming (2000).

Islam, N., "Growth Empirics: A Panel Data Approach", *Quarterly Journal of Economics*, 110 (1995) 1127–70.

Knack, S., and Keefer, P., "Institutions and economic performance: Cross-country tests using alternative institutional measures", *Economics and Politics*, 7 (1995) 207–27.

Kyriacou, G.A., "Level and Growth Effects of Human Capital: A Cross-country Study of the Convergence Hypothesis", C.V. Starr Working Paper, (1991) 91–126.

Levine, R., and Renelt, D., "A Sensitivity Analysis of Cross-country Growth Regressions", *American Economic Review*, 82 (1992) 942–63.

Mankiw, N.G., Romer, D., and Weil, D.N., "A Contribution to the Empirics of Economic Growth", *Quarterly Journal of Economics*, 107, (1992) 407–37.

North, D.C., *Institutions, Institutional Change, and Economic Performance* (Cambridge: Cambridge University Press, 1990).

OECD, *Energy Balances of OECD Countries, 1994–1995* (Paris: OEPD, 1997a).

OECD, *Energy Statistics and Balances of Non-OECD Countries, 1994–1995* (Paris: OECD, 1997b).

Olson, M., *The Rise and Decline of Nations: Economic Growth, Stagflation, and Social Rigidities* (New Haven, CT: Yale University Press, 1982).

Orozco, F., Hultberg, P.T., and Sickles, R.C., "The Convergence Hypothesis: The Latin American Experience", mimeo, Rice University (1996).

Quah, D., "Empirical Cross-section Dynamics in Economic Growth" *European Economic Review*, 37 (1993) 426–34.

Schmidt, P., and Sickles, R.C., "Production Frontiers and Panel Data", *Journal of Business and Economic Statistics*, 2 (1984) 367–74.

Scully, G.W., "The Institutional Framework and Economic Development", *Journal of Political Economy*, 92 (1988), 652–62.

Soligo, R., and Jaffe, A., "The Economics of Pipeline Routes: The Conundrum of Oil Exports from the Caspian Basin", in A. Jaffe and R.C. Sickles(eds), *Unlocking the Assets: Energy and the Future of Central Asia and the Caucasus*, Mimeo, Baker Institute for Public Policy at Rice University, Houston, TX (1998).

Summers, R., and Heston, A., "The Penn World Table (Mark 5.0): An Expanded Set of International Comparisons, 1950–1988", *Quarterly Journal of Economics*, 106 (1991) 327–68.

United Nations, "Production, trade, and consumption of commercial energy", *Statistical Yearbook*, 41 (1995) 592–618.

Part III

National Interests in the Caspian Basin

8
Russia's National Interests in the Caspian Region

Michael Margelov

Introduction

The main interest of the Russian Federation is to build an open and democratic state that is fully integrated into the world community. However, the essential focus is on Russia's internal revitalization and the resolution of its internal problems. These priorities were defined by President Vladimir Putin in January 2001 before the Collegium of the Foreign Ministry. In his speech, Putin stated that: "The recently adopted Foreign Policy Concept clearly outlines our national interests in the international arena. These are closely geared with the country's objectives in such principal areas as defense, national security, the social sphere and economy."[1] This new foreign policy will be multi-directional. In the President's view, "it would be a mistake to start weighing Russia's priorities in Europe against those in Asia. Russia should have neither a western nor eastern bias. In reality, the national interests of a state whose geopolitical situation is similar to Russia's extend everywhere." The key focus of Russian diplomatic energies will be on the creation of a favorable international environment for Russia's internal reform. In Putin's words: "We must see it as our top priority the creation of a stable and secure international environment around Russia that would let the country concentrate its best efforts and maximum resources on meeting the social and economic challenges." However, Putin stressed that this goal would not be pursued by Russia being weak on the international stage. The President drew attention to the importance of "taking a firm but not confrontational stance in upholding Russia's national interests ... It is certainly important to know and take due account of the other party's approach, but you must be unequivocally committed to achieving your one main goal – the effective protection of Russia's national interests." In general, Putin stressed the economic heart of Russia's new foreign policy:

> It is vitally important to create such a system of promoting and protecting our economic interests abroad that would be capable of

> maximizing benefits for the Russian economy and minimizing the risks of our integration into the global market. In my opinion, the Foreign Ministry ought to show greater commitment to supporting major economic projects implemented in co-operation with foreign partners and to ensure that such projects fully match Russian national interests.

The principles set forth in this address are the foundations for a new Russian foreign policy launched at the start of the new century. In contrast to that pursued in the 1990s by Boris Yeltsin, this new policy requires that Russia's integration into the world community work in harmony with Russia's overall state and national interests.

Russia has sought consistently to apply these newly proclaimed principles towards the former Soviet Republics of Central Asia and the Caspian region.[2] This chapter will examine the main vectors in Russian policy toward these regions, including the shifts in Russian policy towards Azerbaijan, the conflict in Chechnya and its impact on Russian policy in the Caucasus, Russian policies toward the conflict in Nagorno-Karabakh, Russian positions in Central Asia, and, finally, Russia's energy diplomacy. The discussion of each of these vectors will focus on the new policy lines set forth by President Putin.

A shift in Russian policy towards Azerbaijan?

Vladimir Putin's visit to Baku in early January 2001 marked a clear shift in Russian policy and led many observers to note that Russia had changed its policies towards Baku, as well as Yerevan and adopted a new approach to the development of the Caspian energy resources. Supporting this shift, many noted also that changes had occurred in Azeri foreign policy. For example, a Russian commentator in the *Ekho Planety* magazine argued that Azerbaijan, which had been on the verge of open confrontation with Russia, had become by 2001 finally ready for constructive dialogue.[3] In touting the riches of the Caspian shelf, it has been argued that Baku had badly overreached itself and misled not only its Western partners but itself. As a result, a number of major international investors announced their withdrawal from the Baku–Ceyhan pipeline project. Russian commentators also noted that the retirement of former Turkish President Suleiman Demirel had led to a distinct cooling-off in the Baku–Ankara relationship. Moreover, the Azerbaijani President, Heidar Aliyev, has been seen to have realized finally that the conflict over Nagorno-Karabakh cannot be settled without close cooperation with Moscow. In addition, in this area, Baku has grown dissatisfied with the West's mediation.

In January 2001, indeed, the Russian and Azeri leaders signed a joint declaration that proclaimed a new level of relations between Russia and Azerbaijan. In the view of the Russian newspaper, *Nezavisimaya Gazeta*:

> Today, Moscow wants to resolve the whole range of the region's major problems, including such burning issues as the Karabakh conflict and the Caspian Sea's legal status. In so doing, Russia hopes to substantially enhance its positions in the Caspian Basin Area on the whole and in Transcaucasia in particular. It is no secret that these positions were badly eroded during Boris Yeltsin's presidency.[4]

The rivalry over influence in the Caspian region has not lost its edge. Vladimir Putin's position on this competition has been more explicit and pragmatic than that of his predecessor. In Spring 2000, speaking before the Russian Security Council, Putin instructed the Foreign Ministry and other relevant state agencies to step up their activity in the Caspian region. Putin also appointed Victor Kalyuzhny as the Presidential envoy in the region to spearhead Russian policy towards the region and ensure its coordination.

In the Russian view, the US Administration led by George W. Bush will continue to promote its influence throughout the Caspian region, which has become a zone of US strategic interests. As Vafa Gulizade, a former aide to Aliyev on international affairs, stated: "Russia and Putin's Administration have understood that the Bush team will be very aggressive in their efforts to wield the commanding influence in the region. That is why the Russians are trying hard to pre-empt such attempts."[5] Russian and American interests in the region have clashed not only in the former Soviet Republics, but also with respect to their policies towards Iran. The primary objective of Russian foreign policy planners has been to avoid any confrontation and pursue a pragmatic approach for the development of multilateral ties with all countries in the region. The effective development of the Caspian natural resources is seen by Russia as being pivotal for the region's economic growth and political stability.

In line with this policy, many observers have noted that Moscow has modified its policy in the Caspian region in favor of Azerbaijan. Russia has retained important leverage over Azerbaijan. Most importantly, it has been estimated that up to 2 million Azeris are working across the Russian Federation, whose remittances sent back to Azerbaijan have reached very important levels. President Aliyev has had to take these circumstances into account and, partly for this reason, he has also adopted a very pragmatic approach to Russia. However, the Russian government has also shifted to a more flexible approach. For one, the government announced that it was prepared to settle the problems caused by Azerbaijan's under-loading of the Baku–Novorossiysk oil pipeline in 2000.[6]

The problem of Azerbaijan's oil transit via the Baku–Novorossiysk pipeline has several aspects. Azerbaijan has built up its oil-refining capacity, which has led to an increased domestic demand for crude oil. The Azeri government has argued against the transportation of "blended" oils as this would impair the quality of its oil exports. However, the existing oil transit scheme through the Baku–Novorossiysk pipeline envisaged the blending of oil from Azerbaijan, Turkmenistan and Kazakhstan en route. For this reason, Azerbaijan has tended to export the bulk of its oil via the Baku–Supsa pipeline. Moscow viewed such actions on the part of Baku as pro-Western and claimed that Baku was infringing on the agreement between Russia and Azerbaijan which stipulated the transit of predetermined volumes of Azeri oil to Novorossiysk. Under Putin, however, Moscow has sought to take the political edge off the problem and has proposed economic options for a solution. According to the Presidential Special Envoy, Victor Kalyuzhny, Russia may start supplying natural gas to Azerbaijan and thus allow the latter to overcome its crude oil shortage on the domestic market. As such, the surplus oil may be used for loading the Baku-Novorossiysk pipeline.

Putin's visit to Baku resulted in Azerbaijan confirming a guarantee to transport 2.2 million tons of oil in 2001 via the Baku–Novorossiysk pipeline.[7] In addition, the Azerbaijan State Petroleum Company and the major Russian oil company, Lukoil, signed an agreement on the rehabilitation, exploration and extraction (on a production sharing basis) of the Zykh-Govsany field's residual oil reserves, which have been estimated at 20 million tons. When speaking to deputies from the parliament of Azerbaijan, Putin stressed that Russia was prepared to cooperate with Azerbaijan in every area of the fuel and energy sector, including participation in oil field development, the purchase of hydrocarbons for domestic consumption, and assistance in hydrocarbons exports.[8] Moreover, Sergei Prikhodko, Deputy Head of the Presidential Administration, characterized the joint statement from Baku on the situation in the Caspian region:

> A substantial step towards an ultimate consensus of all Caspian countries and a tangible expansion of Russia's cooperation with

> Azerbaijan. When considering potential pipeline routes, Russia never resorts to resistance for resistance's sake. We are primarily guided by economic and environmental considerations. At present, the two countries share an understanding that the certain pause which occurred in the bilateral contacts some time ago and the ensuing lack of attention to economic issues was a mistake.[9]

Already in mid-2000, Russia conducted a number of exploratory talks with Azerbaijan regarding the Caspian Sea's legal status. On July 13, 2000, Victor Kalyuzhny made an official visit to Baku to meet with President Aliyev, to discuss the problem of the disputed Azeri and Chirag offshore oil fields, whose ownership rights have been claimed by both Azerbaijan and Turkmenistan. The Presidential Envoy suggested that the disputed oil fields be developed on a fifty-fifty basis.

Summing up the results of the Russian President's visit to Baku, one may conclude that Vladimir Putin has opted for Azerbaijan as one of Russia's chief partners in the Caspian region. With regard to the Caspian Sea's legal status, Moscow has succeeded, albeit tentatively, in harmonizing its position with Azerbaijan and Kazakhstan. Russia has sought the civilized development of the Caspian Sea's legal status in compliance with the appropriate diplomatic practices and procedures. In its view, a final agreement must ensure equitable rules for the effective use of the Caspian Sea's natural resources. Thus, confrontation has not been in Russia's interests.

These views explain the reasons for Russia supporting, together with Azerbaijan and Kazakhstan, a sectoral demarcation of the Caspian's sea bed. The joint memorandum entitled "On the Principles of Cooperation in the Caspian Off-Shore Area" signed at the end of the Baku visit envisaged a stage-by-stage solution to the problem. The first stage will see the Caspian's sea bed divided into predetermined sectors without imposing restrictions on shipping and navigation (all disputed territories ought to be divided up on the fifty-fifty principle). Subsequently, the parties involved will agree on respective quotas for the Sea's bio-resources and work out principles of navigation. In Moscow's opinion, the sectoral demarcation principle may serve also as the basis for discussion with the other two Caspian countries, Iran and Turkmenistan.

Chechnya and the Caucasus

The war in Chechnya has become an open sore for Russia and it has deep implications for Russian policy throughout the Caucasus. With

Azerbaijan, the Chechen war has produced a shift towards pragmatic and cooperative relations with Russia. Russian relations with Georgia, however, took a downturn as a result of the second Chechen war.

All countries that have had to deal with the problem of ethnic separatism are aware of how difficult it is to settle this kind of conflict. The official Russian perspective pursues the following lines of reasoning. Taking advantage of Russia's weakness, its economic instability and an incoherent Caucasus policy, criminal, separatist and terrorist elements managed to create an enclave on the territory of Chechnya. In this view, the regime set up by the enclave's leaders in the republic was based on military force and received lavish financial and material support from foreign terrorist organizations. However, permanent infighting among various clans and groupings within the new structure of power offered little hope for the regime's consolidation. Moreover, there was little promise for solutions to even the most basic social problems faced by local residents. Criminals and terrorists had adopted the disguise of being devout followers of Islam to undermine the positions of more moderate Chechen leaders such as President Maskhadov. These radical groups proclaimed and sought to expand their power across Chechnya's borders. In August 1999, these extremists invaded the neighboring republic of Dagestan. For Moscow, it was imperative that the federal authorities respond to this act of brazen aggression. The situation was seen as being so grave that the government headed by Vladimir Putin deployed Russia's armed forces to assist in carrying out an extensive anti-terrorist operation in Chechnya. In 2001, after his successful election to the Russian presidency, Putin continued his focus on the use of force to crush the threat to Russia posed by terrorism and separatism.

Many Western governments, the international press as well as human rights activists have leveled sharp criticism against Russia for its actions in Chechnya. In the face of this criticism, Putin has adopted a dual strategy. First, the president has pushed for progress in attaining the goals of the counter-terrorist operation. At the same time, Putin has sought to explain clearly on the international stage Russian objectives in Chechnya. The Russian government has always supported open cooperation with international organizations in order to meet the humanitarian challenges that have arisen in Chechnya. Indeed, the people living in Chechnya, are Russian citizens and, naturally, Russia has been concerned for their welfare. The federal authorities, and the interim administration that has been created in Chechnya have sought to reintegrate the Chechen Republic into the Russian Federation as an equal and constituent subject. This policy will depend, however, on the completion of the anti-terrorist operation, with the total elimination of organized groups of terrorists and the end to all channels of financial, material and military support to these groups.

In this context, the Russian government has repeatedly contacted Georgia and Azerbaijan with proposals to block all channels by which organized groups have continued to penetrate into Chechnya and have received financial and material support from extremist organizations abroad. Moscow has also drawn the attention of the authorities of Georgia and Azerbaijan to the fact that Chechen groups were finding refuge and medical treatment on their territories. However, Baku and Tbilisi rejected the positions put forth by Moscow. For example, Georgia refused to cooperate with Russian border guards and armed forces who proposed taking joint steps to enhance control over its border with Chechnya. Georgia saw this proposal as an infringement of its sovereignty and assured Russia that it had effective control over the situation in the Pankissi Valley, an area historically settled by ethnic Chechens. Moscow, however, claimed that this area has become a resting ground not only for Chechen refugees but also for armed militants.

Guided by the need to ensure Russian security, Moscow approached both Georgia and Azerbaijan with a proposal to discuss the introduction of a visa regime, on the assumption that this measure would allow Russian border guards to tighten control over the border areas. Both Baku and Tbilisi, however, interpreted this initiative as a Russian attempt to exert pressure on them. Hundreds of thousands of citizens of Georgia and Azerbaijan live and work in Russia because of a lack of employment opportunities at home. Indeed, it is correct to argue that Moscow was exerting pressure on these two states – but for the purposes of legitimate self-defense.

Following the initial controversy in 2000, Baku and Moscow held a round of diplomatic consultations and managed to find a mutually acceptable solution. Both parties agreed that it would be appropriate to retain the existing visa-free regime. In exchange, in late 2000, Baku made significant moves to confirm its participation in the fight against terrorism. In this context, Vladimir Putin stated in Baku that Russia had no intention of introducing a visa regime with Azerbaijan: "The balanced policy pursued by the President of Azerbaijan made it obvious that Russia should not take any extraordinary one-sided protective measures."[10] Georgia, on the other hand, faced the introduction of a visa regime with Russia. Moscow retained the right to open new talks about the regime with Georgia, but on the condition that Tbilisi established control over a serious problem for Russian security, namely, Moscow's view that Chechen groups have acted freely on the territory of Georgia. On January 21, 2001, President Eduard Shevardnadze announced that the Georgian Foreign Ministry had started work on the draft of a new treaty with Russia. According to Shevardnadze, the Russian Foreign Ministry had received similar instructions from Vladimir Putin. In Shevardnadze's opinion, the signing and ratification of a new treaty would offer a new opportunity for leading the Georgian-Russian relationship out of the deadlock. The Georgian President stated that Georgia sought to develop a new system of relations with Russia.[11] In this sense, an amelioration of Russian–Georgian relations after the degradation of the late 1990s, may be expected under the leadership of Vladimir Putin.

Under Putin, Russia's security requirements in the Caucasus have become the driving force behind Russian policy in the wider region. On this basis, Russian needs in Chechnya have naturally affected Russia's interaction with Azerbaijan and Georgia. The new president has been intent on ensuring a harmonious relationship between internal consolidation and external positions. Therefore, Russian policies towards Georgia and Azerbaijan will continue to be influenced deeply by the development of events in the north Caucasus.

Russia, the West and the conflict in Nagorno-Karabakh

When in Baku, Putin reaffirmed his readiness to act as an intermediary and guarantor of the process of negotiations on a Karabakh settlement. The Russian president stated this willingness both in the Russian capacity of a co-chairman of the OSCE Minsk Group and on a unilateral basis. Putin stated in Baku: "Russia will support any plan for the Karabakh settlement which will satisfy both Azerbaijan and Armenia. Only the presidents of these two countries can find a solution acceptable to both of them." The Baku Declaration stated that Russia and Azerbaijan

> will take efforts to facilitate the settlement of territorial, inter-ethnic, inter-confessional and other conflicts strictly in conformity with the UN Charter and corresponding Security Council resolutions. Russia and Azerbaijan are resolutely against any actions or attempts to interfere in the internal affairs of sovereign states under

> the pretext of human rights protection or other humanitarian purposes.[12]

Russia and NATO have put forth similar positions on this conflict. Both have called upon Baku and Yerevan to reach a compromise solution to the Karabakh problem. On January 16, a few days after Putin's visit to Azerbaijan, Baku played host to NATO Secretary-General George Robertson, who was on his way from Yerevan. It has been argued that the strategic aim of NATO has been to prevent the countries of the Southern Caucasus and Central Asia from "drifting" to the north and to preserve them as potential friends of the West. In a longer-term perspective, the North Atlantic alliance has sought, indeed, to develop ties with the armed forces of these new states through Partnership for Peace. However, while it has been argued by some that NATO may expand eventually into this region, Lord Robertson refuted all allegations about NATO's increased interest in the states of the Caucasus as potential members of the Alliance. But still, following his talks with Robertson, the Azeri President himself did nothing to clarify the situation as he placed significant stress on the role of NATO in maintaining peace in the region:

> There is no peace in the Caucasus today. Unfortunately, the Armenian-Azeri conflict has not been settled because of Armenia's counterproductive position. NATO is a military organization, first and foremost, and it knows who is responsible for one or another conflict. Armenia has started our conflict, and this injustice has since been committed in front of the whole world, including NATO. I think the aim of NATO is to assert peace at least in Europe. It is necessary to put an end to conflicts in the Southern Caucasus.[13]

Robertson had stated that NATO considered the Armenian–Azeri conflict to be a serious problem that affected stability throughout the region. At the same time, however, he stressed that NATO did not wish to assign blame in the conflict or to take sides, and he emphasized that its settlement depended on the parties themselves. Moreover, his reaction to the proposal for Russia to become a guarantor of agreements between Azerbaijan and Armenia was quite positive: "The North Atlantic alliance welcomes all international efforts towards a settlement."

Commenting on the results of Putin's visit to Baku, Naira Melkumian, the Foreign Minister of the self-proclaimed Nagorno-Karabakh Republic, stated there had been no surprises. As a country with its own unsettled ethnic conflict, she argued that Russia was forced to emphasize the supremacy of the principle of territorial integrity. At the same time, Melkumian saw that the Russian president had "in a certain sense managed to single out very diplomatically the Karabakh problem, stressing that it should be settled on the basis of a compromise." In her opinion, Armenian reactions to the shift in Russian–Azeri relations had to be reasonable, "because Russia has its own stakes in the region, which are actually more than just Armenia and Karabakh."[14]

On January 22, 2001, then Secretary of the Russian Security Council, Sergei Ivanov, was dispatched to Baku for a three-hour long conversation with President Aliyev behind closed doors.[15] Ivanov arrived from Yerevan where he had conducted negotiations with President Robert Kocharian and Defense Minister Serge Sarkisian. In Yerevan, the Russian envoy discussed Russian–Armenian relations and the situation in the region in the light of the Russian President's visit to Baku. According to Baku-based media, Ivanov then informed Aliyev about the reaction of Yerevan to Moscow's proposals for the settlement of the Armenian–Azeri conflict.

Therefore, it has already become clear that Russian policy towards the conflict has taken on greater importance under President Putin. The Russian government has stressed the need for the parties themselves to reach an acceptable agreement, and downplayed the role of the external parties. At the same time the Russian government has started to put forth an even-handed approach to conflict settlement. On this basis, there are significant similarities between Russian and Western positions. However, a certain element of anxiety at the active return of Russian influence in the region has arisen in the West and Turkey.

Russia, the West and Central Asia

From the perspective of Moscow, a struggle has started for influence throughout Central Asia as a result of Western policies that have considered the Central Asian region as also a part of the so-called Caspian basin region. All of the former republics of the Soviet Transcaucasus and Central Asia have been lumped together by the West into a "super region,"a policy which has been strengthened by special region-wide projects such as the development of the Caspian basin natural resources, a new Silk Road and TRACECA (Transport Corridor Europe Caucasus Asia), as well as the Partnership for Peace Program. The West has launched into the struggle for a division of the so-called "post-Soviet space," guided by the principles of realism and geopolitics. The increasing strategic rivalry has been centered on a struggle for control over the Central Asian region, its resources and transport routes. Russia, the US and China, as well as Turkey, Iran, Pakistan, India and the countries of the European Union have all developed levers of influence on the development of the geopolitical situation in Central Asia.

Russia has proceeded to develop policies towards Central Asia based on Moscow's recognition of these new states' independence and sovereignty. On an economic plane, Russia has pursued the maximum possible expansion of economic ties, using for this purpose not only the infrastructure that was created in the Soviet era but also modern market-economy instruments. The Russian objective has been set on a course of economic integration between these states. The attainment of this goal will depend on the economic recovery of Russia and its neighbors. External military interference or internal conflicts will obstruct the promotion of Russian interests in the region. Thus, Russia's military presence in Central Asia has been seen as being of critical importance for Russia and wider regional security. Preventing the infiltration of Islamic radicalism from Afghanistan has become a strategically important task for Moscow. For Russia, the Caspian basin region (to adopt the Western term) has emerged as "a belt of instability," stretching from the south to threaten Russia itself. Moreover, in the Russian view, increasing instability on the Central Asian border with Afghanistan has opened a direct threat to the whole of Europe in the form of heavy flows of illegal narcotics supported by the new Afghan regime. Central Asia and Afghanistan have become notorious as the world's leading narcotic drug producers and suppliers. In 1999, Russian estimates were that Afghanistan grew 75 percent of the world's supply of opium-group drugs.[16] According to the Russian Federal Border Services, the amount of narcotics contraband stopped by Russian frontier guards in the past five years more than doubled. In 2000 alone, over 3.1 tons of narcotics were confiscated at the Tajik–Afghan border[17]. In the view of many in Russia and in the West, this particular border has become in reality a "European" border.[18]

In addition, Moscow has placed great importance on the need to counter the rise of terrorism in the region. The Headquarters for the Coordination of Military Cooperation between the CIS member countries sponsored a conference on the problems of counter-terrorism in December 2000. Then Russian Defense Minister, Marshal Igor Sergeyev, argued that terrorism presented a direct security threat to the Commonwealth of Independent States. Lieutenant-General Boris Mylnikov, Head of the CIS Anti-Terrorist Center, informed participants that the international terrorist Osama bin Laden had allocated 20 million dollars for training 4,000 militants from the Islamic Movement of Uzbekistan (IDU) and some 400 Chechen fighters. Mylnikov predicted that in mid-2001 IDU armed units would step up their efforts to destabilize a number of Central Asian states, focusing on regions in Uzbekistan, Tajikistan and Turkmenistan as springboards for further aggressive actions.[19] The consensus in Moscow and throughout Central Asia has crystallized on the need to build a regional security system.

The heads of state of the Central Asian Economic Union met in Almaty on January 5, 2001. The summit stressed the common priorities of the struggle against terrorism and drug trafficking throughout the region. In response to these threats, the Central Asian presidents affirmed that "security is indivisible" and expressed a readiness to fulfill all the obligations they had assumed in the event of new attacks by militants. The Kyrgyz President Akayev argued even that "preventive measures" were needed in order to prevent new attacks. Most notably, the Uzbek President Karimov placed great emphasis on the importance of Russia in the region. In response, the Russian Deputy Foreign Minister Trubnikov stated that Russia was ready to fulfill all of its obligations under the CIS Collective Security Treaty. However, Russia categorically rejected the possibility of air strikes against Afghanistan, arguing that this would constitute "a gross violation of international law."

Despite the elements of common ground, it is clear that the Central Asian states have failed so far to build an effective military-political bloc with Russia. Turkmenistan has continued to pursue a neutral course, whereas Uzbekistan has only recently started to intensify its relations with Russia. All of the Central Asian states have welcomed Russian efforts to prevent the "Afghanization" of the region. However, at the same time, the authorities in the states have feared the extension of Russian influence in their internal affairs. This ambivalence in Central Asia, with pressures pushing Russia and the new states together and concerns dividing them, has opened scope for geopolitical competition in the region. The presence of key strategic reserves in the region has intensified this struggle over influence. However, it is important to not over-state this competition. In the Russian case, in particular, the scope of mutual interests with the Central Asian countries will continue to be wide enough to ensure a long-standing Russian presence in the region.

Energy diplomacy and the clash of interests

During Clinton's presidency, the US affirmed that the main aim of its policies in the Caspian basin and Central Asia was to strengthen the independence and ensure the prosperity of the post-Soviet states.[20] In the Russian view, however, the central thrust of this policy was to diminish Russian influence throughout the region. Following the election of Putin, there were some rhetorical adjustments in the position of the Clinton administration. John Wolf, Advisor to the President stated at hearings before the Senate Foreign Relations Committee in the Spring 2000 that Russia was, is and will be one of the main players in the solution of Caspian energy problems: "We will continue searches for cooperation between Russian and American companies in future Caspian energy projects."[21]

However, the underlying aims of US energy diplomacy remained unchanged. This policy continued to attach major importance to market reforms in the countries of the Caspian basin, partly in a bid to strengthen the positions of American transnational companies in the region. In the Russian view, the US has sought to ensure access to Caspian and Persian oil reserves in order to enhance its geopolitical and economic importance. In a nutshell, the aims of US energy diplomacy have been closely tied with wider American foreign policy objectives. Washington has supported the project of the Caspian Pipeline Consortium, which has taken into consideration Russian interests. However, the US has also backed fully the Baku–Ceyhan project, despite its uneconomic cost. Moreover, the US has lobbied in favor of the project for a trans-Caspian Turkmen gas pipeline via Azerbaijan and Georgia to Turkey. In the Russian view, these projects have become important for the US *only* from the geopolitical standpoint. Indeed, only the geopolitical perspective may explain why the US has sought to discredit the Russian–Turkish Blue Stream project, to which the Russian Foreign Ministry drew the attention of the US Embassy in Moscow in August 1999.

The potential for serious conflicts of interests over these concerns threatens the stability of world energy markets. Moreover, the social and economic development of these new states will depend on whether the energy diplomacies of the US and Russia succeed in finding a balance of interests.[22] The Bush Administration has not paid less attention to the Caspian region than President Bill Clinton and his team did. Moreover, the US government has reiterated its support for the Baku–Ceyhan project in order to strengthen the sovereignty of the Caspian basin countries and their economic independence from Russia. In addition, the pipeline will be a new source of energy for the West. The new Russian government, however, has ruled out any Russian participation in the Baku–Ceyhan project because, in the opinion of the Fuel and Energy Ministry, "it is economically disadvantageous."[23] According to Russian estimates, making this project economically profitable would require 50 million tons of oil a year, a figure well beyond Azerbaijan's reach. At a press conference in Moscow on January 15, 2001, Viktor Kalyuzhny argued that those in favour of the Baku–Ceyhan line had artificially aggravated the restrictions over the capacity for transport through the Bosphoros and Dardanelles Straits. According to Kalyuzhny, an increase in oil transportation would require only simple improvements in the navigation system and a mechanism of sailing directions. Moreover, in a meeting with Turkey's Deputy Foreign Minister, Kalyuzhny explained that Russia would be able to transport an additional 30–40 million tons of oil up to 2015. The Russian Envoy stressed that the Baku–Ceyhan project was not in harmony with the Russian pipeline system.[24]

Conclusions

Significant changes occurred in Russian foreign policy after Vladimir Putin's election. These changes are connected with Putin's bold and clear proclamation of Russian interests and the pragmatism driving his thinking. However, these new policy lines do not signify the start of a confrontational relationship between Russia and the West. Both parties have a clear responsibility towards the other for respect and cooperation. On the US side, much has to be done to rectify the errors of the past. Despite endless talk about partnership, the Clinton Administration did not cooperate with the Kremlin from practically the very beginning. Instead, it relied on pseudo-diplomatic rituals the aim of which was to force Russia to accept American decisions and conditions. This gave birth, on the Russian side, to a growing feeling of indignation, humiliation and mistrust in proposals coming from America – from arms control to agreements on financial questions.

Having created such sentiments, Washington now has to overcome them. From the perspective of the Kremlin, Russian national interests lie in the construction of an open democratic state which is a fully integrated member of the global community. Confrontation with the West would present a danger to this objective.

In terms of Russian foreign policy, the central issue is to ensure the national security and socioeconomic development of the country. Far from choosing directions, the aim of Russian foreign policy is to create a zone of stability around the Russian Federation, which would make it possible to concentrate the country's efforts on crucial domestic tasks. Accusations that the new Russian government has maintained an "imperial syndrome" with regard to the South Caucasus and Central Asia are absolutely groundless. Contrary to these unhelpful claims, the Russian government has stressed that these are historic zones of Russian interests and that it was vital that they avoid becoming strategic "black holes" or lost to other states' geopolitical influence. Moreover, despite their striving for a consolidation of their independence, all of these former Soviet republics have recognized that Russia must play a key role as a main guarantor of security in the region in the event of internal or external threats. There is a geographically and historically preconditioned mutual gravitation between these republics and Russia.

It is important to recognize that the entire region already poses a serious threat to international security. The last years of the 20th century witnessed an intensification of terrorism in Chechnya and on the border between Tajikistan and Afghanistan. Russian troops have played a crucial role in preventing so far the threat of regional instability in Central Asia. However, the threat has not receded and the possibility of a regional "Afghan scenario" cannot be ruled out. Europe itself has started to face the threats posed by developments in the region, in particular the increase of drugs smuggling from sources which can be traced back to Taliban-controlled Afghanistan. In the view from Moscow, the Russian anti-terrorism campaign in Chechnya is part of the international struggle against international terrorism.

After the collapse of the Soviet Union, the Central Asian and Trans-Caucasian republics became targets of close attention on the part of the US, Europe and their neighbors, Iran, Turkey and Pakistan. As a result, the national interests of Russia inevitably have clashed with the polices of these external states and, in particular, the US. In addition, these circumstances have been exacerbated by the region's strategically important oil and gas resources, which have become objects of active energy diplomacy. Relations between Russia and Central Asia are based on centuries-old political, trade and cultural ties. Thus, these relations are historically justified and are economically advantageous. However, the new states of the South Caucasus and Central Asia have made great strides towards consolidating their sovereignty and independence, and in gaining multiple sources of external support. Clearly, the "raw material factor" has played a key role in the process of state formation throughout the region. On this basis, it is important to conclude with the recognition that no single great power will be able to maintain any exceptional degree of influence across these regions.

Notes

1. See www. president.kremlin.ru. 26 January 2001.
2. For an academic view that confirms this shift towards a post-imperial policy, see Menon Radjan, "After the Empire: Russia and Southern CIS States," *USA and Canada: Economy, Politics, Culture* (no. #5, 1999), p. 34.
3. Valery Djalagoniya, "The Orient Does Need a Subtle Approach," *Ekho Planety*, January 19, 2001.
4. See report in *Nezavisimaya Gazeta*, January 31, 2001.
5. See report in *Efir Digest*, January 23, 2001.
6. According to the Intergovernmental Agreement between Russia and Azerbaijan, Azerbaijan's State Petroleum Company was to transport 2.3 million tons of oil via the Baku–Novorossiysk pipeline. The actual volume of Azerbaijan's oil transit, however, totalled slightly more than 500 000 tons. See report in *Nezavisimaya Gazeta*, January 31, 2001.
7. In December 2000, Russia lowered transit tariffs for oil transportation via the Baku–Novorossiysk pipeline, which also contributed to easing the agreement between Russia and Azerbaijan on the volume of the hydrocarbons transit. According to an estimate made by the Transneft (national pipeline operator) and the Russian Fuel and Energy Ministry, Russia may annually receive as much as $350–400 million in revenues for transit of Azerbaijan's oil. Azerbaijan's income is estimated at $2–2.5 billion a year (after 2003). Thus, the pipeline built specifically to bypass the continuing trouble spot of Chechnya is well poised to pay off soon. All the more so that both Turkmenistan and Kazakhstan also use the pipeline to transit their oil via Makhachkala to Novorossiysk. See, for example the discussion in *Rossiyskaya Gazeta*, January 19, 2001).
8. Se *Ekho Planety*, January 19, 2001.
9. See *Vesti.ru*. January 9, 2001.
10. Larissa Buyantseva, "Sea Dividers", *Expert*, January 22, 2001.
11. Mikhail Vygnansky, "Georgia Seeking to Break the Deadlock in Relationship with Russia," *Segodnya*, January 22, 2001.
12. *Bakinsky Rabochiy*, Azerbaijan, January 13, 2001.
13. AssA-Irada Agency, Baku, Azerbaijan, January 16, 2001.
14. MEDIAMAKS Agency, Yerevan, Armenia, January 18, 2001.

15. See report in *Kommersant-Daily*, January 24, 2001.
16. See *Segodnya*, January 6, 2001.
17. Reported in military News Agency, January 18, 2001.
18. See *Nezavisimaya Gazeta*, December 26, 2000.
19. Reported in Military News Agency, December 21, 2000.
20. Sergey Samuilov, "Foreign Policy Discussion in the Course of the Election Campaign", *SshA i Kanada: ekonomika, olitika, kultura* (no. 10, 2000), p. 54.
21. Testimony before the Senate Foreign Relations Committee. Subcommittee on Energy by John S. Wolf, Special Advisor to the President and Secretary of State for Caspian Basin Energy Diplomacy – Washington File, April 12, 2000.
22. S. Zhiznin, "U.S. Energy Diplomacy," *SshA i Kanada: ekonomika, politika, kultura* (no. 2, 2000).
23. PRIME-TASS, Moscow, January 30, 2001.
24. RIA Novosti, Moscow, January 15, 2001.

9

US National Interests: Getting Beyond the Hype

Joe Barnes

Introduction

US relations with the countries of the Caspian Basin are only a decade old, dating to their emergence as independent states following the collapse of the Soviet Union in 1991.[1] The Clinton administration conducted American foreign policy towards the region during eight of those years. Indeed, in a very real sense, Clinton's is the only US policy that the countries of the Caspian Basin have known. The advent of a new administration in Washington in 2001, therefore, marks an important point in US relations with the region. How the Bush administration approaches the Caspian Basin – either by continuing Clinton policies, altering them in part, or making a decisive break with them – will have an important impact, not just on the region, but on US relations with states neighboring it, most notably Russia, now under the firm and less accommodating hand of President Vladimir Putin. It is clearly time for a reassessment of US policy towards the region, within the new administration and outside it.

Any such reassessment must begin with an explanation of the surprising salience achieved by US relations with the Caspian Basin during the Clinton years.[2] After all, the states in question constitute a region that is both geographically remote from the United States and marginal to Washington's traditional strategic interests. This is not to say that the Caspian Basin rose, under Clinton, to the very first rank of US foreign policy; that pride of place continued (and will continue under President Bush) to belong to Washington's relations with Western Europe, East Asia, the Middle East, Russia, China, and Latin America. But for much of the mid- to late-1990s the apparatus of a US diplomatic offensive appears to have been put into high gear. There was a flurry of official visits by regional leaders – Uzbekistan's Karimov (1996), Georgia's Shevardnadze (1997), Azerbaijan's Aliyev (1997), Kazakhstan's Nazarbayev (1997), and Turkmenistan's Niyazov (1998). Senior Clinton administration officials, notably Deputy Secretary of State, Strobe Talbott, delivered well-publicized policy declarations on the importance of the Caspian Basin to the United States.[3] And there was a push to increase Western military cooperation with the countries of the region under the general rubric of NATO's Partnership for Peace Program, including a series of high profile if small-scale joint exercises beginning in 1997.

The Clinton administration took a particular interest in the whole issue of oil and gas pipelines from the region, naming a special Caspian coordinator in 1997. The administration's increased focus on the Caspian Basin – and especially its energy resources – culminated in 1999, when President Clinton attended a ceremony in Istanbul during which leaders of Azerbaijan, Georgia, Turkey, and Kazakhstan signed a protocol committing their countries to construction of an oil pipeline from Baku in Azerbaijan to Ceyhan on the Turkish Mediterranean Coast. (The Bush administration continues to support the Baku–Ceyhan Pipeline.[4])

In the mid- to late-1990s, the American focus on the region was not limited to the diplomatic arena. Seminars and conferences on the Caspian Basin drew ever more interest from academics and businessmen alike. And the American press – whose coverage of the region in the immediate aftermath of independence had been, to put it charitably, spotty – produced a flurry of news reports and opinion pieces on the Caspian Basin, many stressing the need for a more dynamic US policy towards the region.[5]

In short, the Caspian Basin remains the subject of extraordinary interest for a region that the vast majority of Americans would be unable to locate on an atlas, much less name even one of the countries that comprise it. Why? At one level, the answer is simple: oil and gas. The region has both, perhaps lots of them. But there are also complicated political issues in play.

This is true even of international energy companies. Immediately after the fall of the USSR, American and other foreign companies focused their efforts on Russia, with its huge hydrocarbon reserves and extensive, if obsolete, energy infrastructure. The result, with few exceptions, was disillusion. Conflict with powerful domestic monopolies, a chaotic legal climate, and, above all, a deep-rooted Russian suspicion of foreign ownership, caused energy companies to look elsewhere – specifically south to the Caspian Basin.

At one level, American energy companies have enjoyed signal success with their southern strategy. Major deals have been signed, significant investments committed. US companies which have been significantly involved in the region are a veritable "Who's Who" of the American energy sector: Mobil, Chevron, Exxon, Pennzoil, Unocal, and Amoco. They and other international companies figure importantly in international consortia committed to constructing major regional pipelines. But little revenue has been generated. Development of the Caspian Sea itself is entangled in a legal dispute among the littoral states. And the whole issue of transportation routes from the region has proven both economically complex and politically contentious.[6] In particular, construction of the Baku–Ceyhan route – centerpiece of Clinton administration's US energy policy towards the region – has been frustratingly slow to commence, with every year, it seems, bringing further delay.[7]

American energy companies seeking greater involvement by Washington in the region have found no shortage of allies in the US foreign policy establishment. The region, after all, borders not just Russia, but Iran and China. Each of these countries is viewed by influential experts as a current or potential threat to American interests in general.[8] This is particularly true of Russia, still viewed with suspicion by many in the American foreign policy elite. In international affairs, as in so much else, habits die hard; and the habits of the Cold War, with their all-consuming emphasis on countering Moscow, shaped the mind-set of generations of US policy-makers.

The frustration of the American oil companies is not just matched but exceeded by the regimes of the Caspian Basin themselves. The leaders of countries like Ajerbaijan, Kazakhstan, and Turkmenistan – whose political systems range from the autocratic to the unabashedly dictatorial – see the earliest possible flow of energy revenues as important, perhaps decisive determinants of their medium- to long-term legitimacy. Many, if not most, citizens of the Caspian Basin have endured sharp declines in living standards since the end of the Soviet period. They are acutely aware that their material futures will hinge in large part on exploitation of their countries' energy resources. Further delay could lead to public disenchantment with leaders unable to deliver long-promised but much-deferred prosperity.

The regimes of the region also view the early flow of energy revenue as essential in bolstering their countries' sovereignty. While Moscow's attitude toward the region is complex and its ability to intervene there limited, a matter to be discussed at greater length later, there are influential Russian elements that would like to reassert Moscow's traditional dominance in the Caspian Basin. For the oil and gas producing countries of the region, there is a clear appreciation of the role that energy exports can play in buttressing domestic legitimacy and enhancing independence from Moscow.

For the United States government, the 1990s were marked by an evolution of Washington's views towards the region. The independence of these countries in 1991 came, from the first Bush administration's perspective, as an unexpected bonus of the end of the Cold War. In contrast to the liberation of Eastern Europe and the Baltic states, self-determination for the Soviet Republics of the Basin had not been an explicit or even implicit goal of American foreign policy. Independence was a surprise for Washington. It was also a surprise – and at the time a not particularly pleasant one – for a number of leaders in the region. Kazakhstan's Nursultan Nazarbayev, for instance, would have become Prime Minister of the USSR had it survived. He and other then-Communist apparatchiks in the region were literally dragged into independence.

Indeed, after an initial diplomatic effort associated with recognizing these new states and, in the case of Kazakhstan, securing its pledge to forgo the nuclear option, American attention returned to Moscow. The Caspian Basin was not completely ignored. Washington continued to conduct an active, if low-key, diplomacy in the region and to provide a welcome amount of assistance.[9] But the emphasis was clearly on domestic developments in Russia and Moscow's evolving post-Cold War relationship with Washington.

During the first term of the Clinton administration, this focus, if anything, intensified. Deputy Secretary of State Strobe Talbott, in particular, became identified with what could be called a "Russia-first" policy. His role within the administration earned Talbott the enmity not just among those advocating closer American ties to the Caspian Basin but also among foreign policy critics who viewed Russian interests as fundamentally incompatible with those of the United States. Whatever its ultimate merits, the administration's Russia-first policy was indeed plausible. Decisive developments in Russo–American relations – notably Moscow's acquiescence in post-Cold War NATO expansion – suggested prudence when it came to a more ambitious American policy in the Caspian Basin.

By 1997, however, the administration had begun to move, however subtly, towards greater engagement in the region. Russia was safely past its first presidential election. Moscow's acceptance of NATO expansion, however grudging, would be secured that spring. A significant body of opinion within the administration had, in any case, been urging a more assertive policy in the Caspian Basin for some time. Republican criticism of the administration's policy towards Russia had been on the rise for years, and would increase as disenchantment in the late 1990s with the apparent failure of Russia's economic reforms and its harsh policy towards the insurgency in Chechnya. American energy companies therefore found increasingly sympathetic ears within an administration well known – and often criticized – for its emphasis on "dollar diplomacy."

American interests

By most conventional standards, US interests in the region are modest. The countries of the Caspian Basin are physically distant from the United States, militarily insignificant, and sparsely populated. They are also poor. The two Central Asian states most often cited as potential regional leaders – Kazakhstan and Uzbekistan – have GDPs roughly equal to those of Nebraska and West Virginia, respectively.[10]

Nor is this state of affairs likely to change dramatically or soon. Despite talk of a new "Silk Road," their physical remove from important markets and major sea-lanes renders the countries of the Basin unlikely candidates to become, as some optimistically suggest, the new "Tigers" of Asia. A genuine commitment to fundamental economic reform, for instance, has to date been largely absent in the region, home to widespread and high-level corruption. Separated from the Persian Gulf by Iran, dependent on the Bosphorus for access to the Mediterranean, blocked from Europe by the vast expanse of Russia, and bordered to the east and southeast by some of the most inhospitable terrain in the world, the region possesses little obvious geopolitical import. Nor are countries of the Caspian Basin at all appetizing in terms of democratic governance and respect for human rights; indeed, most of their records are no better or even worse than that of Russia.[11]

The idea of another "Great Game" over the region, much bandied about, is dubious. A great game, after all, suggests that there are great interests at stake. For the United States, at least, this is simply not the case. Today, the Caspian Basin would appear to have little claim on the attention, much less affection, of high-level American policy-makers – except, of course, for the region's gas and, especially, oil reserves. The former, it must be noted, is important to regional development. But it is Caspian oil and its potential impact on international markets that have greater impact on the United States.

But even here it is important to get beyond hype. The hydrocarbon potential of the Caspian Basin is significant; but it should not be exaggerated. Loose talk of a second Persian Gulf in terms of oil, for instance, is woefully off the mark. Estimates of proven reserves now run 15–32 billion barrels for the countries of the Caspian Basin, excluding what may be a sizable recent find at the offshore Kashagan field. This pales next to the figure of 260 billion barrels for Saudi Arabia. For the sake of comparison, Russia, the United States, and the North Sea have estimated proven reserves of 47, 29, and 16, billion barrels. In gas, the picture is similar. The Caspian Basin holds roughly 242–372 trillion cubic feet in proven reserves, a fraction of the 1700 and 800 trillion cubic feet estimated for Russia and Iran, respectively.[12]

Two other factors should be recalled in assessing the importance of hydrocarbon reserves in the Caspian Basin. One is their uneven distribution. The lion's share in oil belongs, at 10–22 billion barrels to Kazakhstan, with Azerbaijan, at 4–7 billion barrels, taking up most of the rest. Kazakhstan's share will only increase as firmer figures on the Kashagan field emerge. The distribution of natural gas is less skewed, with Turkmenistan, Uzbekistan, Kazakhstan, and Azerbaijan all possessing significant fields. But the fact remains that a number of countries in the region – Armenia, Georgia, Tajikistan, and Kyrgyzstan – possess no significant hydrocarbons and that only two – Kazakhstan and, to a much lesser extent, Azerbaijan – have important potential in the market that matters most to the United States, oil.

A second important factor to remember is that proven oil reserves, however sizable, do not necessarily mean significant production, at least in the short to medium term. It is critical not to underestimate the geographic and technical difficulties, quite independent of political obstacles, that will be involved with bringing large amounts of new Caspian Basin oil to international markets.[13] Some estimates put regional oil production at perhaps 2.5–3.5 million barrels per day by 2010. This would represent perhaps 2.5–3.5 percent of global demand – a significant but hardly decisive factor in world oil markets.[14]

This sober reality has several implications for American foreign policy. As a major oil consumer the United States has a real interest in seeing Central Asian petroleum enter international markets. But, given the amount involved, that interest is not overriding. Nor is it exclusive. Increased or new production elsewhere – central Africa, Russia, or Mexico to name just a few areas – would serve American interests just as well. Moreover, the centrality of the Persian Gulf, projected to retain 30 percent or more of global oil production, will remain an undeniable fact of economic and military life for Washington. This means that the United States cannot look to increased production of Caspian Basin oil as a way to diminish its costly security presence in the Gulf. Any American security commitments to the Caspian Basin region to facilitate bringing its oil to international markets will have to be in addition to, and not instead of, such commitments in the Gulf.

Even after discounting much of the exaggeration associated with energy in the Caspian Basin, however, the fact remains that development of the region's potential is a worthy goal of US foreign policy. It will create significant commercial opportunities for American firms. Moreover, the flow of the region's petroleum to world markets will tend over time to depress the price of oil or restrain increases in it, a clear advantage to a petroleum-importing country like the United States. Third, and most importantly, bringing the Caspian Basin "on line" will diversify world oil supply and, on the margin, lessen the dependence of global oil markets on exports from the volatile Persian Gulf. It is worth noting that the United States can achieve the last two objectives – downward pressure on prices and diversification in world supply – without American firms being directly involved in the exploitation of energy resources in the Caspian Basin.

Washington's interest in diversification has very specific consequences. Given the potential for instability in the region, it strongly argues for multiple pipelines; and this, indeed, was the stated policy objective of the Clinton administration. Multiple pipelines minimize the possibility of disruption of supply by accident, terrorism, unrest, or action by transit countries. All question of their geopolitical ambitions in the region aside, both Russia and Iran are energy competitors of the countries of the Caspian Basin. All things being equal, a major transit route that avoids both would therefore also serve the US interest in supply diversity. Washington would also prefer an export pipeline that does not go through Iran. This preference, it must be stressed, is independent of Washington's troubled relations with Tehran. Even were those relations to improve rapidly – an unlikely scenario, despite very cautious preliminary steps in that direction – Iran would remain problematic as a transport route. Central Asian oil would still flow to or near the Persian Gulf, the location of two major wars in as many decades.

Unfortunately, cruel economic calculations come into play. Regional oil production may not be sufficient to warrant a multiplicity of export pipelines. As noted, the economics of the Baku–Ceyhan pipeline are highly problematic in themselves. And Iran, by simple geography, may be the most economic export route for a sizable portion of future Kazakhstani production, though US sanctions against Iran have been largely successful, at least to date, in foreclosing this option. US desires in the region, in short, are constrained by economics and, barring an unexpected decision by Washington to subsidize a pipeline project directly and substantially, those constraints will remain in force.[15]

The United States has, of course, other interests in the region. Some, such as Washington's concerns about the Caspian Basin's use in transit of illicit drugs or transfer of controlled technologies, constitute an important part of its bilateral agenda with the various countries in the region. So does the Caspian Basin's integration into the global economy. But all are the stuff of what could be called "normal" American diplomacy. And none today justifies a significantly expanded US role in the region. For that, we must turn to other US interests – real or imagined – in the Caspian Basin.

The Russian threat

One such interest, much bandied about when discussing the Caspian Basin, is strategic. It is a cliché of *Realpolitik* that power abhors a vacuum. The states of the Caspian Basin may represent no threat to the United States. But what of other countries that might seek influence, even hegemony, in the region?[16] At first glance there is no shortage of candidates.

Iran, Turkey, and China all border the countries of the Basin. But all, for a number of reasons, are unlikely to exert decisive regional influence in the short to medium term. It is important to recall that the weakness of individual countries – and those of the Caspian Basin are uniformly weak – does not alone make them candidates for imperial or even hegemonic domination; such domination also requires another state with the resources and will to impose dominance.[17] None of the Basin's neighbors to the south or east currently possesses this combination. For instance, Iran is undergoing an intense domestic conflict between fundamentalists and reformers. In any case, Tehran's appeal in the region is severely limited by the fact that the majority of the region's Muslims are Sunni, not Shia. The exception is Azerbaijan. However, Tehran, fearful of separatism among it own Azeri minority, has played a highly ambiguous game in Baku's conflict with Yerevan over the disputed province of Nagorno-Karabakh. Tehran's policy toward the region, though active, has been remarkably free from any ideological component and focused instead on economic interests and perceived threats to stability.[18] Ankara, itself economically troubled and politically divided along secular and Islamic lines, possesses neither the resources nor prestige to promote "Pan-Turkism" into anything approaching hegemony.[19] And Beijing, despite its much-touted pipeline agreement with Kazakhstan[20] has essentially defensive objectives in the region, above all a desire to limit agitation among its own Muslim minority.[21]

This leaves Russia, which by virtue of its proximity, size, and past domination of the region, is clearly a serious contender for hegemony in the future. At present, Russia is constrained in its ability to exert influence in the region. And Moscow's attitudes toward the Caspian Basin are far more complex and, indeed, contradictory than often assumed. Even the relationship between the Russian government and the country's two major energy firms is both highly ambiguous and constantly evolving. The assumption, still prevalent in certain American foreign policy circles, that there exists a coordinated Russian grand strategy toward the Caspian Basin is over-simplified at best. This is certainly true when it comes to the development of energy resources in the Caspian Basin. There, two major Russian companies – Gazprom and Lukoil – now have major financial stakes in the region, making them less likely to act as simple agents of the Russian government.

Still, there are plainly powerful elements in Russia, both within and outside the government, who would like to see Russia resume its traditional dominant role in the region. This is especially true in relation to the Caucasus, where instability poses a genuine threat on Moscow's ethnically diverse southern flank and where proximity makes Russian military power, though a mere shadow of that possessed by the Soviet Union, easier to project.

President Vladimir Putin has clearly put relations with the countries of the Caspian Basin at the very top of his foreign policy agenda. After assuming office, he moved quickly to name a special presidential representative for Caspian affairs, to commission a strategic study of Russian policy in the region, and to facilitate a consortia of the major Russian energy companies – Lukoil, Gazprom, and Yukos – to develop Caspian Sea resources.[22] His is likely to be a firmer hand than that of former President Yeltsin, under whom foreign policy, like its domestic equivalent, was often not just confused, but chaotic. Putin, moreover, is likely to find a positive response to his overtures in several countries in the region. The rise of a fundamentalist Islamic regime in Afghanistan – the Taliban – has sent shock-waves throughout the region; the Takshent bombings of 1999 and the incursions from Tajikistan and Afghanistan into Kyrgyzstan and Uzbekistan in 2000 are viewed by many there as an ill omen of things to come. For all their distrust of Moscow, regimes in Uzbekistan, Tajikistan, and elsewhere see Russia as able and willing to support them against a perceived Islamic threat. Ironically, Moscow's ruthlessness – some would say savagery – in putting down the rebellion in Chechnya is seen as evidence of Russia's commitment to the anti-Islamic cause. In addition, there may be a growing disenchantment with Washington's policy towards the region, especially its inability to deliver on the Baku–Ceyhan pipeline. It should be noted that not all countries in the region welcome a more assertive Russian role in the region; Georgia, for one, has found itself the subject of increased Russian pressure since Putin came to power.[23]

Whatever the outcome of Putin's initiatives in the Caspian Basin, Moscow will continue to exert influence in the region. In fact, as Russia recovers militarily and economically, that influence is likely to increase. But the precise form of Moscow's influence – its extent, intensity, and intrusiveness – remains an open question. The answer to it will be shaped in part by events within the Caspian Basin itself and by the actions of other powers, including the United States, within the region. But it will essentially be determined in Russia. This is not the place to enter into a discussion of the determinants of Russian foreign policy; the subject has become an intellectual cottage industry in its own right.[24] But it is clear that the final word on Russia's attitude on the so-called "Near Abroad" has yet to be spoken. Still reeling from its sudden fall from imperial center and superpower, Moscow has yet to find its place in the world economic and geopolitical systems.[25]

Recommendations that the United States forcefully counter Russia in the Caspian Basin now, while Moscow is weak – possibly by making Uzbekistan Washington's *de facto* regional surrogate[26] – may only increase the likelihood of a Russian effort to re-exert more direct control over the region. The argument that a firm anti-Russian stand in the Caspian Basin will undermine, rather than embolden, neo-imperialists in Moscow only makes sense if the United States is willing to commit the resources and offer the guarantees necessary to back up its position.[27]

The idea of US security guarantees for the states of the Caspian Basin – ones backed up by the plausible threat of force – is at this time simply laughable. Even supporters of an anti-Russian policy in the region balk at the idea. The United States may be the world's sole superpower. But both its material resources and political will remain finite – only Washington's rhetoric, it seems, is sometimes boundless. Absent real resources and guarantees, for instance, talk of "containing Russia" in the Basin can only be counterproductive. This is especially true were the United States to move forward with expanding NATO to include the Baltic States or with abrogating the Anti-Ballistic Missile Treaty. Combined with a more assertive American stance in the Caspian Basin, such an effort would play into the hands of those in Moscow calling for an aggressive re-imposition of Russian hegemony in the Basin. At this point, a direct Russian takeover of the region is remote; a use of the region by Moscow to threaten American interests elsewhere – for instance in Turkey or the Persian Gulf – is more remote still. There may or may not be a Russian future "threat" to the region and American interests there or elsewhere. But a premature American effort to exclude Russia from influence in the Caspian Basin is likely both to increase the likelihood of such a threat and to intensify its severity should it appear.

In any case, most of the regimes in the region appear to understand the real limits to US engagement in the Caspian Basin. When it comes to their troubled relations with Moscow, the willingness of Washington to intercede is modest; the likelihood of a direct US military intervention to protect their independence approaches zero. Calls in Georgia and Azerbaijan for their countries to join NATO are either ill informed or cynical; given the long queue of would-be NATO members in line before them, their membership lies far in the future. Membership, moreover, assumes that other NATO countries would be willing to take on major security responsibilities in a highly unstable region, a proposition that is highly unlikely in the short to medium term.[28]

The Islamic threat

In all but two countries of the region – Armenia and Georgia – Muslims are a majority of the population. This has prompted predictable – and predictably alarmist – talk about an Islamic threat in the region. In the early 1990s, this talk centered on Iran's possible role in fomenting radical fundamentalism; in recent years it has focused on the role of the Taliban regime in Afghanistan.[29] It is true that Islam, after decades of suppression under Communist rule, is undergoing revival throughout the Caspian Basin. But talk of Islamic fundamentalism sweeping the region is dangerously exaggerated. The Muslims of the region are anything but monolithic; they are, in fact, a body of striking diversity.

Islam in the Caspian Basin is divided along religious, ethnic, and linguistic lines.[30] And all countries boast strong secular elements, particularly among governmental elites.[31] The unique experience of the Muslim peoples of the Basin under 70 years of Communist control makes drawing close parallels between fundamentalist movements there and areas outside the former Soviet Union highly problematic.[32] The sizable majority of Muslims in the region are moderate in their religious beliefs and unlikely to be attracted to radically politicized Islam, though there are enclaves – parts of Tajikistan and Uzbekistan's Fergana Valley – where fundamentalism has already demonstrated real strength.[33]

That said, there is, in fact, a real threat of a broader fundamentalist movement in the medium to long term. It arises from the corrupt and authoritarian nature of most of the regimes in the region. In time, radical Islam could become a form of alternate personal allegiance and a vehicle for political opposition, as it did in pre-Revolutionary Iran and does today in Egypt. This appears already to be the case in Uzbekistan, where the Karimov regime's harsh suppression of moderate Islamic opposition groups appears to have radicalized them.[34] Notwithstanding the incursions that so alarmed the region in 2000, the chief threat of radicalization is not external but internal, though the regimes affected will no doubt claim otherwise as they seek assistance from Moscow or Washington.

Ironically, those who call for closer American ties to the regimes of the Caspian Basin – whether to ensure stability, contain Russian influence, or both – may actually be encouraging the rise of radical Islamic fundamentalism. At present, there is little anti-Western sentiment in the region. Too intimate an American relationship with secular but authoritarian local regimes could feed it. Nearly two decades later, some in the American foreign policy establishment still seem unable to draw the obvious lessons of the Iranian Revolution. In the Persian Gulf, at least, one might argue that US vital interests justified the choice of regional strongman, whatever the risks the United States ran should he fall from power. But in the Caspian Basin, we have no such vital interests – and no need to pick a favorite from among the potential Shahs of the region.

Stability and sovereignty

Finally, what of two other supposed American interests in Caspian Basin – stability and independence? Both would appear, on first glance, to be unexceptionable. Who after all, is against stability and independence? But both, on inspection, are slippery concepts and dubious guides to American action.

Given its current unchallenged pre-eminence, the United States is an essentially conservative power. The reason is simple: Washington has more to lose than gain by a change in the international *status quo*. As such, Washington's preference – all other things being equal – is for stability. (Needless to say, other things sometimes are not equal and the United States has been quite prepared to foster instability, in Afghanistan in the 1980s and in Iraq in the 1990s, when greater interests are perceived to be at stake.) This general conservatism explains in part the first Bush administration's hesitant approach to the break-up of the Soviet Union. Even there, however, stability was essentially a derivative goal, related to other American interests involved – notably a concern that progress on arms agreements be consolidated and that unified command over the Soviet nuclear arsenal maintained. Stability, therefore, is important less in itself than for the other interests it either protects or promotes. This is as true of the Caspian Basin as it is elsewhere. American interest in central African stability, to choose one example from many, has been slight to non-existent. In Tajikistan, for instance, those interests are similarly modest and Washington's response to date has been unsurprisingly minimal. The Armenian–Azerbaijani dispute is qualitatively different. There, potential for conflict between Turkey, a NATO ally, and Russia, Washington's partner in a dialogue on arms control and other critical issues, does raise US interests in a peaceful resolution to a higher plane. Despite Congress's title towards Armenia, the United States has been able to play a useful role in mediating the conflict through its membership in the Minsk Group.

The US interest in stability in the Caspian Basin, therefore, is case-specific, not general. And it nowhere rises to Washington's critical stakes in stability in North America, Western Europe, or East Asia. Talk of America's "vital interests" in the region raises an interesting question.[35] If American interests there are vital, what does that make Washington's interests in, say, Japan, Germany, or Mexico? Super-vital?

The United States should, as a matter of course, encourage where possible the peaceful resolution of disputes and foster regional security arrangements that minimize the risk of conflict. However, absent direct involvement of other American interests, Washington should limit its role to low-cost, low-risk support of international initiatives by organizations such as the Organization for Security and Cooperation in

Europe. To suggest anything more is to raise patently false expectations. Washington's extreme reluctance under both the first Bush and Clinton administrations to intervene in Bosnia, only a few hundred miles from the heart of Europe, illustrates the narrow limits of the US commitment to stability even when other, arguably important interests are involved; many of President George W. Bush's advisors opposed even Washington's late and limited role in the Balkans. Cooperation under the general rubric of the Partnership for Peace should continue to be severely limited, lest it send a wrong signal to both Moscow and the capitals of the region.[36]

Like stability, support for sovereignty has often been cited as an American interest in the region. It has clearly served as the rhetorical centerpiece of Washington's policy towards the Caspian Basin. This has made sense in both specific and general terms. There was much fear at the time of independence that Moscow might reassert its formal claim to the states of the Caspian Basin or that the region itself might fall into chaos. And, as a general principle, the United States does support national sovereignty.

But "sovereignty" is a very elastic concept, indeed. Lebanon is sovereign but a client state of Syria; dozens of countries around the world, most recently in East Asia, have found themselves under the strict tutelage of the IMF; Mexico is sovereign but profoundly dependent on Washington's whims in such areas as immigration and trade. Indeed, since its inception in the Westphalian Treaty in 1648, the ideal of national sovereignty as been breached as much as it has been observed.[37]

Given the reality, however unfortunate, of their relative weakness, the states of the Caspian Basin can expect to see their sovereignty constrained. Moreover, they will see it limited in different ways, depending on their size, wealth, demographic composition and proximity to Russia.[38] Uzbekistan, for instance, will clearly enjoy a far greater freedom of action than Kazakhstan with its long border with Russia and large Russian minority population. Again, the questions are the form and extent of autonomy and independence. There is clearly a great difference, for the region as a whole and for individual countries, whether Russian influence takes the form of Syria's over Lebanon or the United States' over Mexico.

To the extent that Washington seeks diversity of supply to world oil markets, it would clearly prefer that Azerbaijan and Kazakhstan enjoy energy policies free from Russian control, if not influence. One thing, however, is clear: making an idealized form of sovereignty the heart of

American policy towards the region is both intellectually untenable and – insofar as it might foster unrealizable hopes – potentially dangerous.

The second Bush administration

Some believe that the administration of George W. Bush may assume a more aggressive posture towards the Caspian Basin region and, in specific, exert a firmer hand with perceived Russian meddling there. There is plausibility to this view. After all, the President, Vice President Dick Cheney, and Secretary of Commerce Don Evans are all men with extensive experience in the energy industry. American companies eager to realize profits from their investments in the region's hydrocarbons will certainly find senior members of the administration both informed about the issues and sympathetic to their desires. Moreover, the Bush administration is perceived, here and abroad, to be less inclined to accommodate Russia than its predecessor. To be sure, Congressional Republicans were harshly critical of what they believed to be the soft line taken towards Russia by President Clinton and his advisors, a tone taken over, somewhat muted, by candidate Bush himself. And President Bush includes among his senior advisors a number of individuals – his Vice President, Secretaries Donald Rumsfeld and Colin Powell, their deputies Paul Wolfowitz and Richard Armitage, as well as National Security Advisor Condoleezza Rice – who all cut their foreign policy teeth during the anti-Soviet years of the Cold War. Not least, by his support for the rapid development of national missile defense, President Bush has signaled a willingness to confront Moscow if it is in what he perceives to be the American national interest. The first months of the Bush administration – marked by diplomatic expulsions and public scolding of Moscow on proliferation issues – certainly suggest that it will indeed take a tougher line towards Moscow.

But it is important not to overdraw the case. The actual statements of candidate Bush and his advisors prior to the election were actually quite circumspect when it came to Russia.[39] And, as new administrations always discover, it is far easier to criticize a policy while out of office than to administer it while in power. Within weeks of assuming office, for instance, National Security Advisor Rice was quoted as saying, "The people who think a weak Russia is a good thing for the United States are wrong. A weak Russia will only be a problem for the international community."[40] This is the kind of reassuring statement that either of her predecessors under the Clinton administration could have made and often did. Moreover, the very high importance the new administration attaches to national missile defense means that it may be loath to add yet another bone of contention – an expanded American role in the Caspian Basin – to an already lengthy and difficult Russo–American bilateral agenda. Not least, candidate Bush's call for a "humble" foreign policy that does not overextend American resources is hard to reconcile with a dramatically heightened involvement in a remote region tangential to the traditional American interests that Bush advisors consistently stress. As noted earlier, the Bush administration has retained the policy centerpiece of the Clinton's administration's energy policy in the Caspian Basin: support for the Baku–Ceyhan pipeline.

In short, American policy towards the Caspian Basin may not change as much under a Bush administration as many in the region, Moscow, or indeed Washington may think.

Conclusion

Much of this chapter has been an attempt to bring perspective to US interests in the Caspian Basin – to get beyond the hype that has clouded much of the American debate about it. Such hype is perhaps understandable. American energy companies have huge sums at potential stake in the region. Foreign policy experts are keen to put their personal stamp on US strategy in a region largely unencumbered by past policies or current commitments.[41] And many regional specialists, in government and academia, feel a deep personal attachment to the long-suffering peoples of the Caspian Basin. Money, influence, passion: the combination is not one likely to lead either to sobriety of analysis or modesty of ambition.

Two points should be made clear: to speak of limited American interests in the Caspian Basin is not to suggest that they are non-existent. And to stress the constraints circumscribing US freedom of action in the region is not to argue that the United States need take an entirely passive approach. But Washington should, nonetheless, exercise great caution as it reassesses American policy towards the region – and particularly as it contemplates a shift towards an explicitly or even implicitly anti-Russian policy in the Caspian Basin.

Some critics have argued that the United States has unduly neglected the Caspian Basin because of Washington's fixations elsewhere –

notably Russia and the Persian Gulf. This may have some truth to it. Washington clearly cannot view the Caspian Basin exclusively through the prism of US policies toward Russia and the Persian Gulf. At a minimum, our interest in an additional independent supply of oil to world markets argues otherwise. But the United States will – and should – continue to view its policies in the region largely through those prisms.

For instance, US interests in the Caspian Basin pale in comparison to Washington's vital interest in working towards a continued orderly reduction of Moscow's nuclear arsenal. That arsenal, though much reduced by arms control agreements and general disrepair, remains capable of effectively destroying the United States. Washington's interests in the Caspian Basin are also modest compared to its interests in the Persian Gulf, where just a decade ago the United States fought a major war to maintain our dominant position in the region. With or without oil from the Caspian Basin, the Persian Gulf will remain by far the most important supplier of petroleum to world markets.

This is not to argue that Washington confronts an either/or decision – a choice, say, between cooperation with Moscow and an American role in the Caspian Basin. Rather, it suggests that United States should continue to put Moscow's relationship with the region on its broader bilateral agenda. Washington's object should not be to exclude Russia from the region, but to shape its role there in ways that advance America's own interests, most notably in an independent supply of oil to world markets. And the United States should never forget that its policies outside the Caspian Basin – especially any attempt further to expand NATO or abrogate the ABM Treaty – will directly affect Washington's ability to shape Moscow's behavior in the region.

The same complexity will hold true for Washington's dealings with Tehran – even if a thaw occurs in US–Iranian relations. The idea that the differences between the United States and Iran are the result of bitterness and misunderstanding alone is misguided. All question of the Islamic revolution aside, Iran is a large, populous, and potentially rich country with a strongly nationalist population and clear regional ambitions. American domination of the Persian Gulf – dramatically illustrated by Washington's defeat of Saddam's bid for regional hegemony – will clearly cause strains between Washington and Tehran. There is much to be said for a dialogue between the United States and Iran. But even the resumption of full diplomatic relations will leave, as with Moscow, a long, complex, and contentious bilateral agenda of which the Caspian Basin will be only part.

As the United States approaches its policy toward the region it should above all avoid the easy assumptions that implicitly color much of the debate about the Caspian Basin.

The first is that the regimes of the region are plucky little democracies struggling to free themselves from Moscow's cruel yoke. They are, almost without exception, autocratic, corrupt, or both. Like our interests, American values are only tangentially served by supporting the regimes of the Caspian Basin. The second assumption is that their problems are largely external in origin. External problems do exist: countries of the region are rightly worried about the possible destabilizing role that can be played by the Taliban regime in Kabul. And Georgia, for one, has genuine cause for complaint at Moscow's meddling and bullying. But the fundamental problems of the region – poverty, authoritarian regimes, unreformed economies, and ethnic divisions – are not the creation of external actors. The third assumption is that the flow of oil revenues to the region is a panacea for every economic, strategic, and political ill in the Caspian Basin. Oil may improve the welfare of the region's populations – but only if revenues are not siphoned off by corrupt elites or channeled into unproductive, if impressive, pet projects. It may enhance stability – but only if revenues are not used to fuel a regional arms race. And oil revenues might actually, in the short to medium term, diminish the prospects for more open political systems by providing authoritarian regimes with the external recognition and internal resources necessary to maintain power. Certainly, there appears to be little relationship, worldwide, between possession of major oil reserves and the protection of human rights.

Washington should avoid too close an association with the regimes in the Caspian Basin. The United States does not require a surrogate in the region; nor could it control such a surrogate if it had one. Washington should be particularly chary of anything beyond the current small-scale bilateral military exchange and training programs and an occasional joint exercise under NATO's Partnership for Peace Program. The idea of an expanded American role in providing the states of the Basin with the means necessary to protect their borders is particularly problematic; one state's defensive weaponry is, notoriously, its neighbor's offensive threat. And, as always, Washington should be wary of intelligence cooperation that may give the appearance of American support for indigenous secret police.

Any *de facto* alliance would in any case lock the United States into a relationship in a region whose independence is still in its infancy and whose future course remains breathtakingly open. Washington would be wise to remember how new the states of the Caspian Basin really are. They have hardly begun the process of building enduring post-Communist institutions; they are still forging their post-colonial national identities.[42] Washington's relative lack of interests in the region is, in the final analysis, a great advantage: it enjoys the luxury of influence without entangling commitment.

Acknowledgement

A number of individuals provided invaluable assistance in the preparation of this paper. Amy Meyers Jaffe was chief among them. Any errors, however, remain the author's alone.

Notes

1. "Caspian Basin" is admittedly imprecise. A number of countries under discussion, after all, do not border the Caspian Sea. But I will use the term instead of "Central Asia and the Caucasus" for brevity and because it suggests the centrality of oil and (to a much lesser degree) gas to American interests in the region. The states of the Caspian Basin are the former Soviet Republics of Armenia, Georgia, Azerbaijan, Turkmenistan, Kazakhstan, Kyrgyzstan, Uzbekistan, and Tajikistan.
2. See Ian Bremmer's "Oil Politics: America and the Riches of the Caspian Basin", *World Policy Journal*, Spring 1998 for a good summary of US policy towards the region since 1991; less analytic, but fact-filled, is Jim Nichol's *Central Asia's New States: Political Developments and Implications for US* Interests (Washington, DC: Congressional Research Service, IB93108, 2000).
3. See Strobe Talbott's "A Farewell to Flashman: American Policy in the Caucasus and Central Asia," an address delivered at the School for Advanced International Studies at Johns Hopkins on July 21, 1997. Ironically, Talbott was very much the *bête noire* of those who seek a more assertive US role in the Caspian Basin.
4. See "Energy Policy: Report of the National Energy Policy Group" – the so-called "Cheney Report." The reference to Baku–Ceyhan may be found in Chapter 8 of the report (Washington, DC: The Government Printing Office, May 2001).
5. By 2000, there was some evidence that academic and media interest in the region may have peaked. There were a number of pieces that argued that the importance of the Caspian Basin had been exaggerated. An earlier version of this essay, published by the Baker Institute for Public Policy in 1998, is only one example. Also see Anatol Lieven's "The (Not So) Great Game," in *The National Interest*, Winter 1999/2000; and Robert Ebel and Rajan Menon's (eds) introduction to *Energy and Conflict in Central Asia and the Caucasus*, (New York: Rowman and Littlefield, 2000), pp. 1–20. Michael Lelyveld in "Caspian Gridlock: Failures of Policy and the Press" argues that there was also a sharp decline in American press interest in the region. His

piece may be found in Belfer Center for Science and International Affairs, *Succession and Long-term Stability in the Caspian Region* (Cambridge, MA: BCSIA, 2000).

6. See Chapter 5.
7. Consortium members, led by BP, say that construction could begin as early as 2002, with completion in 2005–6. See "Chevron Talks to Azerbaijanis about Pipeline," *The New York Times*, February 10, 2001. In private conversation, other industry experts remain unconvinced that the project is economically viable or, at a minimum, that it will be built in the timeframe suggested. The author is among the skeptics: see Joe Barnes and Ronald Soligo's "Baku-Ceyhan Pipeline: Bad Economics, Bad Politics, Bad Idea" in the October 26, 1998 edition of *Oil and Gas Journal*.
8. The foreign policy literature on the general threats posed by Russia, Iran, and China is voluminous. Anatol Lieven provides a useful taxonomy of post-Cold War views on Russia in "Against Russophobia," *World Policy Journal*, Winter 2000/1. Ray Takeyh's "Pragmatic Theocracy" provides a relatively recent and highly representative example of the view that Iran, reform or not, is an abiding strategic opponent of the United States. It may be found in *The National Interest*, Spring 2000. The same issue, interestingly, contains an article by Daniel Pipes, "Islam and Islamism: Faith and Ideology," that paints an alarming picture of the threat posed to the West by politicized Islam. Perhaps the most noteworthy product of the "China Threat School" is Richard Bernstein and Ross Monro's "The Coming Conflict with China," in *Foreign Affairs*, March/April 1997. The title says it all. Samuel Huntington, whose essay and later book "The Clash of Civilizations" is perhaps the most influential general assessments of post-Cold War foreign policy, would presumably argue that Russia, Iran, and China are all threats. Each, after all, represents major non-Western cultural blocs: the Slavic-Orthodox (Russia), the Islamic (Iran) and the Confucian (China). Huntington's thesis first appeared in *Foreign Affairs*, Fall 1993.
9. To be sure, American aid to the Caspian Basin during the 1990s was not trivial. Between 1992 and 1997, Washington funneled roughly $1.65 billion in civilian assistance to the region under the auspices of the Freedom Support Act, chief US conduit for aid to the successor states of the Soviet Union. This compares with $2.26 and 1.21 billion for Russia and the Ukraine, respectively, under the Act during the same period. The assistance is less impressive than at first glance, however. The aid was unevenly distributed. $530 million, or roughly a third of it, went to one country, Armenia, largely reflecting the influence of the Armenian–American constituency with the US Congress. Kazakhstan and Georgia followed with $312 and 236 million, respectively. Moreover, we are speaking of a seven-year period, making average annual American civilian assistance to the countries of the Caspian Basin, though welcome to its recipients, modest in comparison to American commitment to Israel, Egypt or, for that matter, Russia. Direct military assistance to the region during the same period was smaller, at $141 million, almost all of it going to Kazakhstan under the Nunn-Lugar program for dismantlement and safe storage of nuclear materials. Assistance from the US Department of Energy is even smaller and similarly skewed towards Kazakhstan. Direct US military cooperation was largely

limited to small exchange and training programs. Indirect funding of cooperation through NATO's Partnership for Peace Program was also modest. This analysis is drawn from *US Government Assistance to and Cooperative Activities with the New Independent States of the Former Soviet Union*

10. Data available in the CIA's *World Fact Book 2000* (Washington, DC: CIA , 2000).
11. See Freedom House's *Country Ratings for 1999–2000* (Washington, DC: Freedom House, 2000).
12. See Chapter 1.
13. See Chapter 5.
14. See the US Department of Energy's *International Energy Outlook 2000* for predictions of global oil production (Washington, DC: DOE, 2000).
15. See Laurent Ruseckas' "US Policy and Caspian Politics: The Two Faces of Baku-Ceyhan" for a scathing attack on the Clinton administration's support of the pipeline project. It may be found in *Succession and Long-Term Stability in the Caspian Region*, (n.5).
16. The term "hegemony" is admittedly slippery. Michael Doyle makes a useful point when he suggests that it is a substantial degree of control over the external as opposed to the internal affairs of the subject state; the imperial relationship includes both. See his *Empires* (Ithaca, NY: Cornell University Press, 1986), pp. 129–30.
17. See Doyle, Empires, pp. 123–138.
18. See "Islam, Iran and Prospects for Stability in the Caspian Region," by Brenda Shaffer in *Succession and Long-Term Stability in the Caspian Region*, (n.5).
19. See "Turkey's Caspian Interests: Economic and Security Opportunities" by Sabri Sayari in Ebel and Menon, (n.5), pp. 225–47, for a balanced look and the strengths and weaknesses that Turkey brings to its Caspian policy.
20. With an estimated price tag of up to $10 billion, the pipeline is unlikely to be built soon. It should be viewed as a diplomatic symbol of Beijing's interest in the region, rather than a practical short- to medium-term possibility.
21. See Evan A. Feigenbaum's "China's Strategy of Weakness", *The Far Eastern Economic Review*, March 1, 2001.
22. See Carol R. Saivetz's *Putin's Caspian Policy* (Cambridge, MA: BSCIA, 2000).
23. See "Georgia Wriggles in Russian Orbit", *The Christian Science Monitor*, February 13, 2001.
24. See Peter Rutland's "Paradigms for Russian Policy in the Caspian Basin," in Ebel and Menon, (n.5), pp. 163–88, for an overview of theoretical approaches to Moscow's policy in the region.
25. See Zbigniew Brzezinki's "Living with Russia" and a response to it, Stephen Sestanovich's "Where Does Russia Belong?" in *The National Interest*, Fall 2000 and Winter 2000/1, respectively, for a lively discussion of the many imponderables shaping Russia's future geopolitical role.
26. See S. Frederick Starr's "Making Eurasia Stable", Foreign Affairs, January/February 1996.
27. For instance, William E. Odoms's "US Policy Towards Central Asia and the South Caucasus", pp. Caspian Crossroads, Vol. 3, No. 1, 1997, 2–5, calls for a more assertive US role in the region without mention of any additional resources required to undertake one.

28. See Richard Sokolsky and Tanya Charlick-Paley's *NATO and Caspian Security: A Mission Too Far* (Santa Monica, CA: RAND, 1999).
29. In a reminder – and a much needed one – that neither Islam in general nor even "fundamentalist" Islam is monolithic, countries in the region are finding Tehran a willing partner in containing the perceived Taliban menace.
30. Shirin Akiner's *Islamic Peoples of Central Asia*, though out of date, remains an immensely useful source on the extraordinary complex picture presented by the Muslims of the Caspian Basin (London: Kegan Paul International, 1983).
31. See Chapter 4.
32. See Yaacov Roi's *Islam in the Soviet Union* (London: Hurst, 2000).
33. See Roi, (n.32) p. 729.
34. See Anatol Lieven (1999/2000), (n.5).
35. See Senator Sam Brownback (R-Kansas), "US Economic and Strategic Interests in the Caspian Sea Region", *Caspian Crossroads*, Vol. 3, No. 2. The Senator refers to the "vital political, economic and social importance" of the region for the United States.
36. See Robin Bhatty and Rachel Bronson's "NATO's Mixed Signals in the Caucasus and Central Asia", *Survival*, Autumn 2000.
37. See Steven D. Krasner's *Sovereignty: Organized Hypocrisy* (Princeton, NJ: Princeton University Press, 1999).
38. Martha Brill Olcott, "Facing the Future: Twelve Myths about Central Asia," a paper presented at the Central Asian Conference on Regional Cooperation, Bishkek, Kyrgyzstan, 1995.
39. See, for instance, "Promoting the National Interest" by now-National Security Advisor Condoleezza Rice in *Foreign Affairs*, January/February 2000. Nonetheless, one passage in her article, though carefully hedged, no doubt raised hackles among those in Moscow determined to play a greater role in the Caspian Basin: "The war (in Chechnya) is a reminder of the vulnerability of the small, new states around Russia and of America's interest in their independence. If they can become stronger, they will be less tempting to Russia. Much depends on the ability of these states to reform their economies and political systems – a process, to date, whose success is mixed at best."
40. "Don't Let Them Spook You," by Robert G. Kaiser, *The Washington Post*, February 25, 2001.
41. Both Ebel and Lieven (1999/2000) mention personal ambition as one of the forces behind the surprisingly high salience achieved by Caspian policy under the Clinton administration. Certainly, the emergence of the independent states of the Caspian Basin in the wake of Soviet collapse represented a unique and exhilarating opportunity for regional experts to create a whole new realm of US foreign policy from the ground up and to advance their careers while they did so.
42. See Chapter 2.

10

Turkish National Interests

Gareth M. Winrow

Introduction

With the break-up of the Soviet Union, Turkish officials were eager to develop close ties with the newly independent Turkic states. Encouraged by a US administration suspicious of Iranian ambitions, there were those in Ankara who hoped that Turkey could lead some form of Turkic Commonwealth. But the Turkic states, reluctant to be led by a new Turkish Big Brother, and soon aware of Turkey's economic shortcomings and political difficulties, sought also to cultivate relations with other states. In Turkey, with the right-wing Nationalist Action Party (MHP) in the coalition government, which took office in 1999, a warm sentiment toward the Turkic states lingers. However, most Turkish officials and businessmen have come to pursue more pragmatic policies. Closer ties with non-Turkic states of the former Soviet Union have been fostered, including with Russia, Turkey's traditional rival.

Ethnic conflicts in an increasingly volatile Caucasus neighbouring Turkey have also forced policy-makers in Ankara to focus on immediate security concerns. It was feared that Russia could exploit tensions in Chechnya, Abkhazia, South Ossetia, and Nagorno-Karabakh, for instance, to reassert more influence if not dominance in the area – although by spring 2001 Moscow appeared more willing to help finalize a peace settlement over Nagorno-Karabakh. Seeking to assuage Russian anxieties over Turkish interests in the Caspian region, while also aiming to check Moscow's ambitions there, Turkey has proposed initiatives to enhance regional security, which would include Russia. After successfully sponsoring the organization, Black Sea Economic Cooperation (BSEC), Turkey has lobbied for a Black Sea Cooperation

Naval Task Group (BLACKSEAFOR) – officially launched in April 2001 – and for a so-called Caucasus Stability Pact.

In spite of these initiatives, continuing suspicions of Moscow's intentions have heightened the already deep-rooted concerns of the Turkish military and the Turkish Ministry of Foreign Affairs (MFA) with regard to Russian – and previously Soviet – geopolitical aims. As of spring 2001, Russian armed units were in Chechnya, and remained based in Armenia and Georgia. Russian troops also patrolled the Armenian–Turkish frontier. Many in Moscow suspected that Turkey provided covert support for Chechen guerrillas. The Russian military were uncomfortable with the large-scale modernization programme of the Turkish armed forces. Nevertheless, Turkey and Russia are major commercial partners in trade, investment, and in the energy sector. Turkey and Iran are also longstanding rivals in the Caspian region. Ideological differences, Ankara's concerns that Tehran is lending support to Kurdish rebel forces and to the extremist Islamic group Turkish Hezbullah, and an apprehension in Turkey over Iran's missile development programme, have created problems for Turco–Iranian relations. Again, though, Turkey and Iran are business partners too.

The Caspian region is also important for Turkey, because oil from Azerbaijan and Kazakhstan, and gas from Azerbaijan, Turkmenistan, Iran, and Russia can be imported to meet Turkey's expanding energy needs. Here, geopolitics and demands for energy are to some extent intertwined. Many Turkish officials are keen to ensure that not all pipelines are routed through Russia, as this could allow Moscow to exert further influence in the region. Russia – and Iran to a lesser extent – appears destined to become a key exporter of gas to Turkey. Turkey will import substantial amounts of Russian natural gas by means of the so-called Blue Stream project. But many in Ankara are eager also to tap other gas suppliers to avoid too much economic dependence, and thereby possibly political dependence, on Moscow. Turkey's geopolitical importance could be enhanced if substantial amounts of Caspian oil and gas are delivered to outside markets via pipelines crossing Turkey. Ankara has developed closer ties with Tbilisi largely because Georgia has become a notable energy transit state.

With regard to Turkey and Caspian energy, therefore, geopolitical factors as well as commercial, technical, environmental, and legal issues must be considered. This chapter will also examine the value of Caspian energy for the Turkish consumer, while acknowledging that Caspian energy reserves will probably be only of marginal significance for the global market. The Caspian region is important to Turkey on both geopolitical and economic grounds.

Turkish foreign policy-making and the Caspian region

It is not possible to separate completely foreign policy from domestic issues and economic matters. With regard to Turkey and the Caspian region, various official and non-official actors within Turkey influence policy-making. Some of these emphazise more either geopolitical concerns or energy needs. What Turkey's national interests are is thus often open to debate. Pipeline politics is a particularly contentious issue given that geopolitics and energy issues are involved. The jurisdictions of the MFA and the Energy Ministry inevitably overlap. Frequent changes of coalition governments in Turkey in the 1990s and replacement of key personnel may also have hindered the development of a more coherent policy, particularly with gas projects.

Concentrating on geopolitics, the Turkish military and the MFA have cultivated close ties with the Turkic states and Georgia. Diplomatic support for Azerbaijan over the disputed enclave of Nagorno-Karabakh, and tensions over whether the massacres of Armenians in 1915 by the Ottoman government constituted a "genocide", have prevented the MFA from normalizing relations with Armenia. Security issues – external and domestic – are discussed in the influential National Security Council (NSC), which is largely controlled by the Turkish armed forces. However, in NSC meetings the Turkish General Staff has not always prevailed. Immediately before the visit to Ankara of Russian Prime Minister Viktor Chernomyrdin in December 1997 to finalize the agreement to construct gas pipelines to connect Russia and Turkey via the Black Sea, this Blue Stream project was debated in the NSC. In spite of the military's fears that Turkey may become too dependent on Russia for gas imports, the project was given the go-ahead. Chernomyrdin had warned that failure to realize the project could result in Turkish companies no longer being awarded lucrative construction contracts in Russia (Baran, 2000, pp. 141–2). Caspian energy could feature on the agenda of future NSC sessions. Renewed concerns over Turkey's energy dependence on Russia, or apprehension for the safety of Istanbul should the number of tankers transiting the Bosporus substantially increase, could be discussed in the NSC.

The Energy Ministry and affiliated state agencies such as the Turkish Petroleum Corporation (TPAO) and the Turkish State Pipeline

Corporation (BOTAŞ) focus on energy. Handling exploration and production, TPAO has stakes in oil fields in Azerbaijan and Kazakhstan, including a 6.75 percent share in the Azeri, Chirag and Guneshli offshore fields in the Caspian. These Azerbaijani fields are managed by the Azerbaijan International Operating Company (AIOC), an international consortium led by BP. BOTAŞ has had a monopoly over the transportation, distribution and marketing of oil and gas in Turkey, but legislation to liberalize the Turkish gas market may be enacted in 2001. Although these bodies are primarily concerned with satisfying Turkey's energy needs, officials at BOTAŞ have repeatedly stressed that Turkey will not be dependent on Russia for more than 60 percent of its gas imports. Leading the government in office since 1999, Prime Minister Bülent Ecevit of the Democratic Left Party (DSP) has had to balance the interests of his coalition partners. The MHP is wary of Russia and sympathetic toward the Turkic states. The Motherland Party (ANAP), which has had control of the energy portfolio under Cumhur Ersümer – until Ersümer's forced resignation in April 2001 over allegations of corruption – is regarded in some quarters as being in league with the so-called "Russian lobby" in Turkey.

The Russian lobby evidently consists of large Turkish construction companies, such as GAMA, ENKA, and Tekfen, which have extensive investments in Russia. These companies are helping upgrade and build pipelines connecting Russia and Turkey to provide gas for power stations they are constructing in Turkey. It is worth noting that trade turnover between Turkey and Russia in 2000 totalled around $4.5 billion, compared to $1.8 billion for Turkey's trade with all of the Turkic states (*Turkish State Institute of Statistics*, 2001). The opposition Virtue Party (FP) in Turkey has complained that the powerful ANAP–Russian lobby alliance led to the Blue Stream project taking priority over the Trans-Caspian Gas Pipeline project, which intends to deliver Turkmen gas to Turkey. The FP leader, Recai Kutan, a former Energy Minister, has declared that Russia plans to purchase Turkmen gas and resell it to Turkey at a higher price by means of Blue Stream (Pamir, 2000, p. 37).

Less influential non-official actors include Caucasian ethnic lobbies. The Turkish parliament, often the target of these groups, does not have a decisive impact on foreign policy-making. Environmental protest groups have paraded on the Bosporus to demonstrate against increased tanker traffic. Supporting these actions Turkish officials have argued that the construction of a Baku–Ceyhan oil pipeline will relieve traffic congestion on the Straits. Ultranationalist Mafia groups in Turkey, linked with rogue elements in the Turkish intelligence services, have attempted to influence decision-making. These forces were alleged to be behind the failed attempt to overthrow Azerbaijani President Haydar Aliyev in March 1995 and replace him with his predecessor Ebulfez Elchibey, who had been more supportive of the Baku–Ceyhan project (*Turkish Probe*, 22 February 1998).

External actors also influence Turkish policy-making. US administrations have underlined Turkey's geopolitical importance. There is presumably a Turkish lobby in Russia, centred on Gazprom. Turkmen President Saparmurad Niyazov attempted to influence Turkish public opinion in October 1999 when he publicly upbraided visiting Energy Minister Ersümer and threatened to abandon the Trans-Caspian Gas Pipeline project because of Ersümer's support for Blue Stream (*Radikal*, 7 October 1999).

Turkey's energy needs

It is not possible to assess accurately Turkey's rising energy needs. Projections may only be based on certain assumptions, such as likely annual rates of economic growth. The economic crisis, which struck Turkey in spring 2001, when the Turkish lira devalued overnight by 30 percent, means that the Turkish economy will probably contract by 2 percent in 2001. In the longer term, the privatization of electricity and gas distribution networks in Turkey may generate growth. The FP deputy Veysel Candan has charged that official figures on Turkey's energy needs are inflated to suit the interests of the Russian lobby and ensure that the Blue Stream project is realized (*Turkish Daily News*, 27 November 1999). Investigations commencing early in 2001 into serious scandals in the Turkish energy industry give more credence to these allegations. Serious irregularities in the allocation of energy tenders resulted in the arrest of several prominent officials and culminated in the forced resignation of Energy Minister Ersümer. In the wake of these developments, the procedures by which a consortium was awarded the contract to build the land section in Turkey of the Blue Stream pipeline have come under close scrutiny (*Turkish Daily News*, 4 May 2001).

Oil consumption will become less important as Turkey uses cleaner forms of energy including gas. According to the Turkish Energy Ministry, in 2000 Turkey would have imported around 35 million tons of oil, mainly from Saudi Arabia. By 2010 Turkey intends to procure 49 million tons, of which 20 mt may come from the Caspian region and Russia.

According to Gökhan Yardim, the Managing Director of BOTAŞ in 2000 Turkey would have imported 15.5 billion cubic metres (bcm) of gas (*Turkish Daily News*, 20 September 2000). This amount would consist of 12 bcm of Russian natural gas delivered along a pipeline crossing south eastern Europe – the "Western route" – and smaller quantities of liquefied natural gas (LNG) from Algeria and Nigeria. The Energy Ministry has estimated that in 2010 Turkey will need to import 55 bcm. Officials from the US administration and the International Energy Agency believe Turkey would only need to import 30–40 bcm.

How will Turkey meet its gas import requirements? Agreements have been concluded with Russia for the delivery of 30 bcm/yr – 14 bcm/yr via the Western route and 16 bcm/yr via Blue Stream. Turkey is also contracted to import 10 bcm/yr from Iran, 16 bcm/yr from Turkmenistan, and 6.6 bcm/yr from Azerbaijan. Deals have been finalized to receive more expensive LNG – 4 bcm/yr from Algeria and 1.2 bcm/yr from Nigeria. According to a memorandum of understanding of 1997, Turkey may import 10 bcm/yr of Iraqi natural gas once UN sanctions are lifted. Problems in the Middle East, though, may compel Turkey to abandon hopes of receiving 4 bcm/yr of Egyptian natural gas. It appears that if most of these agreements were fully implemented, Turkey would have over-contracted. In practice, though, Turkey may not receive Turkmen gas because the Trans-Caspian Gas Pipeline may not be built. Turkey is only obliged to honour its contracts once gas is delivered to the Turkish border.

Gas may also be redirected via a possibly saturated Turkish gas market to Europe. The demand for gas in western Europe is expected to increase by 50 percent, from 350 bcm/yr to 525 bcm/yr in the period 1995–2010. However, because gas is a network-bound product, deliveries to western Europe are fully contracted until at least 2005. Gas consumption needs in central and eastern Europe will also rise (Skagen, 2000, pp. 67-8). Redirected gas exports via Turkey would require a connecting gas pipeline system in southeastern Europe. A tentative agreement to develop such a system was signed by the European Commission, Greece and Turkey in Brussels in July 2000. The intention is to build a southern European gas ring to pipe gas from the Caspian region to Turkey, Greece, and Italy (Lelyveld, 2000a). Much more work is needed to realize this project. If Turkey became a major gas transit state, its geopolitical importance would be enhanced.

Turkey may also become a valuable energy bridge for Caspian oil if the Baku–Ceyhan project is realized.

The significance of Baku–Ceyhan

As of spring 2001 the AIOC had still to decide if a main export pipeline was necessary to transport oil from their fields. The Turkish and US governments have vigorously lobbied for a Baku–Ceyhan pipeline connecting the Caspian Sea with the Turkish Mediterranean. In a shift in policy in October 1999 BP declared that Baku–Ceyhan was a "strategic project" which could deliver oil to Europe (*Turkish Daily News*, 21 October 1999). BP did not want to jeopardize its hopes of selling gas on the Turkish market. Significant reserves had been discovered in the Shah Deniz gas field in Azerbaijan, and BP led the consortium working there. In November 1999 Azerbaijan, Georgia and Turkey concluded four inter-governmental agreements which provided the necessary legal framework for Baku–Ceyhan. A sponsoring group of eight companies – including TPAO – was formed in October 2000 to undertake a basic engineering study on the feasibility of a Baku–Ceyhan main export pipeline. If the results of this study were favourable a more detailed one-year engineering study would begin in summer 2001. Assuming another positive report and the immediate availability of financing, a Baku–Ceyhan pipeline could then be constructed within 32 months. However, not convinced of the commercial attractiveness of Baku–Ceyhan, LUKoil and ExxonMobil, both AIOC members, declined to participate in the sponsoring group.

In Turkey a consensus has emerged in favour of Baku–Ceyhan. According to the Turkish Energy Ministry, Turkey could consume 15 million tons per year of oil carried to Ceyhan, thereby meeting much of the Caspian oil planned to be imported by 2010. Pipeline construction would provide employment for an economically deprived region of Turkey. Turkey would also benefit from transit fees – the estimates vary from $100 million to $300 million annually (See, for example, *Turkish Daily News*, 5 September 2000 and 23 June 2000 respectively).

Concerned about tanker traffic, Turkish officials have repeatedly stressed that the Bosporus is not a pipeline. According to Turkish official figures, in 2000 91 million tons of oil was transported through the Bosporus. The Turkish Maritime Pilots Association noted that 4937 tankers navigated the Straits in the same year

(Oral, 2001, pp. 2 and 4). Substantially more oil will most probably have to be transported through the Bosporus once the Caspian Pipeline Consortium (CPC) conveys Kazakh oil to Novorossiysk. Moscow has argued that CPC oil would only necessitate the passage of 1–4 additional tankers each day. It has also been noted that a 40 million tons per year Baku–Ceyhan pipeline would mean only one less tanker transiting the Straits each day (Soligo and Jaffe, 1998). Various figures may be employed to support a particular argument. For example, Turkish officials could contend that an additional 4 tankers each day could lead to an extra 1460 tankers having to navigate the Bosporus each year once the CPC's pipeline is fully operational. Ankara could insist on the double hulling of tankers, impose stricter traffic regulations, and charge higher transit fees to make the tankering of oil through the Straits less commercially attractive. A collision or other accident involving a tanker may result in the NSC taking up the issue.

Proposed Bosporus-bypass routes through pipelines across Bulgaria, Romania, or Ukraine could reduce tanker traffic. Bypass options through Turkey have also been suggested. These include pipelines connecting Zonguldak on the Black Sea coast to the refinery at Izmit, east of Istanbul; a link from the Black Sea port of Samsun to Ceyhan; and a pipeline across Turkish Thrace connecting the Black Sea and Aegean Sea. These options would be cheaper than Baku–Ceyhan (Soligo and Jaffe, 1998; Jaffe, 1998; Roberts, 1996, pp. 59-60). However, they would be cumbersome and time-consuming involving the loading–offloading–loading of oil. Tankers could pollute the Aegean coastline, a major tourism area (Roberts, 1996, p. 59; Iskit, 1996, note on p. 68). The Thrace option would involve laying pipes near sensitive military zones. Bypass options avoiding Ceyhan would mean that a terminal with excellent deepwater facilities would not be fully exploited. Most significantly, the capacity of each of the Bosporus-bypass options through Turkey would be scarcely comparable to that of a Baku–Ceyhan main export pipeline. In this context, the geopolitical value of Baku–Ceyhan warrants further consideration.

The Turkish military and MFA believe that Baku–Ceyhan would boost Turkey's prestige and influence at the expense of Russia and Iran. Moscow and Tehran are eager to thwart the pipeline's construction because of its geopolitical value. On the same grounds, since 1995 US administrations have staunchly backed Baku–Ceyhan. Suspicious of Russian ambitions, Turkey and the US have spearheaded NATO's engagement with states in the Caspian region through its Partnership for Peace programmes, and have encouraged the emergence of the

GUUAM grouping of Georgia, Ukraine, Uzbekistan, Azerbaijan, and Moldova. The formation of a GUUAM joint battalion to guard pipelines in the Caucasus has been discussed (Pavliuk, 2000, pp. 42-3). Apparently, Turkey is interested in supplying Georgia with military training, equipment, and surveillance systems to provide security for a Baku–Ceyhan pipeline (*Turkish Daily News*, 29 February 2000). Most strikingly, evidence of a Turkish forward military presence in Georgia came to light in January 2001. Turkish experts are manning the control tower of the Marneuli airfield in Georgia, which the Turkish military had renovated (*Radikal-on-line*, 2001). Given Turkey's heightened interest in the security of Georgia and also Azerbaijan, in the face of possible Russian attempts to reassert control in the Caspian region, the Turkish and US governments will continue to perceive Baku–Ceyhan as a project involving high geopolitical stakes.

Problems and prospects for Baku–Ceyhan

A minimum throughput guarantee of 50 million tons a year is required to make Baku–Ceyhan viable. The AIOC-managed fields will have a peak production of 35–40 million tons a year in 2010. Some oil here is committed to be piped to Novorossiysk and to Supsa in Georgia. Turkish officials hope Kazakhstan may provide 20 million tons a year from the Kashagan field. In spite of pressure from Ankara, Kazakhstan has still to commit itself to an Aktau–Baku–Ceyhan route. Presumably, Kazakh officials are waiting for the results of the feasibility studies on Baku–Ceyhan. The transportation of Kazakh oil to Baku by barge or underwater pipeline would increase project costs.

Ankara would have been encouraged by suggestions from BP that Baku–Ceyhan could be filled even without Kazakh crude (Lelyveld, 2001b). Oil from other Azerbaijani fields could be added. This could explain Chevron's interest in joining the Baku-Ceyhan sponsoring group given Chevron's 30 percent stake in the Absheron field (*New York Times*, 9 February 2001; and Lelyveld, 2001a). The first results of the test well being drilled at Absheron will not be known until at least May 2001.

Turkish officials have agreed to cover any additional costs for the section of pipeline to be laid in Turkey – that is, expenses in excess of $1.4 billion (Lelyveld, 1999). Up to $300 million in additional costs is envisaged. The total cost of Baku–Ceyhan, though, may surpass $3 billion. Most funds would have to come from international energy companies. If the economic difficulties in Turkey persist, Ankara would struggle to raise $300 million.

Possible problems over the security of Baku–Ceyhan are exaggerated. In a worst case scenario, the recommencement of full-scale hostilities between Armenia and Azerbaijan would seriously jeopardize the project. However, other security risks are much less threatening. Abkhaz units are unlikely to sabotage the pipeline in Georgia because that would endanger the lucrative trade in smuggled goods between Trabzon and Sukhumi. After the imprisonment of Abdullah Öcalan, demoralized Kurdish rebels no longer threaten southeastern Turkey. The impoverished Armenian minority in Javakhetia, in Georgia, could sabotage the pipeline, but damaged oil pipes are usually quickly repaired.

The Baku–Novorossiysk pipeline, which bypasses Chechnya, carries oil produced by the State Oil Company of Azerbaijan. The AIOC no longer delivers its oil to Novorossiysk due to the high transit fees, and the practice of mixing poorer quality Urals crude with Azerbaijani oil at the Russian port. The facilities at Novorossiysk will not be able to handle both CPC and AIOC oil. An alternative export route via Ukraine is possible. Work on a terminal at Odessa and on a 40 million tons per year pipeline connecting Odessa with Brody in Ukraine is expected to be completed by early 2002. Oil delivered to Supsa and Novorossiysk could be shipped to Odessa. An export route through Romania will not materialize in the foreseeable future because of lack of funds and an obstructive bureaucracy in Romania. Greek, Bulgarian and Russian officials have yet to agree on the terms of operation of a Burgas–Alexandropoulis pipeline. Tensions in the Balkans have seriously damaged the prospects of a pipeline linking Bulgaria, Macedonia, and Albania.

In practice, smaller scale export options, which are cheaper and quicker to build or operate, may lead energy companies to decide that a main export pipeline is unnecessary. The Baku–Supsa pipeline, which carries around 5 million tons a year of AIOC oil, could be upgraded to transport 15 million tons a year President Eduard Shevardnadze has been lobbying for a second Baku–Supsa pipeline with a capacity of 15 million tons a year (*Radio Free Europe/Radio Liberty Newsline*, 4, 137, pt. 1, 19 July 2000). Iran is promoting swap arrangements where Caspian oil is delivered to refineries in northern Iran, and equivalent amounts are shipped to markets from Iranian ports. Tehran has reduced the cost of swap fees and in early 2001 completed an 18.5 million tons a year pipeline connecting Neka on the Caspian coast to refineries near the Iranian capital (Lelyveld, 2000b). More ambitiously,

Iranian officials are supporting a feasibility study to be conducted by TotalFinaElf on a 50 million tons a year pipeline connecting Iran with the Kashagan field in Kazakhstan (*Turkistan Economic Bulletin*, 101, 112, 9 December 2000).

Most of the oil piped to Ceyhan would need to be sold on the European market. Turkey could become an energy bridge. However, oil demand in Europe over the next 10–15 years will only increase by 1 million barrels per day (b/d) (*United States Energy Information Administration*, 2000). In contrast, in the developing countries of Asia, demand is projected to increase from 11.1 million b/d in 1995 to 24.9 million b/d in 2015 (Amineh, 1999, pp. 29-30). Superior quality but more expensive Caspian oil must compete with Middle Eastern and African crudes on the European market.

Turkish officials stress that Baku–Ceyhan is economically sound and necessary on environmental grounds. In practice, the Turkish armed forces and MFA, together with successive US administrations, have been promoting the project primarily for geopolitical reasons. A Baku–Ceyhan pipeline may not be the most commercially attractive project. However, fierce lobbying from Turkish and US politicians may result in its building if energy companies are persuaded that the project is at least viable. Moreover, the discovery of gas at Shah Deniz may boost the prospects for Baku–Ceyhan.

The significance of Caspian gas

With regard to Caspian gas and Turkey's national interests, geopolitical concerns and energy needs must be considered. Turkey's traditional rivals, Russia and Iran, are or will be supplying gas to the Turkish market. The Turkish armed forces and MFA will be eager to import gas from other sources so that Turkey's geopolitical interests may not be compromised. Turkey's strategic importance would be enhanced if Caspian gas would be transported to European markets via Turkey.

Since 1987 Turkey has imported Russian natural gas along the Western route. The capacity of this pipeline is being upgraded to carry 14 bcm/yr. In December 1997 Turkey agreed to import a further 16 bcm/yr of Russian natural gas. This Blue Stream project involves laying two parallel pipes under the Black Sea. In spite of questions over financing and technical feasibility, work has progressed largely due to support from the Italian company ENI, which has a strategic alliance with Gazprom. Blue Stream may become operational by late 2001. Turkish construction firms are involved in both these projects.

In 1999 Ed Smith, the head of the PSG International consortium formed to construct a Trans-Caspian gas pipeline to carry Turkmen gas to Turkey, declared that the size of the Turkish market meant that either Blue Stream or a Trans-Caspian gas pipeline could be developed, but not both. Work on the losing project would have to be delayed for 5–10 years (Pamir, 2000, p. 38). Apparent cooperation between the ANAP-led Energy Ministry and the Russian lobby, and difficulties between Niyazov and the consortium, has resulted in the acceleration of work on Blue Stream and the near collapse of the Trans-Caspian Gas Pipeline project. In the short term, Turkey could thus become over-dependent on Russia for gas imports. Could Moscow exploit this advantage and, for example, persuade Ankara not to implement measures to restrict increased tanker traffic on the Bosporus?

Ignoring opposition from the US administration, Turkish energy officials are determined to purchase Iranian gas. In August 1996 the coalition government in Ankara, led by the Islamist Welfare Party (RP), had agreed to procure 228 bcm for $20 billion over 25 years. Work on the Turkish leg of the pipeline from the Iranian border to Erzurum has been delayed. The Clinton administration had blocked the sale by an American company of a $35 million compressor station (*Radikal*, 21 April 2000). In the face of Iranian threats to impose penalties, Turkish energy officials promised to complete their sections of the pipeline by July 2001. In the first year 3 bcm would be delivered, rising to 10 bcm by 2007 (*Turkish Daily News*, 31 August 2000). The pipeline does not violate the Iran–Libya Sanctions Act passed by the US Congress in 1996, which had threatened to impose sanctions on companies investing in energy projects within Iran. However, the Iranian economy would clearly benefit from the pipeline, and this aroused Washington's ire. Here, Turkey's energy needs prevailed over geopolitical concerns. The Turkish armed forces and the MFA, and the US administration, may have decided to tolerate the project, as Turkey would only be importing a maximum of 10 bcm/yr.

In May 1999 Turkmenistan and Turkey finalized a deal whereby Turkmenistan would deliver 16 bcm/yr to the Turkish border. An additional 14 bcm/yr would be transported to Europe via Turkey (*Radikal*, 22 May 1999). Ankara had apparently tapped a new source of gas, and it appeared that Turkey would become an important energy bridge. However, by spring 2001, the Trans-Caspian Pipeline Project had virtually collapsed.

Niyazov accused PSG International of seeking excessive profits, and of failing to honour a $500 million offset payment (Aliriza, 2000) By

October 2000, G.E. Capital and Bechtel withdrew from the consortium leaving only Shell committed to the project. Disputes between Turkmenistan and Azerbaijan over the ownership of Caspian oil fields have not helped. The discovery of gas in the Shah Deniz field caused further complications. Azerbaijan insisted that gas from Shah Deniz should make up half of the volume carried along a Trans-Caspian gas pipeline to Turkey. Niyazov was only prepared to allocate 20 percent of the pipeline's capacity for Azerbaijani gas (*Radio Free Europe/ Radio Liberty Newsline*, 4, 14, pt.1, 20 January 2000). Probably overplaying his hand, instead of delivering gas to the Turkish and European markets at a higher price, Niyazov has been forced to sell gas on less favourable terms to Iran, Russia, and Ukraine.

Turkey could import Shah Deniz gas, and this gas could also be delivered to Europe via Turkey. Talk was of initially upgrading and extending the pipelines in Azerbaijan and Georgia to carry limited amounts of gas to Turkey, before preparing a new pipeline network to deliver substantial volumes to Turkey and Europe. In June 2000 officials from Statoil – a member of the consortium developing Shah Deniz – outlined a plan for Azerbaijan to supply Turkey 16–30 bcm/yr and southeastern Europe a further 10–20 bcm/yr over 15–20 years. In November 2000 Statoil announced it would form a joint venture with the Turkish business Koç Holding to sell Azerbaijani gas in Turkey after the liberalization of the Turkish market (*Middle East Economic Survey*, 2000, p.A16). In March 2001, after delays, Turkey and Azerbaijan signed agreements whereby Turkey pledged to import initially 2 bcm of gas from Shah Deniz in 2004, and eventually 6.6 bcm/yr. The gas would be delivered along a pipe running parallel to a Baku–Ceyhan oil pipeline (*Financial Times*, 13 March 2001).

The March 2001 agreement raised several questions. The volumes are substantially less than those envisaged by Baku and by members of the Shah Deniz consortium. Turkish energy officials may have realized that there is not a large market in Turkey for Azerbaijani gas. This suggests that Russia may have already succeeded in cornering a sizable stake in a not quite so large Turkish gas market. If so, the political repercussions could be serious given that the Turkish armed forces and the MFA have been emphasizing the geopolitical importance of Caspian energy. Surprisingly, perhaps, there was also no mention in the agreement of transporting Azerbaijani gas to Europe via Turkey. The question of upgrading and extending the pipeline in the Caucasus to the Turkish border remains unresolved. Presumably, companies in the Shah Deniz consortium would provide finance, but their hopes of selling large volumes of gas on the Turkish and European markets seem to have been dashed at least for the foreseeable future. These uncertainties may adversely affect the Baku–Ceyhan project.

It is generally believed in Turkey that BP's eagerness to sell Shah Deniz gas on the Turkish market led that company to become more supportive of Baku-Ceyhan. Laying parallel oil and gas pipelines would reduce costs. There are reports of 1.8–2 billion barrels of gas condensate – the liquid hydrocarbon recovered on the surface during gas production – at Shah Deniz, and possibly much larger amounts of oil beneath the gas column (*Turkish Daily News*, 20 October 2000. Article by Ferruh Demirmen titled "Baku–Tbilisi–Ceyhan: The Project Enters a New Phase. Part 1"). This condensate and liquids could be used to raise the quality and quantity of oil carried to Ceyhan. It remains to be seen, though, how the questions posed by the March 2001 agreement may affect how BP and Statoil – both AIOC members – regard the Baku–Ceyhan project.

Conclusion

Great Game scenarios concerning the Caspian region often refer to two competing blocs – Russia, Iran, and Armenia, and a US/Western-backed Turkey, Azerbaijan, and Georgia – participating in a zero-sum game for influence, power, and prestige. In these depictions so-called "pipeline politics" assume great importance. Although Great Game advocates usually fail to consider properly the role of energy companies, and presume that states are rational and monolithic actors pursuing a predetermined set of national interests, the geopolitical relevance of pipeline politics in the Caspian region cannot be totally dismissed. In Turkey, the geopolitical value of a Baku–Ceyhan oil pipeline is generally recognized either explicitly – by the Turkish military – or at least implicitly – by energy officials, for instance. But, to realize national interests, Turkey must also import more natural gas from the Caspian region. Geopolitical concerns and energy needs must somehow be balanced. This will not be easy given the influence of the so-called Russian lobby in Turkey, which appears to have close ties with certain politicians. Ministries, state agencies and institutions, business groups and other lobbies in Turkey, at times have different views on what they believe to be Turkey's national interests.

With regard to Caspian energy, the assumption that there are two rigid and opposing blocs is somewhat simplistic. Russia and Iran are commercial partners as well as geopolitical rivals of Turkey. Encouraged by the European Commission, Armenia, Iran, and Greece are considering a scheme to construct a gas pipeline to carry Iranian gas to Greece and Italy via a route connecting Iran, Armenia, and Turkey (*New Europe*, 11–17 March 2001). This plan is in line with the memorandum signed in Brussels in July 2000 by representatives of Turkey, Greece and the European Commission. The actual details of what would be a highly ambitious and expensive project remain to be hammered out, and, in practice, it may not materialize. Shevardnadze's attempts to convince energy companies to deliver more oil to Supsa, possibly by means of a second pipe, could seriously endanger the Baku–Ceyhan project. Moreover, officials of GUUAM member states, when underlining the importance of a Baku–Supsa–Odessa–Brody oil export route, have even suggested that the continued existence of GUUAM will depend on whether Caspian oil will be transported to Europe via Ukraine.[1] Competition over oil export routes could therefore damage relations between Turkey and GUUAM member states.

Given the intricacies of pipeline politics and the divisions among Turkish decision-makers, it would be foolish to predict how Turkey will react to developments in the Caspian region. Clearly, though, changes of regime in Azerbaijan and Georgia could have repercussions. The prolonging of the economic crisis in Turkey may make Ankara more dependent on Moscow for its gas needs. This would be due to the contraction of the Turkish economy and because Turkey will most probably receive up to 30 bcm of Russian natural gas. It seems unlikely that Turkey will import Turkmen gas via a Trans-Caspian pipeline, and Azerbaijani gas may only be imported in small quantities. In these circumstances, Turkey could become dangerously dependent on Russia for satisfying its energy needs, and the fears of the Turkish military and MFA could then materialize. A failure to realize the Baku–Ceyhan project could also have serious consequences given the value Turkish officials have attached to it. Turkish–US relations would suffer. What contingency plans does Ankara have in place if a Baku–Ceyhan pipeline is not constructed? What would be the impact on tanker traffic through the Straits? In the near future Turkish policy-makers may have to address very sensitive issues with regard to Caspian energy and Turkey's national interests.

Note

1. These were the views expressed by several officials and other delegates attending the conference titled "GUUAM-Problems and Prospects for the Development of Transportation and Communication Corridors" organized by the National Institute of Ukrainian-Russian Relations, Yalta, Ukraine, 4–5 July 2000.

References

Aliriza, Bülent (2000) "US Caspian Pipeline Policy: Substance or Spin?" *CSIS Caspian Energy Update*, 24 August.

Amineh, Mehdi Parvizi (1999) *Towards the Control of Oil Reserves in the Caspian Region*, New York, St Martin's.

Amirahmadi, Hooshang (ed.) (2000) *The Caspian Region at a Crossroad: Challenge of a New Frontier of Energy and Development*, New York, St Martin's.

Baran, Zeyno (2000) "Corruption: The Turkish Challenge", *Journal of International Affairs*, 54, 1, pp. 127-46.

Dwan, Renate and Oleksandr Pavliuk (eds.) (2000) *Building Security in the New States of Eurasia – Subregional Cooperation in the Former Soviet Space*, Armonk, NY, M.E. Sharpe.

Financial Times, 13 March 2001.

İskit, Temel (1996) "Turkey: A New Actor in the Field of Energy Politics?" *Perceptions*, 1, 1, pp. 58-82.

Jaffe, Amy (1998) *Unlocking the Assets: Energy and the Future of Central Asia and the Caucasus: Main Study*, James A. Baker III Institute for Public Policy, Rice University, Houston, TX.

Lelyveld, Michael (1999) "OSCE: Caspian Pacts Don't Guarantee Project", *Radio Free Europe/Radio Liberty Report*, Boston, 23 November.

Lelyveld, Michael (2000a) "Caspian: Turkey and Greece Open Talks on Pipeline Connection", *Radio Free Europe/Radio Liberty Report*, Boston, 11 July.

Lelyveld, Michael (2000b) "Iran Seeks to Improve its Caspian Sea Interest", *Radio Free Europe/Radio Liberty Report*, Boston, 18 December.

Lelyveld, Michael (2001a) "Azerbaijan: Baku-Ceyhan Pipeline Gets a Boost", *Radio Free Europe/Radio Liberty Report*, Boston, 13 February.

Lelyveld Michael. (2001b) "Caspian: Russia Softens Opposition to Baku-Ceyhan Pipeline", *Radio Free Europe/Radio Liberty Report*, Boston, 6 March.

Middle East Economic Survey (2000) 43, 48, 27 November p. A16.

New Europe, 11-17 March 2001 Issue No. 407.

New York Times, 9 February 2001.

Oral, Nilufer (2001) "Oil and Water: Caspian Oil and Transportation Challenges Facing the Turkish Straits", paper presented at the 25th Annual Conference of the Center for Oceans' Law and Policy (University of Virginia, School of Law), Hamburg, 16–19 March.

Pamir, Necdet (2000) "Is there a Future for the Eurasian Corridor?" *Insight Turkey*, 2, 3, pp. 31-44.

Pavliuk, Oleksandr (2000) "GUUAM: The Making of a Political Grouping into Economic Cooperation", in Renate Dwan and Oleksandr Pavliuk (eds.), pp. 33-56.

Radikal, 22 May 1999; 7 October 1999; 21 April 2000.

Radikal-On-Line, www.radikal.com.tr/2001/01/30/dis/01dus.shtml

Radio Free Europe/Radio Liberty Newsline, 4, 14, pt.1, 20 January 2000; 4, 137, pt.1, 19 July 2000.

Roberts, John (1996) *Caspian Pipelines*, London: Royal Institute of International Affairs, Former Soviet South Project.

Skagen, Otto (2000) "Survey of Caspian's Oil and Gas Resources", in Hooshang Amirahmadi (ed.), pp. 55-74.

Soligo, Richard and Jaffe, Amy Myers (1998) "The Economics of Pipeline Routes: The Conundrum of Oil Exports from the Caspian Basin", *Baker Institute Working Paper*, Rice University, Houston, TX.

Turkish Daily News, 21 October 1999; 27 November 1999; 29 February 2000, 23 June 2000, 31 August 2000, 5 September 2000, 20 September 2000, 20 October 2000, 4 May 2001.

Turkish Probe, 22 February 1998.

Turkish State Institute of Statistics (2001), Tables 7.9 at:
www.die.gov.tr/English/sonist/Disticist/27020007.gif
www.die.gov.tr/English/sonist/Disticist/27020008.gif
www.die.gov.tr/English/sonist/Disticist/27020009.gif

Turkistan Economic Bulletin, 101, 112, 9 December 2000.

United States Energy Information Administration (2000) "Caspian Sea Region, June, at www.eia.doe.gov/emeu/cabs/caspfull.html

Conclusion

Dov Lynch

Money, influence and passion

In the conclusion to his chapter on US national interests in this volume, Joe Barnes notes: "Money, influence and passion: the combination is not one to lead to sobriety of analysis or modesty of ambition." Indeed, since the collapse of the Soviet Union, discussions of energy in the Caspian region have been prone to both over-simplification and over-ambition, mixed in with a heavy dose of potential wealth and geopolitical competition. A region that had previously been closed to the world, and even surrounding regional influences, was suddenly opened wide for foreign involvement, investment as well as scholarly analysis. The magnet attracting the surge of foreign interest has been the existence of large reserves of oil and gas in the Caspian region. Without these reserves, the new states of this area might have pursued very different paths, and international perspectives on the importance of the region would have been very different. Energy is a primary reason for many of the distortions of understanding that have arisen about the new states of the Caspian region. Energy reserves have skewed expectations in the new states themselves, and also increased the propensity for international misunderstanding about the nature of the region.

Ten years after the collapse of the Soviet Union, sufficient time has passed to analyse developments in the Caspian region with a degree of historical detachment and objectivity. This volume, *Energy in the Caspian Region*, has sought to discuss soberly the various dimensions that affect the development of resources of this area of the post-Soviet "space." In this, it seeks to develop further a number of important themes elaborated in the first volume of the Euro-Asian Studies Series, *The Euro-Asian World: A Period of Transition*. The chapters incorporated in the present volume draw on the expertise of the James Baker Institute in conjunction with the Centre for Euro-Asian Studies. The result of this cooperation is a volume that seeks to throw some clear light over the political, economic, geological, technical and geopolitical dimensions of energy resources in the Caspian region.

Complexity and diversity

The studies in this volume lay to rest a number of common assumptions and simplifications about the Caspian region.

First, the chapters by Michael Margelov, Joe Barnes and Gareth Winrow demystify the often claimed notion that the Caspian region is the target of a new Great Game. The Great Game of the 19th century was played out between two great empires, Britain and Russia at the height of the age of imperialism. The stakes in that Game were territorial, and the region over which the Game stretched, mainly Central Asia, was seen as a weak cipher with little power or role to play. After the Soviet collapse, the existence of energy reserves in the Caspian region led many commentators to seize upon the image of a Great Game in order to explain the nature of contemporary international relations in the area. In the words of one respected analyst, "similar to the Great Game of the early twentieth century, which pitted the British interests against those of the Russian empire and the German Reich, today's struggle involves geopolitics and oil."[1] The use of the image in much analysis is based on the assumption of competition between coherent and solid rival blocs, led by either the US or Russia, in a Game that encompasses all the new states of the region in a race for the exploitation and development of their purported vast resources. In reality, there is no Great Game in the Caspian region. The situation is far more complex and prosaic than this romantic image might lead one to assume.

In a pertinent article in 1998, William Odom argued that the utility of the image of the Great Game resided more in the differences that existed than in the similarities between the current situation and that of the past.[2] In particular, Odom defined four differences with the past. First, the past Great Game was played between two players. In the twenty-first century, the number and type of actors interacting in the Caspian region have become far more complex. These actors range from states, and most prominently the new states themselves, international organizations (NATO, the UN, the OSCE) to multi-national corporations (Shell, British Petroleum, ENI). The bipolar Game has become more than simply multi-polar, it has become multi-leveled. Second, the past Great Game was one of competing imperialisms. Today, imperial objectives no longer lead the main players in the region. While the new Russia has never existed in its current shape, the authorities of the Russian Federation have abandoned imperialist designs on the former Soviet Union. Russia has interests in the so-called "near abroad" and these interests have been pursued actively. However, imperialism has not been the objective leading Russian policies.[3]

Linked to this, the third difference resides in the objectives pursued by actors in the region. These objectives are no longer those of territorial gain but include "national independence, profits from oil and gas production, an Islamic cultural revival and many lesser ones."[4] Finally, the Caspian region is no longer a borderland caught between rival empires, with little power and few resources. The new states of the region underwent the strenuous process of Soviet modernization in the last century, which left them with literate populations, local industries, and large urban centers. Perhaps most importantly, these new states are led by new political elites intent on building new states and nations from the bare administrative vehicles that they inherited from the Soviet collapse. The new states are active and dynamic players in the region, and no longer ciphers that are purely functional to external interest and power.

The chapters in this volume also clarify another important point: The stakes in the region are important but they are not "great." Discussions of the amount of energy reserves that exist in the Caspian region have been stretched beyond realism in the past. The new states themselves had an interest in amplifying the scale of these projections in order to attract foreign interest and investment. For a sober understanding, the energy resources of the Caspian region must be seen in comparison to other energy-rich areas. In fact, it is clear that these reserves stand far behind those of the Persian Gulf, and are comparable at best to those of the North Sea. These amounts are far from negligible. However, their impact on world energy markets has yet to be determined. The discussion in this volume by Patrik Hultberg and Robin C. Sickles is insightful on this point. Using their projection model, the Caspian region oil reserves will at the most "play a significant role as a marginal supplier" in a scenario based on high demand. A scenario based on lower projections would decrease the role potentially played by Caspian reserves in the world market.

In addition, as noted in the chapter by Ronald Soligo and Amy Myers Jaffe, the exploitation of these reserves faces deep problems not least because of a dearth of drilling rigs and other necessary equipment in the region. In their words, "the Caspian Basin still remains one of the most difficult oil prospecting territories in the world." The uncertainty surrounding production and exploitation has complicated further the difficulties regarding the export of Caspian region energy, in both natural gas and oil.

The chapters in this volume also elucidate the role played by major external states in the Caspian region: that is, Russia, the United States and Turkey. All of the present analyses stress the complex nature of international interplay in the region. The Caspian region has featured a degree of geopolitical competition between these states. In particular, the agreement to construct a pipeline from Baku to Ceyhan on the Turkish Mediterranean coast has been imbued with a geopolitical significance that has overshadowed its commercial competitiveness in relation to other potential export routes. The possibility of a Baku – Ceyhan pipeline (still uncertain) has obscured areas of significant cooperation that have developed between external powers in the region.

In discussing this region, it is important not to confuse a focus on geopolitical competition between external players, which undeniably exists, with its significance. This competition is not the only feature of international interplay. As noted by Gareth Winrow in his chapter in this volume, the relationship between Russia and Turkey, as well as the ties between Turkey and Iran, are based as much on mutually beneficial commercial trade and energy cooperation as they are on geopolitical competition. In his chapter, the Russian analyst Michael Margelov noted the changes that have occu -rred towards more determination and increased coordination in Russian policy towards the Caspian Region under President Putin. Russian policy is intent on a course of defending its historic interests in this region. However, Margelov stressed that the heart of Russian policy resided in the desire to build a benign international environment that will be propitious for Russia's internal revitalization. On this note, he argued that Russia will continue to play a key role in the region and cannot be discounted. However, confrontation with the West will be avoided at all cost. In his discussion of US policy, Joseph Barnes threw cold water over the notion that the US had vital interests in the region. The relationship with Moscow and the US commitment to the Persian Gulf were seen as being more important. International affairs in the Caspian region, therefore, are far more complex than has been implied by the zero-sum notion of the Great Game.

In addition, the chapters in this volume have highlighted the diversity of this region. The chapter by Andrei Belopolsky and Manik Talwani provides detailed analysis of the five geological basins that make up the Caspian region, ranging from the South Caspian, North Caspian, North Usturt, Mangyshlak to the Amu-Darya basins. Each of these basins has different resources, reservoir types, geological histories and types of hydrocarbons. From this perspective, the region must be seen as more than simply the Caspian Sea itself, and as encompassing large sectors of territory and including non-littoral states such as Uzbekistan. This volume also focuses on an issue that is often ignored in much discussion of energy in this region: that is, the state of oil refineries and gas processing in these states. The Caspian region faces a real challenge in the domestic infrastructure that was inherited after the Soviet collapse, which became inappropriate for the needs of new domestic markets. As argued by Andrei Kalyuzhnov, Julian Lee and Julia Nanay, in addition to developing export routes for their energy resources, these new states must seek to strengthen their domestic markets and also to develop a regional processing market. These markets will also be critical for the longer term development of these economies.

Moreover, the analysis in this volume has highlighted the diversity of the new states themselves that emerged from the Soviet collapse. In her contribution, Martha Brill Olcott argued for a clear distinction between the Central Asian states, which form a distinct political space, and Azerbaijan in the South Caucasus. Olcott disputed the very existence of a so-called "larger Caspian region", and underlined the very different histories of these states, their religious compositions, geographical and economic orientations and experiences with independence. In the late 1980s, the South Caucasian states were driven to independence by large popular movements that were bent on throwing off the shackles of rule by Moscow. By contrast, independence was thrust upon the Central Asian republics, which left them unprepared and shocked.

Moreover, the religious make-up of the peoples of the Caspian region is diverse. As discussed in the chapter by Mehrdad Haghayeghi and Fred R. von der Mehden, the Central Asian states mostly follow the Sunni Islamic faith, while the Azeri people are Shi'i. Tajikistan contains a small Ismaili population living in the Badakhshan region high in the Pamir mountain range. Moreover, the nature of politics has varied significantly across the Caspian region, ranging from the tentatively democratic Kyrgyzstan to the thoroughly autocratic Turkmenistan. The political regime of Heider Aliyev in Azerbaijan has definite authoritarian features, and serious questions have been raised about respect for human rights and election fraud. However, at the same time, Azerbaijan also has the region's most vibrant opposition parties.

Similarities and weaknesses

Thus, as noted by James Baker in his Preface, a central conclusion of this volume is the diversity and complexity of the Caspian region. At the same time, all of the chapters in this volume have noted significant similarities between the new states making up this region. These similarities reside mainly in the weakness of these states. These studies of the Caspian region highlight the critical idea that energy resources are not a panacea to the problems faced by these new states. In fact, these resources may even create more problems than they resolve.

The concept of state weakness is insightful for understanding the problems faced by the new states of the Caspian region. In the general literature, there are two broad understandings of the notion of state weakness.[5] The first understanding concentrates upon the institutions and individuals that make up the state, as well as the capacities of state agencies. In the words of Joel S. Migdal, the relative strength of a state must be considered in light of its capacity to "penetrate society, regulate social relationships, extract resources and appropriate or use resources in determined ways."[6] From this perspective, state weakness is interpreted as a syndrome, that is characterized by widespread corruption, the collapse of state coercive powers, the rise of "strongmen" and the segmentation of the political community into several "publics."

A second approach to understanding state weakness focuses on more than political-institutional concerns. For one, Barry Buzan has stressed the importance of the "idea" of the state in terms of perceptions of its nature and legitimacy.[7] If widely held, this "idea" may act as an organic binder, that links the state and its parts with coherence and building mechanisms to allow for popular subordination to its authority. Without such an "idea" and in circumstances of institutional weakness, Buzan raised the possibility of the "disintegration of the state as a political unit."[8] On a related point, Kalevi Holsti, in his discussion of the link between the nature of states and war, argued that the fate of states was determined "in the realm of ideas and sentiments."[9] In his view, state weakness consisted of patterns of flawed legitimacy, in which the state became personalized or "captured," and uniform "rules of the game" are contested.

The chapters in this volume draw a number of conclusions that are relevant to these notions of state weakness. First, at the institutional level, a number of the authors stress that the existence of energy resources may not strengthen these new states. In the words of Martha Brill Olcott, the new states of Central Asia may "become trapped in the classic third world cycle of selling off non-renewable resources while failing to invest in productive capacity to sustain the economy once the resources are gone." Moreover, she expects that the benefits from the exploitation of the resources will not be evenly spread. This revenue may entrench the poverty of the majority of these populations, and the weakness of state services and capacities, and lead to higher levels of corruption.

In her chapter, Yelena Kalyuzhnova highlighted the economic difficulties these new states face in dealing with the exploitation of energy resources. Their exploitation must be embedded in an appropriate macroeconomic framework and a healthy economy in order for these states to avoid the dangers of "Dutch disease." This macroeconomic framework must include, most importantly, a strong legal structure that establishes clear rules and guidelines. Without this framework, Kalyuzhnova states, "increased income from oil industry windfall leads to increased demand, exchange rate appreciation and loss of competitiveness in the economy as a whole." The key issue that is highlighted by Kalyuzhnova is that revenues must be carefully channeled by these states to ensure that they serve to strengthen the institutions of good governance. The creation of trust funds in Kazakhstan and Azerbaijan is a first small step in the right direction.

A number of authors in this volume stressed the dangers that may arise if the current "social bargain" that has been struck in the states of the Caspian region comes undone. Since the collapse of the Soviet Union, the bargain in these new states has been built on political stability, not to say authoritarianism, in exchange for social stability and the promise of future prosperity derived from foreign investment and energy incomes. However, as these states fail to provide for their sides of the bargain, there is a danger that, in the words of Martha Brill Olcott, "political change when it finally comes will be convulsive and violent."

This danger is linked to the second understanding of state weakness. Thus far, the basic "idea" behind these new states of the Caspian region has remained unchallenged. Azerbaijan has been the exception in this respect. The Armenians in the Nagorno-Karabakh region have rejected the very idea behind the new Azeri state. In response, the separatist Armenian authorities have struck out on their own and declared their own independent, if still unrecognized state, called the Nagorno Karabakh Republic. However, in Central Asia, stability since 1992 has been founded on the Central Asian populations agreeing to the basic idea behind their new states, citizenship within them and the boundaries inherited from the Soviet collapse. Even in the case of Tajikistan, where a vicious civil war raged from 1992 until the peace agreement of 1997, most of the parties to the conflict agreed to the fundamental notion of a Tajik state. The parties in the civil war were fighting for power in Tajikistan and not to destroy or exit Tajikistan. In this sense, while the Central Asian states have been weak in institutional terms, they have maintained degrees of strength in terms of the legitimizing ideas supported by their populations. This may not last.

As the socio-economic situation deteriorates and political repression is maintained across the region, the rise of potential challenges to the basic ideas behind these states cannot be ruled out. Thus far, the basic idea driving these states has been that of a secular model of economic and political development. This model may very well be abandoned. Mehrdad Haghayeghi and Fred van der Mehden noted the long-term potential of a rise of Islamic fundamentalism, until now largely absent from the region, as a rallying call of the discontent that would fundamentally threaten the basic political and economic consensus in the new states that emerged after the Soviet collapse.

Thus far, the states of the Caspian region have made significant progress in the process of transformation from the difficulties of the Soviet collapse. However, the future remains uncertain and dangers lie ahead for these states. It is imperative that the energy reserves of the Caspian region be used to support stability and good governance across these states. Failing this, the weaknesses of these states may become ever deeply entrenched. In these circumstances, far from a region of opportunity, the Caspian area will become a zone of instability.

Notes

1. Ariel Cohen, "The New Great Game: Pipeline Politics in Eurasia," *Caspian Crossroads*, Vol. 2, Issue 1, Spring-Summer 1996.
2. William Odom, "The Caspian Sea Littoral States: The Object of a New Great Game?" *Caspian Crossroads*, Vol. 3, Issue 3, Winter 1998.
3. For a discussion of Russian policy in the former Soviet Union, see the author's *Russian Peacekeeping Strategies in the CIS: The Cases of Moldova, Georgia and Tajikistan* (Macmillan-now Palgrave- and RIIA: London, 2000)

4. *Ibid.*
5. This discussion of state weakness draws from previous work by the author in "Euro-Asian Conflicts and Peacekeeping Dilemmas," in Y. Kalyuzhnova and D. Lynch (eds), *The Euro-Asian World: A Period of Transition* (Macmillan-now Palgrave : London, 2000) and Dov Lynch, "The Tajik Peace Process," *Civil Wars* (forthcoming, 2001), and Dov Lynch, "De Facto States and Eurasian Security," Forth coming.
6. See, for example, Joel S. Migdal, *Strong Societies and Weak States, State-Society Relations and States Capacities in the Third World* (Princeton University Press, Princeton: 1988), Mohammed Ayoob, "State-Making and Third World Security," in J. Singh and T. Berhauer, *The Security of Third World Countries* (UNIDIR, Dartmouth: 1993); William Zartman (ed.), *Collapsed States: The Disintegration and Restoration of Legitimate Authority* (Lynne Rienner, London: 1995).
7. Barry Buzan, *People, States and Fear: An Agenda for International Security Studies in the Post-Cold War Era* (Harvester Wheatsheaf: Hemel Hempstead, 1991).
8. *Ibid.*, p. 82.
9. Kalevi J. Holsti, *The State, War and the State of War* (Cambridge University Press: Cambridge UK, 1996), p. 84.

Index

The manufacturer's authorised representative in the EU is Springer Nature Customer Service Centre GmbH, Europaplatz 3, 69115 Heidelberg, Germany. If you have any concerns regarding our products, please contact ProductSafety@springernature.com

Printed and bound by CPI Group (UK) Ltd, Croydon, CR0 4YY

13/10/2026

02232378-0015